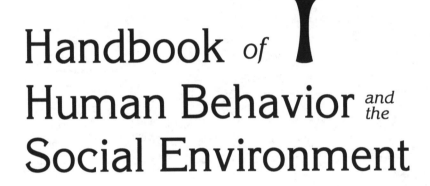

Handbook *of*
Human Behavior *and the*
Social Environment

Handbook *of* Human Behavior *and the* Social Environment

A Practice-Based Approach

Roberta R. Greene
Joe M. Schriver

Transaction Publishers
New Brunswick (U.S.A.) and London (U.K.)

Library of Congress Catalog Number: 2016005379
ISBN: 978-1-4128-6284-4 (hardcover); 978-1-4128-6321-6 (paper)
eBook: 978-1-4128-6234-9
Printed in the United States of America

Library of Congress Cataloging-in-Publication Data

Names: Greene, Roberta R. (Roberta Rubin), 1940- author. | Schriver, Joe M., author.
Title: Handbook of human behavior and the social environment : a practice-based approach / Roberta R. Greene and Joe M. Schriver.
Description: New Brunswick : Transaction Publishers, 2016. | Includes bibliographical references and index.
Identifiers: LCCN 2016005379 (print) | LCCN 2016005990 (ebook) | ISBN 9781412862844 (hardcover) | ISBN 9781412863216 (pbk.) | ISBN 9781412862349 (eBook) | ISBN 9781412862349
Subjects: LCSH: Human behavior. | Social service.
Classification: LCC HM1033 .G74 2016 (print) | LCC HM1033 (ebook) | DDC 302--dc23
LC record available at http://lccn.loc.gov/

2016005379

Contents

This chapter introduces the Handbook, *a state-of-the-art compendium of key theories applied in the social work profession. The chapter also describes the current social work curriculum developed by the Council on Social Work Education Commission on Educational Policy and Accreditation Standards. In addition, it discusses the Council's 2015 mandate that* human behavior and the social environment *(HBSE) be used to inform and guide the processes of client engagement, assessment, intervention, and evaluation with individuals, families, groups, organizations, and communities.*

This chapter discusses the ecological perspective—the unifying conceptual base of HBSE. Also known as the person–environment construct, its key assumptions and terms offer a means of applying HBSE theories differentially, depending on client system size, context, and needs throughout the processes of engagement, assessment, and intervention.

This chapter describes the use of HBSE theory to support social workers in engaging diversity and difference in practice. The theory and models presented are guided by the ecological systems perspective and symbolic interaction theory. These are contrasted with Afrocentric concepts intended to inform micro- and macropractice with individuals, families, groups, organizations, and communities. Major concepts include power, oppression, and identity formation. Strategies to try and eliminate personal bias and to promote human rights are discussed.

This chapter presents selected developmental theories and reviews how they inform the social work practice processes of engagement, assessment, and intervention. The strengths and limitations of developmental theory in regard to difference are also discussed.

This chapter presents HBSE theory for engaging, assessing, and intervening with individuals in social work practice. It first outlines the historical evolution of the cognitive movement, applying the terms and assumptions of behavioral, social learning, and cognitive behavior theory—part of the positivist scientific paradigm. These ideas are then contrasted with social constructionism, a school of thought linked to the shift in paradigm to postmodern thinking. Each theory provides a different way of viewing the social work helping process.

This chapter presents the use of structuralist HBSE theory to engage, assess, and intervene with families. The primary assumptions discussed are derived from general systems theory and are augmented with selected theoretical frameworks and practice strategies taken from the family therapy literature. The knowledge, attitudes, and skills necessary for competency-based practice are applied to illustrate family-centered social work practice.

This chapter presents HBSE theories for social work practice with groups. Mutual aid in social work groups and Yalom's existential group therapy processes are contrasted, illustrating the sociohistorical context of theory construction. Transtheoretical content is also explored.

This chapter presents HBSE theory for social work practice with organizations (occupational social work). It outlines HBSE theory that informs social work practice with workers and their families at the job site (employee assistance programs). The chapter also provides HBSE theory to guide social workers in carrying out organizational change strategies. It then discusses the application of leadership theory for social workers who carry out administrative or managerial roles as part of organizational change.

This chapter presents HBSE theories for social work practice with communities. It traces the historical development of how people relate to one another as members of a society. It then provides an overview of macrolevel social work practice approaches for community assessment and asset-building interventions.

This chapter presents a metatheory of the risk and resilience approach to practice with individuals, families, groups, organizations, and communities. It suggests that when the risk and resilience approach to social work practice is amplified by the ecological perspective and other related theoretical frameworks, the combination of precepts constitutes an HBSE theory and practice model that bridges the gap between genetics and the global ecology.

Tables and Figures

Figures

Chapter 1

Chapter 2

Chapter 3

Preface

Human Behavior and the Social Environment (HBSE) Handbook: A Practice Approach is a compendium of theories for social work practice with individuals, families, groups, organizations, and communities. It synthesizes the widespread knowledge base on this topic, tracing the sociohistorical evolution of its content and the accompanying role of the social worker in serving clients and constituencies. The *Handbook* is based on an ecosystems person–environment point of view. The intent is to assist the social worker in fostering human well-being and social functioning to enhance competence.

Chapter 1 introduces the *Handbook* and describes the current social work curriculum developed by the Council on Social Work Education Commission on Educational Policy and Accreditation Standards. It demonstrates how client and constituency engagement, assessment, intervention, and evaluation are guided by knowledge of HBSE theory (Council on Social Work Education 2015). It also integrates ethics, research, and policy content as well as diversity and Human Rights and Social, Economic, and Environmental Justice issues.

Chapter 2 discusses the ecological perspective—the unifying conceptual base of HBSE. Also known as the *person–environment construct,* its key assumptions and terms offer a means of applying HBSE theories differentially, depending on client system size, context, and needs.

Chapter 3 describes the use of HBSE theory to support social workers in engaging diversity and difference in practice. Major concepts include power, oppression, and identity formation. Strategies to try and eliminate personal bias and to promote human rights are presented.

Chapters 4, 5, and 6 focus on HBSE for microlevel social work practice, emphasizing how social workers enhance personal and interpersonal functioning. Chapter 7 discusses two examples of HBSE for mesolevel practice in social group work, allowing the social worker to focus on personal and interpersonal meaning and functioning within a group setting (Sheafor and Horejsi 2012).

Chapter 8 covers HBSE theory for social work practice with organizations. It outlines HBSE theory that informs social work practice with workers and their families at the job site, HBSE theory for carrying out organizational change strategies, and the application of leadership theory for social workers in administrative or managerial roles.

Chapter 9 presents HBSE theories for social work practice with communities. It traces the historical development of how people relate to one another as members of a society. It then provides an overview of macrolevel social work practice approaches for community assessment and asset-building interventions.

Chapter 10 offers a metatheory of the risk and resilience approach to practice with individuals, families, groups, organizations, and communities. It suggests that when the risk and resilience approach to social work practice is amplified by the ecological perspective and other related theoretical frameworks, the combination of precepts constitutes an HBSE theory and practice model that bridges the gap between genetics and the global ecology.

References

Council on Social Work Education. 2015. *Educational Policy and Accreditation Standards*. Alexandria, VA: Council on Social Work Education.

Sheafor, B. W., and Horejsi, C. J. 2012. *Techniques and Guidelines for Social Work Practice*. 9th ed. Boston, MA: Allyn & Bacon.

1

Introduction: Theory-Informed Social Work Practice

> ➤ *This chapter introduces the HBSE* Handbook, *a state-of-the-art compendium of key theories applied in the social work profession.*
>
> ➤ *The chapter also describes the current social work curriculum officially developed by the Council on Social Work Education Commission on Educational Policy and Accreditation Standards.*
>
> ➤ *In addition, it discusses the CSWE 2015 mandate that* human behavior and the social environment *be used to inform and guide the processes of client engagement, assessment, intervention, and evaluation with individuals, families, groups, organizations, and communities.*

This handbook is a compendium of *human behavior and the social environment* (HBSE) theories that fall under the rubric of person and environment. The theories chosen illustrate the current use and application of prevalent conceptual frameworks, reflecting the state of the profession's widespread HBSE knowledge base.

Selected theories illustrate the historical changes in HBSE content that have evolved over time depending on the social work profession's practice needs and values and the scientific advances of the day. In addition, the theories emphasized demonstrate how changes in HBSE resulted in modifications in the social worker's role as practitioners applied HBSE theory under various practice and sociohistorical conditions.

Social Work Practice Competency

The intent of the *Handbook* is to promote social workers' practice competency by proposing theory-informed strategies that address the processes of client engagement, assessment, intervention, and evaluation with individuals, families, groups, organizations, and communities as reflected in the Council on Social Work Education (CSWE) curriculum standards (CSWE 2015a). Because the CSWE curriculum rationalizes the social work practice process, an overview of the Educational Policy and Accreditation

Standards (EPAS) can help you step back and prepare to interact with your clients and constituencies.

Upon graduation, you will be expected to have demonstrated the mastery of nine interrelated competencies outlined in Table 1.1. You will be required to "demonstrate the level of competence necessary to enter professional practice" and exercise judgment in regard to unique practice situations (CSWE 2015a, 3).

Table 1.1.
2015 Educational policy and accreditation standards competencies
and practice behaviors

Competency 1	**Demonstrate ethical and professional behavior**
	a Make ethical decisions by applying the standards of the NASW *Code of Ethics,* relevant laws and regulations, models for ethical decision-making, ethical conduct of research, and additional codes of ethics as appropriate to context
	b Use reflection and self-regulation to manage personal values and maintain professionalism in practice situations
	c Demonstrate professional demeanor in behavior; appearance; and oral, written, and electronic communication
	d Use technology ethically and appropriately to facilitate practice outcomes
	e Use supervision and consultation to guide professional judgment and behavior
Competency 2	**Engage diversity and difference in practice**
	a Apply and communicate understanding of the importance of diversity and difference in shaping life experiences in practice at the micro, mezzo, and macro levels
	b Present themselves as learners and engage clients and constituencies as experts of their own experiences
	c Apply self-awareness and self-regulation to manage the influence of personal biases and values in working with diverse clients and constituencies
Competency 3	**Advance human rights and social, economic, and environmental justice**
	a Apply their understanding of social, economic, and environmental justice to advocate for human rights at the individual and system levels
	b Engage in practices that advance social, economic, and environmental justice
Competency 4	**Engage in practice-informed research and research-informed practice**
	a Use practice experience and theory to inform scientific inquiry and research
	b Apply critical thinking to engage in analysis of quantitative and qualitative research methods and research findings
	c Use and translate research evidence to inform and improve practice, policy, and service delivery
Competency 5	**Engage in policy practice**
	a Identify social policy at the local, state, and federal level that impacts well-being, service delivery, and access to social services
	b Assess how social welfare and economic policies impact the delivery of and access to social services
	c Apply critical thinking to analyze, formulate, and advocate for policies that advance human rights and social, economic, and environmental justice

(Continued)

Table 1.1. (Continued)

Competency 6	**Engage with individuals, families, group, organizations, and communities**
	a Apply knowledge of human behavior and the social environment, person-in-environment, and other multidisciplinary theoretical frameworks to engage with clients and constituencies
	b Use empathy, reflection, and interpersonal skills to effectively engage diverse clients and constituencies
Competency 7	**Assess individuals, families, groups, organizations, and communities**
	a Collect, organize, and apply critical thinking to interpret information from clients and constituencies
	b Apply knowledge of human behavior and the social environment, person-in-environment, and other multidisciplinary theoretical frameworks in the analysis of assessment data from clients and constituencies
	c Develop mutually agreed-on intervention goals and objectives based on the critical assessment of strengths, needs, and challenges within clients and constituencies
	d Select appropriate intervention strategies based on the assessment, research knowledge, and values and preferences of clients and constituencies
Competency 8	**Intervene with individuals, families, groups, organizations, and communities**
	a Critically choose and implement interventions to achieve practice goals and enhance capacities of clients and constituencies
	b Apply knowledge of human behavior and the social environment, person-in-environment, and other multidisciplinary theoretical frameworks in interventions with clients and constituencies
	c Use inter-professional collaboration as appropriate to achieve beneficial practice outcomes
	d Negotiate, mediate, and advocate with and on behalf of clients and constituencies
	e Facilitate effective transitions and endings that advance mutually agreed-on goals
Competency 9	**Evaluate practice with individuals, families, groups, organizations, and communities**
	a Select and use appropriate methods for evaluation of outcomes
	b Apply knowledge of human behavior and the social environment, person-in-environment, and other multidisciplinary theoretical frameworks in the evaluation of outcomes
	c Critically analyze, monitor, and evaluate intervention and program processes and outcomes
	d Apply evaluation findings to improve practice effectiveness at micro, mezzo, and macro levels

Note. Council on Social work Education (2015).

Enhancing Our Professional Purpose and Well-Being

The overarching professional role of social work can be understood by examining the statements of its professional purpose: to promote human and community well-being. Both major social work organizations, the National Association of Social Workers (NASW) and CSWE, have a similar definition of the purpose of social work. NASW has espoused a historical interest in individual and community well-being and the empowerment of vulnerable, poor, and oppressed populations, whereas CSWE has had a similar focus on human and societal well-being.

> ➤ *Social work's mission is to enhance human well-being and help meet the basic human needs of all people, with particular attention to the needs and empowerment of people who are vulnerable, oppressed, and living in poverty. A historic and defining feature of social work is the profession's focus on individual well-being in a social context and the well-being of society. Fundamental to social work is attention to the environmental forces that create, contribute to, and address problems in living. (NASW 2008, 1)*
>
> ➤ *The purpose of the social work profession is to promote human and community well-being. . . . [Moreover], social work's purpose is actualized through its quest for social and economic justice, the prevention of conditions that limit human rights, the elimination of poverty, and the enhancement of the quality of life for all persons. (CSWE 2015a, 1)*

Improving Human and Community Well-Being

It is not surprising that the purpose of social work corresponds with social workers' primary practice goals: That is, the social work helping process usually begins when factors in the client (system) interfere with health and well-being, necessitating professional help. This suggests that one of the social worker's first considerations is learning what can be done to enhance client and constituency functioning. What are the client's psychosocial needs? Does the client require basic life necessities (Sheafor and Horejsi 2012)?

Improving Societal Conditions

Achieving the professional purpose of improving societal conditions requires that the social worker take action to guarantee that people have "human rights such as freedom, safety, privacy, an adequate standard of living, health care, and education" (CSWE 2015a, 5). Social workers are also expected to attend to social, economic, and environmental justice issues—that is, circumstances that limit human rights, contribute to poverty, or diminish people's quality of life. Principles of fairness and equity oblige social workers to try and bring about a society in which each individual has equal access to resources and opportunities.

Ways in which the social worker can carry out these ideal purposes—for both individuals and society—are embedded in theories and concepts throughout the *Handbook*.

Applying *Abraham Maslow's Hierarchy of Needs*. Another way of thinking about improving well-being is through Abraham Maslow's (1970) hierarchy of needs. A humanist who was interested in people reaching their full potential, Maslow proposed a priority of human needs: (a) *physical and life-sustaining needs,* such

Figure 1.1.
Maslow's hierarchy of needs. (From Huitt 2007).

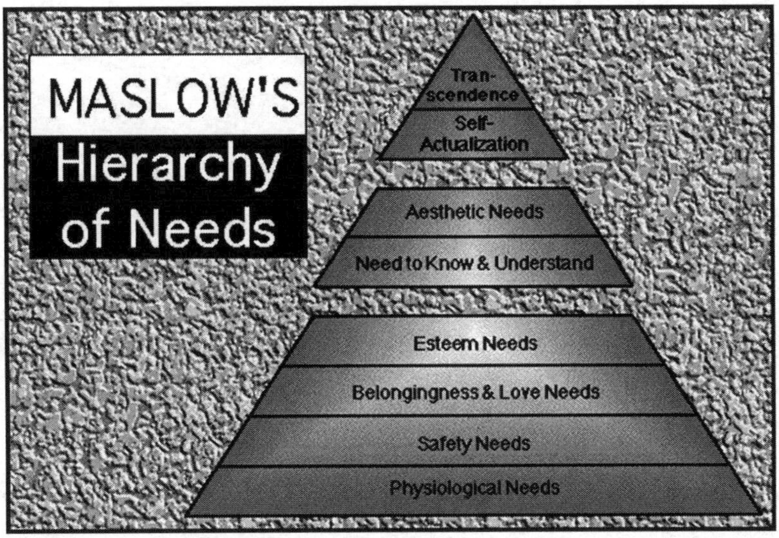

as the need for food, water, and shelter; (b) *physical safety,* including the need for protection from physical attack, bodily harm, and disease; (c) *love,* involving the need to be cherished and supported; (d) *self-esteem,* including the need for family members to have a sense of personal worth; and (e) *self-actualization,* or the need to be creative and productive (Figure 1.1). His humanistic philosophy and values are infused into most social work practice approaches.

Applying a *strengths and resiliency perspective.* In the following chapters, you will see that theories differ in their perspective on what constitutes and how to achieve well-being. However, generally speaking, social workers "recognize, support, and build on the strengths and resiliency of all human beings" (CSWE 2015a, 10). According to Saleebey (1993), the strengths-based approach is not a model, paradigm, or theory. Rather, it is a set of principles, ideas, and techniques that represents a shift in the professional social work role that emphasizes the resourcefulness of clients. Building on client attributes enhances social functioning, calling the social worker's attention to personal and community resilience (Table 1.2; see also Chapter 10 for a discussion of resilience).

Theory-Informed Social Work Practice with Individuals, Families, Groups, Communities, Organizations, and Societies

Chapters throughout the *Handbook* present multitheoretical content to guide engagement, assessment, and intervention with individuals and systems of all sizes—families, groups, communities, organizations, and societies. Some of the practice questions that may be answered in the *Handbook* include the following:

- My client is hoping to be understood. What are the right questions to ask?
- What will happen in the first meeting?
- What ideas does the client have about what would make things better?

Table 1.2.
To what extent do I assess client strengths?

Using a Likert scale, answer the following questions about your approach to social work practice. When I meet with a client, I . . .

1. Give preeminence to client's understanding of events

Low 1	2	3	4	5 High

2. Believe the client

Low 1	2	3	4	5 High

3. Discover what the client needs

Low 1	2	3	4	5 High

4. Move the assessment toward person–environment strengths

Low 1	2	3	4	5 High

5. Make the assessment of strengths multidimensional

Low 1	2	3	4	5 High

6. Use the assessment to discover uniqueness

Low 1	2	3	4	5 High

7. Use language the client can understand

Low 1	2	3	4	5 High

8. Make assessment a joint activity between social worker and client

Low 1	2	3	4	5 High

9. Reach a mutual agreement on the assessment and intervention plan

Low 1	2	3	4	5 High

10. Avoid blame and blaming

Low 1	2	3	4	5 High

11. Assess, not diagnose

Low 1	2	3	4	5 High

Note. Adapted from Cowger (1994).

- Will I, as a social worker, be a good listener?
- Will I know in what ways I can be helpful?
- Will I have the ability to help the client—individual, family, organization, or community—clarify and assess the issues at hand?
- What will be the area of our mutually defined work and strategies for intervention?
- Will I be able to effectively advocate for and against policies affecting my clients and constituencies?
- Will I be able to practice in culturally sensitive ways at all system levels?
- Will I be able to understand and respond, in partnership with the client system, to contextual issues of social and economic justice, discrimination, and oppression that have a negative impact on achieving our mutually agreed upon outcomes?

Interviews: Clients

The makeup of the interview varies depending on the HBSE theory or paradigm chosen by the social worker. When you read practice textbooks that describe techniques for working with clients and constituencies, you will see that many traditional methods were originally derived from HBSE theory (Hepworth et al. 2010). For example, Carl Rogers (1957) suggested a classical approach to an effective interview in which the social worker affirms the client's worth and dignity and fosters client self-determination. In contrast, postmodern theorists such as White and Epston (1990) or Dean and Fenby (1989) have suggested that helping professionals and clients coauthor the meaning of life events (see Chapter 5).

Furthermore, Freudian or psychoanalytically based interview principles suggest that the social worker listen to client feelings, interpret hidden meanings, develop client insight, assess client behaviors and motivation, and maintain professional authority and control in the interview (Freud 1956; see Chapter 4). In each instance, the nature of the interview and of the questions the social worker asks will be different (Tomm 1994).

Interviews: Constituencies

Interviews at the group, organizational, and community level take still other forms (see Chapters 6 to 8). Attention is given to systemic needs and resources. Participation by various stakeholders is needed, as are methods of collecting information, such as focus groups, forums, or surveys.

Engagement with Individuals, Families, Groups, Organizations,
and Communities

As a social worker, you can prepare to engage clients and constituencies before you even meet them. Agencies and various practice settings, including schools, hospitals, and courts, have a professional culture and tend to serve a particular population or populations. The social worker must differentiate these factors to gain self-awareness.

In addition, the competencies and practice behaviors in Table 1.1 reveal several areas related to engagement that you should be ready to infuse into practice, including the following:

- What personal and societal factors may negatively impact client and constituency social functioning and quality of life?
- What ethical decision-making models are you ready to use to try and resolve ethical dilemmas that arise in practice?
- Have you engaged in self-reflection about the diverse clients and constituencies you may serve? Are you aware of clients you may have difficulty serving effectively?
- Will you recognize and work to eliminate social, economic, and environmental abuses that occur in your practice area?

- Have you read and critically analyzed journal articles on your client population? Have you sought out master practitioners?
- What health and social welfare policies would help or hinder the well-being of your clients and constituencies?

Carl Rogers's Core Conditions and the Relationship

The client–social worker relationship may also vary by choice of theory. Client engagement has historically been based on the formation of the client–social worker relationship. Human behavior theorist Carl Rogers proposed that the relationship is facilitated through three core conditions: (a) *warmth,* or acceptance of the client; (b) *empathy,* or acceptance of the client's feelings and experiences as if they were one's own; and (c) *genuineness,* or authenticity (Rogers 1957, 1961).

More than forty years of outcomes research have confirmed that Rogers' core conditions make a major contribution to client improvement. This research suggests that the helping process is a form of healing, with the core conditions necessary to any type of successful intervention (Hubble, Duncan, and Miller 1999; Lambert 1992).

Constituency Relationships

Building trust with constituencies at meso- and macrolevels of practice necessitates the social worker being able to connect with the community and the community members being ready to form a collaborative among themselves. The process of community building also requires that the social worker pay attention to power and ethnic dynamics (Bayne-Smith, Garcia, and Mizrahi 2009; see Chapter 3).

Assessment with Individuals, Families, Groups, Organizations, and Communities

The CSWE EPAS suggest that assessment requires the social worker to "collect and organize data, and apply critical thinking to interpret information from clients and constituencies" (CSWE 2015a, 7). Regardless of whether a problem originates with an individual, family, or group, the purpose of an assessment is to bring together the various facets of the client's situation, and the interaction among them, in an orderly, economical manner and then to select salient and effective interventions (Greene 2008).

Meyer (1982) first called for the need for a set of human behavior assumptions as a system for collecting data and a means of making decisions in practice. She wisely suggested that "what one is trained to see one addresses in assessment and intervention" (pp. 19–20). This viewpoint enables the "social worker to develop mutually agreed-on intervention goals and objectives based on the critical assessment of strengths, needs, and challenges within client and constituencies" (CSWE 2015a, 7). Community-level assessment also requires an agreement about which social, economic, and political factors can facilitate sustainable community change (see Chapters 8 and 9).

Intervention with Individuals, Families, Groups, Organizations, and Communities

Assessment and intervention are not separate phases of the helping process. It may be said that intervention in the way of self-healing begins when the client or constituency asks for help.

According to Shulman (2005), the social work helping process includes increasing people's problem-solving and coping capacities, obtaining resources and services, facilitating interaction among individuals and their environments, improving interpersonal relationships, and influencing social institutions and organizations. You will see in the following chapters that each HBSE theory assumes that social workers will engage in different interventions relevant to the individual or social system involved. Therefore, practitioners will want to know the relative adaptiveness of their respective constituencies.

Because most human circumstances are complex, practitioners might need to use more than one theory to achieve their intervention plan. This is known as an *eclectic orientation* or sometimes a *transtheoretical process*. In addition, whenever possible, social workers are required to implement evidence-informed interventions to achieve client goals. Furthermore, social workers recognize that a beneficial practice outcome may require collaboration with professionals from other disciplines.

Additional Competencies in Social Work Practice

Although this handbook emphasizes the valuable link between HBSE theories and practice, it is necessary to critique the interrelationships between other EPAS curriculum standards and how they inform and are infused into practice (CSWE 2015a). Five other curriculum areas encompassed in competent practice are infused into later chapters: The ability to (a) demonstrate ethical and professional behavior; (b) engage diversity and difference in practice; (c) advance human rights and social, economic, and environmental justice; (d) engage in practice-informed research and research-informed practice; and (e) engage in policy practice.

Demonstrate Ethical and Professional Behavior

Ethical dilemmas invariably arise in social work practice, such as how to balance an older adult's right to self-determination with his or her safety. The increasing use of technology in social work practice can also present ethical dilemmas. Social workers who are on agency committees that try to resolve these dilemmas should be familiar with ethical decision-making models. Engaging in social work supervision is another positive way to go about resolving such issues and understanding the client–social worker relationship.

Social work organizational mandates. Social work professionals may turn to the two major social work organizations, CSWE and NASW, to learn about ethical issues. As previously mentioned, CSWE values human rights; social, economic, and environmental justice; and diversity. It is also committed to a strengths/resilience perspective, evidence-based practice, and equal access to social services.

In addition to abiding by relevant laws and regulations, social workers can turn to the NASW *Code of Ethics* for help in resolving practice dilemmas (Table 1.3).

Table 1.3.
National Association of Social Workers *code of ethics* **preamble**

The primary mission of the social work profession is to enhance human well-being and help meet the basic human needs of all people, with particular attention to the needs and empowerment of people who are vulnerable, oppressed, and living in poverty. A historic and defining feature of social work is the profession's focus on individual well-being in a social context and the well-being of society. Fundamental to social work is attention to the environmental forces that create, contribute to, and address problems in living.

Social workers promote social justice and social change with and on behalf of clients. "Clients" is used inclusively to refer to individuals, families, groups, organizations, and communities. Social workers are sensitive to cultural and ethnic diversity and strive to end discrimination, oppression, poverty, and other forms of social injustice. These activities may be in the form of direct practice, community organizing, supervision, consultation administration, advocacy, social and political action, policy development and implementation, education, and research and evaluation. Social workers seek to enhance the capacity of people to address their own needs. Social workers also seek to promote the responsiveness of organizations, communities, and other social institutions to individuals' needs and social problems.

The mission of the social work profession is rooted in a set of core values. These core values, embraced by social workers throughout the profession's history, are the foundation of social work's unique purpose and perspective:

- service
- social justice
- dignity and worth of the person
- importance of human relationships
- integrity
- competence

This constellation of core values reflects what is unique to the social work profession. Core values, and the principles that flow from them, must be balanced within the context and complexity of the human experience.

Note. From National Association of Social Workers (2008, 1).

The Preamble to the *Code of Ethics* states that the core historical values embraced by social workers are service, social justice, the dignity and worth of the person, the importance of human relationships, integrity, and competence (NASW 2008, 1). The NASW *Code of Ethics* also includes a brief guide for dealing with ethical issues or dilemmas in social work practice as well as specific ethical standards to guide social workers' conduct and to provide a basis for adjudication (NASW 2008).

Ethical decision making can be made more difficult because HBSE theories are not necessarily neutral. Therefore, each theory selected for practice "involves a thinking paradigm or a process of asking questions continually about what the information we send and receive reflects about ourselves and other's views of the world" (Schriver 2012, 27). This idea is congruent with the EPAS requirement that students "use reflection and self-regulation to manage personal values and maintain professionalism" (CSWE 2015a, 4).

Engage Diversity and Difference in Practice

Intersectionality. Human diversity, another curriculum component, is a multidimensional concept that has evolved over time. It is now understood as the "intersectionality of multiple factors including, but not limited to, age, class, color, culture, disability and ability, ethnicity, gender, gender identity and expression, immigration status, political ideology, race, religion/spirituality, sex, sexual orientation, and tribal sovereign nation" (CSWE 2015a, 4). These various aspects of diversity and the cultural milieu in which people live influence their identity formation and shape how they express their difficulties in social functioning. Recognizing that a social worker's subjective experiences and emotional reactions may negatively impact his or her ability to effectively engage with diverse client systems, social workers may use self-regulation to counter this possibility (Table 1.4).

Knowledge, attitudes, and skills. Perhaps one of the major challenges facing the profession is to define the knowledge, attitudes, and skills necessary for effective culturally competent social work practice (Greene and Watkins 1998). In cross-cultural practice, social workers must assume that they can become more knowledgeable about a client's culture. Because clients are experts on their own experiences, the social worker needs to take a learning stance while gathering client information (CSWE 2015a; see Chapter 3).

Non-neutral theory. When you are evaluating HBSE theories, it is important to recognize that they may be culture bound. According to Schiele (1996), traditional Eurocentric theories dominate in social work practice. Schiele contended that Eurocentric theories of human behavior focus on concepts developed in Europe and mainstream America and "are implicitly oppressive," emphasizing mainstream cultural values (p. 286). In contrast, "Africentricity" (as spelled by Schiele) infuses the values of people of color—the collective nature of human identity, the spiritual/

Table 1.4.
Ethnic-sensitive inventory

In working with ethnic minority clients, I . . .

- realize that my own ethnic and class background may influence my effectiveness
- consider it an obligation to familiarize myself with their culture, history, and other ethnically related information
- clearly delineate agency functions
- am able to explain clearly the nature of the interview
- make an effort to ensure privacy and/or anonymity
- am sensitive to their fears of racism or prejudiced orientations
- am aware of the systematic sources (racism, poverty, and prejudice) of their problems
- can identify the links between systemic problems and individual concerns
- learn whether the issue(s) involved is (are) of an individual or a collective nature
- am able to engage them in identifying major progress that has already taken place
- am respectful of their definition of the problem to be solved
- am sensitive to treatment goals consonant with their culture
- am able to mobilize social and extend family networks
- am able at the termination phase to help them consider alternative sources of support

Note. Adapted from Ho (1991, 60–61).

faith component of people's lives, and the validity of emotions/effect in understanding life events.

Trader (1977) long ago suggested that practitioners use the following four criteria to evaluate theory for effective social work practice with oppressed minorities:

1. *Pathology–health balance:* Does the theory have a balance among well-being, strengths and illness, and deficits?
2. *Practitioner–client control balance:* Does the theory allow for shared control of the helping process?
3. *Personal–societal impact balance:* Does the theory take into account historical, political, and economic influences on behavior?
4. *Internal–external change balance:* Does the theory emphasize internal change in preference to societal change?

In addition, social workers should communicate to their clients that they understand that diversity and difference shape the clients' life experiences. Clients who have faced discrimination and oppression may have different power positions in society and limited access to resources. Community-based social workers and others may be leaders in combating these barriers through such methods as building alliances that foster human rights.

Advance Human Rights and Social, Economic, and Environmental Justice

Discrimination and oppression create structural barriers that limit human rights. However, "social workers [need to] understand that every person regardless of position in society has fundamental human rights such as freedom, safety, privacy, an adequate standard of living, health care, and education" (CSWE 2015, 6). For example, the 2010 NASW Delegate Assembly Action to support the Affordable Care Act was saved by the U.S. Supreme Court action on June 25, 2015 (King v. Burnell; www.cnn.com/2015/06/25.../supreme-court-ruling-obamacare/).

To eliminate oppressive structural barriers and to ensure that social goods and responsibilities are distributed equitably, social workers need to be familiar with and apply theories of social and economic justice and their policy implications. These theories discuss how resources should be allocated in society and what an individual may owe his or her society.

There are three major philosophies of social and economic justice:

1. The utilitarian view examines the relative benefits and harms or costs of various social policies and determines which provides the greatest good.
2. The libertarian perspective focuses on the natural distribution of goods within a society, suggesting that if left to their own devices (with less government), people will naturally have societal equity.
3. The egalitarian point of view suggests that because all people are born equal, they have the same basic rights, which are to be ensured by societal institutions.

It is important for social workers to reflect on their own political views so that they do not impose them on their clients (Table 1.5).

Table 1.5.
Utilitarian, libertarian, egalitarian, liberal, or conservative:
what definition best fits me?

---

1. I believe in a utilitarian approach to social justice, which suggests that we examine the relative benefits and harms or costs of social policy as well as which policy provides the greatest good.

   Low 1   2   3   4   5 High

2. I believe in a libertarian approach to social justice, which emphasizes that there is a natural distribution of goods in society and that governments should provide citizens with maximum freedom.

   Low 1   2   3   4   5 High

3. I believe in the egalitarian approach, which contends that all people are born equal and have the same basic rights to freedom, equal opportunity, access to goods and resources, and self-respect.

   Low 1   2   3   4   5 High

4. I would define myself as a liberal, or someone who believes in government advancing the public good and providing a safety net.

   Low 1   2   3   4   5 High

5. I would define myself as a neoliberal, or someone who has a more cautious view of government and is somewhat skeptical of universal entitlements.

   Low 1   2   3   4   5 High

6. I believe that government should invest in human capital or programs that invest in education, research, and job training.

   Low 1   2   3   4   5 High

7. I would like to see a self-reliant society in which there is no poverty and all people have what is required for survival.

   Low 1   2   3   4   5 High

8. I would describe myself as a classic conservative, or one who believes in economic, social, and political freedom, including the separation of church and state.

   Low 1   2   3   4   5 High

9. I would see myself as a neoconservative, or someone who would arrest the growth of government programs and give responsibility to the private sector.

   Low 1   2   3   4   5 High

10. I am a cultural conservative who believes that the state is often the cause of, not the solution to, social problems.

   Low 1   2   3   4   5 High

A global perspective. One can also take a global perspective on what constitutes human rights. In 1966, the Charter of the United Nations recognized the inherent dignity and equal and inalienable rights of all members of the human family, making social and economic justice a global consideration (CSWE 2008). Among the key articles of the charter are the right to work and receive fair wages, the right to live without discrimination, equal rights for men and women, freedom from hunger, access to facilities that promote health and education, and the conservation of local cultures (see Chapter 10).

Engage in Practice-Informed Research and Research-Informed Practice

Master practitioners. The EPAS encourage the use of knowledge based on scientific inquiry in social work practice (CSWE 2015a). Social workers should obtain evidence that informs practice—quantitative or qualitative—often from multidisciplinary sources. Evidence may also be garnered from master practitioners, suggesting that professional social work practice involves the interpretation of complex situations and reflection (Schon 1983, 1987). From this point of view, knowledge involves a process in which one learns from "lived experience" and from master practitioners, infusing this knowledge into his or her practice (Weick 1993, 11).

Evidence-based practice. CSWE (2015a) requires that social workers use and translate research findings to inform and improve practice, policy, and service delivery. CSWE has a section on its website called the "Teaching EBP Web Bibliography" to assist in this task (http://www.cswe.org/CentersInitiatives/CurriculumResources/TeachingEvidence-BasedPractice/TeachingEBPWebBibliography.aspx). The Web contains the following definition of evidence-based practice:

> Evidence-based practice (EBP) has been described as the "conscientious, explicit and judicious use of current best evidence in making decisions about the care of individual [clients]" (Sacket et al. 1996, 71). As stipulated by these same authors, this definition requires a process that is comprised of several steps for finding and employing appropriate interventions for every client, and also requires that the client's preferences and actions, as well as their clinical state and circumstances, be a part of the decision-making process. Specifically, the steps [the social worker takes] involve:
>
> 1. Formulating a client, community, or policy-related question;
> 2. Systematically searching the literature;
> 3. Appraising findings for quality and applicability;
> 4. Applying these findings and considerations in practice;
> 5. Evaluating the results (CSWE 2015b).

Practice evaluation. Another way in which social workers can be systematically accountable for their work is to evaluate their practice. Practice evaluation is "a process of determining if a given change effort was worthwhile" (Kirst-Ashman and Hull 2008, 311). At the microlevel, the social worker wants to know whether the intervention with the client had a successful outcome. Was it effective? At the mesolevel, the social worker wants to know whether the intervention met its purpose. At the macrolevel, the social worker asks whether the entire program has met its purpose. In short, the social worker wants to know whether his or her professional practice is effective (Rubin and Babbie 2013). Finally, it should be noted that social workers act as researchers in their practice activity, hoping to gain knowledge to improve client functioning.

Engage in Policy Practice

To understand the role of policy in service delivery, you must become familiar with your agency's policies even before you engage with the client. What local, state, and national laws and regulations affect your clients and constituencies?

To accomplish this task, you should understand the history and current structures of social policies and services and how they affect well-being.

Policy practice is a form of practice in its own right, just like community organization. Social workers who practice in the policy arena emphasize how social welfare and economic policies impact the delivery of and access to social services. Especially when working in such settings as legislative staff, they are also concerned with and analyze how a policy affects welfare; human rights; and social, economic, and environmental justice. In short, all social workers need to be aware of how policy impacts clients' daily lives.

In sum, when taken together, the nine competencies discussed in this chapter provide a foundation for "purposeful, intentional, and professional" social work practice (CSWE 2015a, 2). Knowledge of human behavior theory and the social environment (person and environment) is necessary for that work.

Glossary

Afrocentricity. A paradigm emphasizing African culture and the contribution of Africans to the development of Western civilization. The focus is on the human collective.

Carl Rogers. An American psychologist who was among the founders of a humanistic and client-centered approach to psychology. He is known for the core conditions of therapy.

Competency. A measurable successful behavior that is composed of knowledge, values, skills, and cognitive and subjective processes.

EPAS. The Educational Policy and Accreditation Standards, which intend to promote academic excellence by establishing thresholds for professional competence.

Eurocentric theory. A theory with a worldview centered on Western civilization.

Global perspective. A personal outlook that considers contexts from diverse and broader viewpoints.

NASW Code of Ethics. Guidelines for the everyday professional conduct of social workers.

Resilience. Markedly successful adaptation following an adverse event.

Social work competence. The ability to perform complex practice behaviors in the professional service of promoting human and community well-being.

Strengths-based approach. A social work practice approach that emphasizes people's self-determination and strengths.

References

Bayne-Smith, M., Garcia, M., and Mizrahi, T. 2009. "Comparative Perspectives on Interdisciplinary Collaboration from Academia and the Community." *Community Development* 39 (3): 1–15.

Council on Social Work Education. 2008. *Educational Policy and Accreditation Standards.* Washington, DC: Council on Social Work Education.

Council on Social Work Education. 2015a. *Educational Policy and Accreditation Standards*. Washington, DC: Council on Social Work Education.

Council on Social Work Education. 2015b. *Teaching Evidence-based Practice*. Retrieved from http:// www.cswe.org/CentersInitiatives/CurriculumResources/TeachingEvidence-BasedPractice.aspx.

Cowger, C. D. 1994. "Assessing Client Strengths: Clinical Assessment for Client Empowerment." *Social Work* 39 (3): 262–68.

Dean, R. G., and Fenby, B. L. 1989. "Exploring Epistemologies: Social Work Action as a Reflection of Philosophical Assumptions." *Journal of Social Work Education* 25:46–53.

Freud, S. 1956. "On Psychotherapy." In *Collected Papers*, edited by Hogarth, Vol. 1, pp. 256–68. London: Hogarth.

Greene, R. R. 2008. *Human Behavior and Social Work Practice*. New Brunswick, NJ: Aldine Transaction Press.

Greene, R. R., and Watkins, M. 1998. *Serving Diverse Constituencies: Applying the Ecological Perspective*. Hawthorne, NY: Aldine de Gruyter.

Hepworth, D. H., Rooney, R. H., Larsen, J., Rooney, G. D., and Strom-Gottfried, K. 2010. *Direct Social Work Practice: Theory and Skills*. 9th ed. Belmont, CA: Wadsworth.

Ho, M. K. 1991. "Use of Ethnic-Sensitive Inventory (ESI) to Enhance Practitioner Skills with Minorities." *Journal of Multicultural Social Work* 1(1): 57–68.

Hubble, M. A., Duncan, B. L., and Miller, S., eds. 1999. *The Heart and Soul of Change*. Washington, DC: American Psychological Association.

Huitt, W. 2007. *Maslow's Hierarchy of Needs*. Retrieved from http://www.edpsycinteractive.org/topics/ regsys/maslow.html.

Kirst-Ashman, K., and Hull, G. 2008. *Understanding Generalist Practice*. Independence, KY: Cengage Learning.

Lambert, M. J. 1992. "Implications of Outcome Research for Psychotherapy Integration." In *Handbook of Psychotherapy Integration*, edited by J. C. Norcross and M. R. Goldfried, 3–45. New York: Basic Books.

Maslow, A. H. 1970. *Toward a Psychology of Being*. New York: Longman.

Meyer, C. 1982. "Issues in Clinical Social Work: In Search of a Consensus." In *Treatment Formulations andCclinical Social Work*, edited by P. Caroff, 19–26. Silver Spring, MD: National Association of Social Workers.

National Association of Social Workers. 2008. *Code of Ethics*. Washington, DC: Author.

Rogers, C. R. 1957. "The Necessary and Sufficient Conditions of Therapeutic Personality Change." *Journal of Consulting Psychology* 21:95–103.

Rogers, C. R. 1961. *On Becoming a Person*. Boston, MA: Houghton Mifflin.

Rubin, A., and Babbie, E. R. 2013. *Research Methods for Social Work*. Monterey, CA: Brooks/Cole.

Sacket, D. L. January 13, 1996. "Evidence-based Medicine: What it Is and What it Isn't." *BMJ* 312 (7023): 71–72.

Saleebey, D. 1993. "Notes on Interpreting the Human Condition: A Constructed HBSE Curriculum." In *Revisioning Social Work Education: A Social Constructionist Approach*, edited by J. Laird, 197–217. New York: Haworth Press.

Schiele, J. H. 1996. "Afrocentricity: An Emerging Paradigm in Social Work Practice." *Social Work* 41 (3): 284–94.

Schon, D. 1983. *The Reflective Practitioner: How Professionals Think in Action*. London: Temple Smith.

Schon, D. 1987. *Educating the Reflective Practitioner*. San Francisco, CA: Jossey-Bass, 1987.

Schriver, J. M. 2015. *Human Behavior and the Social Environment: Shifting Paradigms in Essential Knowledge for Social Work Practice*. 6th ed. New York: Pearson.

Sheafor, B. W., and Horejsi, C. J. 2012. *Techniques and Guidelines for Social Work Practice*. 9th ed. Boston, MA: Allyn & Bacon.

Shulman, L. 2005. *The Skills of Helping Individuals, Families, Groups, and Communities*. New York: Wadsworth.

Tomm, K. 1994. "Interventive Interviewing: Part III. Intending to Ask Lineal, Circular, Strategic, or Reflexive Questions?" In *Constructivism and Family Therapy*, edited by K. Brownlee, P. Gallant, and D. Carpenter, 117–56. Thunder Bay, ON: Canada: Lakehead University.

Trader, H. 1977. "Survival Strategies for Oppressed Minorities." *Social Work* 22 (1): 10–13.

Weick, A. 1993. "Reconstructing Social Work Education." In *Revisioning Social Work Education: A Social Constructionist Approach*, edited by J. Laird, 11–30. New York: Haworth Press.

White, M., and Epston, D. 1990. *Narrative Means to Therapeutic Ends*. New York: Norton.

2

Human Behavior and the Social Environment: An Ecological Base

> ➤ This chapter discusses the ecological perspective—the unifying conceptual base of human behavior and the social environment (HBSE). Also known as the person–environment construct, its key assumptions and terms offer a means of applying HBSE theories differentially, depending on client system size, context, and needs throughout the processes of engagement, assessment, and intervention. Multilevel ethical concerns are described.

Human behavior and the social environment (HBSE) theory is primarily derived from social sciences that have evolved over sociohistorical time. Social workers have adopted theories deemed relevant to the profession's historical mission to both improve societal conditions and enhance social functioning of and between individuals, families, and groups. Because of this dual allegiance, there has been an inherent tension around whether change strategies should address the person, the environment, or both (Boehm 1958, 1959; Richmond 1917).

Because social work's knowledge base continues to be a "mosaic of methods and skills based upon many kinds of knowledge and guided by multiple theories" (Meyer 1987, 409), this chapter discusses how the *ecological perspective* serves as a unifying force. It also discusses how HBSE theory provides a knowledge base to explain the human condition and suggests ways to take action on behalf of client and constituencies (Bloom 1984). It is followed by Chapter 3, which presents additional conceptual frameworks for culturally sound social work practice. Taken together, these two chapters provide a foundation for a theory-based approach to client engagement, assessment, and intervention.

Professional Purpose and Well-Being

The ecological construct offers several avenues for achieving social work's professional purpose, including a means of conducting multilevel assessments, providing a comprehensive view of case situations, and choosing intervention strategies. Furthermore, practice from an ecological perspective addresses the development of individual well-being across the life course in juxtaposition with the collective functionality of social systems (see Chapter 10).

Defining Person and Environment

Person and environment, or the ecological perspective, is a blend of concepts that explain how people and their social systems mutually influence one another (Bertalanffy 1968; Buckley 1968). This focus directs the social worker's attention to the complicated network of forces that positively affect the individual in his or her natural setting and, at the same time, explores how individuals can positively influence social systems.

The Evolution of the Person and Environment Perspective

The person and environment view is dynamic and evolves depending on historical, social, economic, organizational, environmental, and global influences (Council on Social Work Education [CSWE] 2015). By reviewing this changing context, social workers can decide whether and how to modify their change strategies.

The Four Forces of Psychology

An example of the reformulation of microlevel theory and how it influences practice was provided by Cowley (1996). He categorized the evolution in psychological thought into four stages known as the *Four Forces of Psychology. (*These as well as other shifts in focus can be followed throughout the *Handbook.)*

The *First Force* was primarily based on a Freudian deterministic view of personality development. According to this point of view, the role of the practitioner was to assess psychopathology or mental distress. People were generally thought of as guilt ridden and repressed. Practitioners hoped to discover and modify the client's unconscious motives for socially unacceptable behaviors. The *Second Force* emphasized helping clients find relief from symptomatic, observable behavior. Social workers could collect evidence of client progress, with the outcome of interventions being paramount. As described in Chapter 5, cognitive treatments stressed practitioner and client accountability.

The *Third Force,* which is addressed later, gave attention to a client's search for self-fulfillment and self-actualization. It encompassed *humanistic theory* (including the human innate potential for love, creativity, and spirituality) and *existential theory* (encompassing the search for meaning in a seemingly meaningless world), thereby extending psychological thought to humanistic, less observable, and measurable subjects (Maslow 1959; Yalom 1980; Yalom and Leszez 1995; see Chapter 7).

In the *Fourth Force* theorists and clinicians extended their models to transpersonal and spiritual concerns. There was an interest in how technology and its ability to provide global connections and multiple perspectives impacted people's ability to relate to one another. The aim of treatment was to reconnect the seemingly autonomous self with a "completion or fulfillment of self in communion with others"

(Robbins, Chatterjee, and Canda 2006, 389); thus, building on earlier humanistic ideas of how people can achieve peak experiences or *self-actualize.*

Community Building

Just as microlevel practice has expanded, changing with sociohistorical conditions, so has practice in the community. Although community building is accomplished through the collaborative efforts of professionals from a variety of fields, social workers also join in these efforts to improve the standard of living for disadvantaged populations (Mondros and Staples 2008). This method of practice that promotes well-being is "designed to eliminate oppressive structural barriers to ensure that social goods, rights, and responsibilities are distributed equitably and that civil, political, environmental, economic, social, and cultural human rights are protected" (CSWE 2015, 5).

> ➤ *Well-being as positive person and environment fit.*

Well-Being and Person–Environment Fit

As seen here, well-being from the ecological perspective is defined as goodness of fit. *Goodness of fit* is the "extent to which there is a match between an individual's adaptive needs and the qualities of his or her environment over time" (Greene 2008, 215). The ecological approach suggests that the attainment of personal well-being is a lifelong process of positive person and environment exchanges. However, stress can occur when environmental demands are greater than a client's or constituency's resources or social supports (Lazarus and Folkman 1984).

Social systems can also be disrupted by the stress of everyday demands. In both instances, the overarching goal of intervention is to increase coping/adaptive skills and help clients and constituencies solve problems of living. (Chapters 5 and 10 describe how social workers foster a system's naturally ability to adapt.)

The Ecological Perspective: Applying Terms and Assumptions in Social Work Practice

The ecological perspective's multifaceted theory base draws on many disciplines, such as psychology, sociology, and economics. Theories range from Darwinian theory (2009) to role theory (Table 2.1). In addition, the perspective is often paired with systems theory. Both share a focus on person–environment exchanges, the need to see the whole picture, different levels of systems, and stress and balance within and between systems. Ecological assumptions emphasize people's ability to negotiate their environment and become increasingly competent (White 1959; Table 2.2). In contrast, systems assumptions explain people's connectedness to others (Garbarino 1983) and how systems *adapt* or change, become more complex, and maintain a steady state (Greene 2008). (Adaptation and how systems respond to the demands of the environment are discussed in detail in Chapter 10.)

Table 2.1.
Selected theoretical foundations of the ecological perspective

Time adopted	Major theorist(s)	Theme	Concepts for practice
1829	Darwin: Evolutionary theory	There is an ongoing match between organisms and their environment.	Goodness of fit
1959	Boehm: Curriculum and social work's purpose	Curriculum defines social work's domain and boundaries.	Person-in-environment
1917	Richmond: Social diagnosis	Social functioning involves improving socioeconomic conditions through personal adjustment.	Social functioning and basic needs
1984	Lazarus and Folkman: Positive nature of coping	Coping with the biopsychosocial aspects of environmental stress is innate but can be disrupted.	Meaning ascribed to stress
1959	Maslow: Humanism	There is a hierarchy of human needs. The helping process can be growth inducing.	Nurturing environments
1959	White: Personal competence	Competence is a person's ability to interact effectively with the environment.	Competence
1995	Goldstein: Ego psychology	Ego functioning is improved through attention to both intrapsychic issues and environmental factors.	Ego functioning
1968	Bertalanffy: General systems theory	People form relationships through active transactions with social systems.	Life course relatedness
1968	Buckley: Human systems	Systems that are disrupted by stress attempt to regain balance; they are adaptive in their own right.	Homeostasis, equilibrium
1979	Bronfenbrenner: Multisystemic development	People develop in an ecological environment, a set of ever-widening nested structures.	Micro-, meso-, exo-, and macrosystem interventions
1980	Germain and Gitterman: Problems in living	The ecological social work approach helps people mitigate problems in living.	Life space interventions
1983	Garbarino: Social supports	Day-to-day social networks support well-being.	Connectedness

Table 2.2.
Basic assumptions of the ecological perspective

- The capacity to interact with the environment and to relate to people is innate.
- Person and environment form a unitary system in which humans and the environment mutually influence each other (forming a reciprocal relationship).
- Goodness of fit is a reciprocal person–environment process achieved through transactions between an adaptive individual and his or her nurturing environment.
- People are goal directed and purposeful. Humans strive for competence. Individuals' subjective meaning of the environment is key to their development.
- People need to be understood in their natural environments and settings.
- Positive change can result from life experiences.
- Problems of living need to be understood within the totality of life space.
- To assist clients, the social worker should be prepared to intervene anywhere in the client's life space.

Defining the Ecological Perspective

The *ecological perspective* is a "scientific study of the progressive, mutual accommodation, throughout the life course between an active, growing human being and his or her environment" (Bronfenbrenner 1979, 188). The emphasis is on the person–environment as a unitary system in which humans and environments reciprocally shape each other. Throughout the helping process, the social worker can observe that a change in a person or a change in his or her environment brings about change within the person–environment unit. This principle of mutual influence is referred to as *reciprocal causality*. The use of the ecological metaphor can hopefully help the social worker avoid "dichotomizing person and situation and direct attention to the transactions between them" (Germain 1979, 326).

Defining Theory

As already emphasized, HBSE content provides knowledge for social work practice, including client engagement, assessment, and intervention (Schriver 2014; Zastrow and Kirst-Ahman 2009). However, there is no consensus about how to define theory. For example, Newman and Newman (2005) defined theory as a logical system of concepts that offer a framework for organizing and understanding observations. In contrast, Saleebey (1993), coming from a postmodern perspective, contended that theories are not truths. Rather, they are perspectives, texts, narratives, or interpretive devices.

Transtheoretical Approaches

The ecological perspective, or person–environment construct, is used as an overarching framework in conjunction with other theories to shape social work practice. For example, ego psychology may be paired with the person–environment construct as part of the clinical social work *armamentarium,* or the collection of techniques available to the practitioner (Goldstein 1995).

In short, no single theoretical framework can be chosen to achieve social work's professional purpose to promote both individual and community well-being. However, unity of purpose can be strived for by adopting the person-in-environment construct as a guide or conceptual reference point (CSWE 2015; Greene 2005; Greene and Watkins 1998).

Choosing a Theory

Another question under debate among social work theorists is what constitutes the best theoretical approach to apply in practice. However, by their very nature, theories are selective about the factors they emphasize and those they ignore (Laird 1993; Turner 1995). Among the differences between theories is how their assumptions address well-being; the impact of historical, political, and economic influences on behavior; and the balance between internal and external change. Should social workers try to help individuals change, or should practitioners attempt to improve societal conditions or the environment? Or can they do both?

Although this debate continues, by selecting a theory that fits under the umbrella of the person-in-environment context, the social worker may obtain a more comprehensive view of the client's circumstances and can better deal with the complexity of life concerns at play (Mattaini and Meyer 1988).

Compton, Gallaway, and Cournoyer (2005) suggested that theories be selected using six criteria:

1. Select theory that is supported by empirical testing.
2. Use theory that has been proven effective.
3. Choose theory that is less abstract and given to interventions.
4. Pick theory that is congruent with social work values.
5. Choose theory that is applicable to diverse constituencies (see Chapter 3).
6. Critique theory for its historical and person-in-environment context.

> ➤ Engagement can occur with individuals, families, groups, organizations, or communities depending on the presenting difficulties and the social worker's professional judgment.

Engage With Individuals, Families, Groups, Organizations, and Communities

From an ecological perspective, the mutually agreed-on work—whether with individuals, families, groups, organizations, or communities—emphasizes human relationships and the connections between all aspects of the *ecological space.* This means that the social worker must obtain the *whole picture* or an understanding of the individuals and social systems involved in the presenting difficulty. From this point of view, the social worker is contemplating how he or she will approach the client even before the helping process begins.

> ➤ Assessment content addressed is multilevel.

Assess Individuals, Families, Groups, Organizations, and Communities

Person–Environment Multilevel Assessment

The social worker who uses the ecological perspective in assessment asks whether there is *goodness of fit* between a person and the environment and, if not, how this fit can be improved. This requires using multilevel assessment "to collect and organize data, and apply critical thinking to interpret information from clients and constituencies" to sort out the primary concern (CSWE 2015, 7).

With what systems do people interact? How do people interact within systems? Systemic thinking is at the heart of the ecosystems perspective. This mindset allows the practitioner to identify the interconnections present in a case and to conceive of interventions. In sum, when working with an ecological perspective, the social worker will follow the principle of exploring and critically analyzing the totality of a client's life space.

Figure 2.1.
An ecological model of human development. (From Bronfenbrenner 1979).

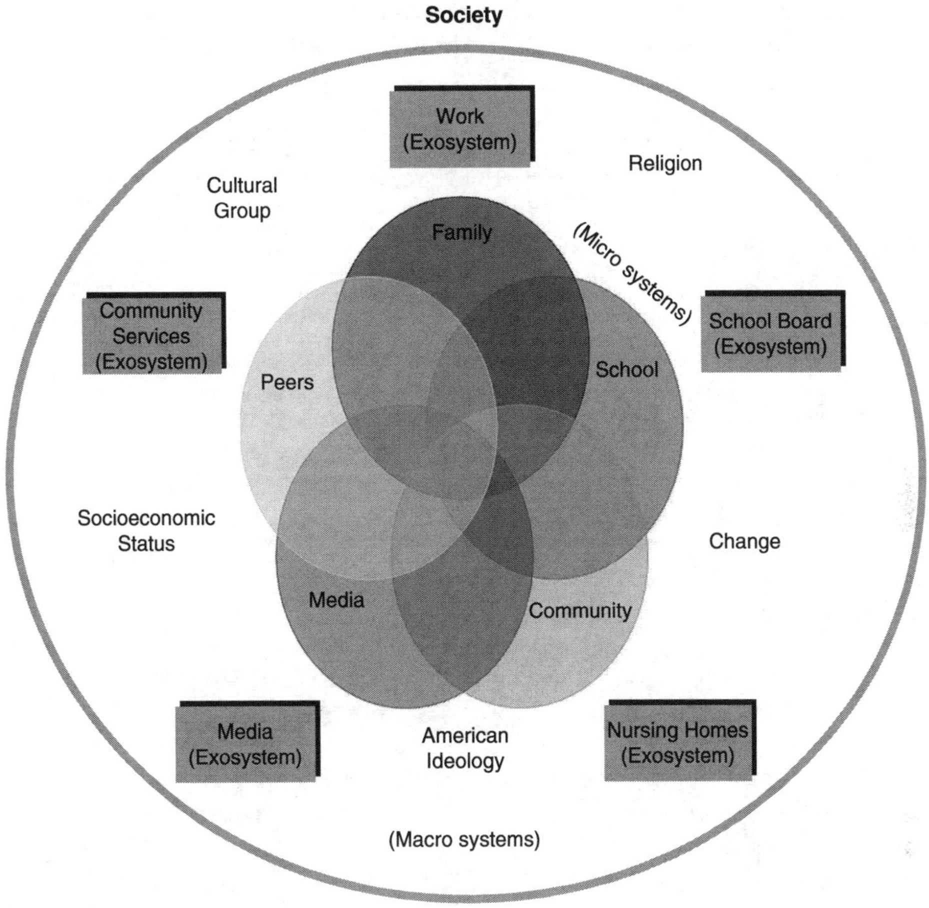

Society

Principles and Schema

Although the ecological perceptive does not offer the social worker specific techniques, it does provide principles and schema to guide critical thinking, reflection, and self-regulation (CSWE 2015). These schemas can be used by the social worker to bring together the totality of coexisting facts that otherwise might be viewed independently. This understanding involves the practitioner having a mental picture of person-in-environment, such as Bronfenbrenner's (1979) ecological model of human development (Figure 2.1). This image is a series of concentric circles that depict the social systems in which people live, any of which may be the source of client stress, including

- *microsystems,* made up of interpersonal face-to-face relationships, such as families and small groups;
- *mesosystems,* composed of the interaction between two microsystem environments, such as the connection between a child's home and Girl Scout troop;

- *exosystems,* related to the environment in which a developing individual is not directly involved and that is external to his or her experience but nonetheless affects him or her, such as a parent's workplace; and
- *macrosystems,* associated with the broader social context, such as cultural values, media, and legislation.

> ➤ *Assessment content addresses sources of stress.*

To understand the source(s) of client stress, the social worker can also use Carter and McGoldrick's (1999) (2011 throughout) flow of stress schema (Table 2.3 and Figure 2.2). Figure 2.2 tracks time on the horizontal axis and social systems of various sizes on the vertical axis. Horizontal stressors on the schema include

- *developmental events,* such as life cycle transitions and migration;
- *unpredictable events,* such as the untimely death of a friend or family member, chronic illness, accident, and unemployment; and
- *historical events,* such as war, economic depression, political climate, and natural disasters.

Vertical stressors illustrated include

- racism, sexism, classism, ageism, consumerism, and poverty;
- the disappearance of community, more work, less leisure, the inflexibility of the workplace, and no time for friends;
- family emotional patterns, myths, triangles, secrets, legacies, and losses;
- violence, addictions, ignorance, depression, and lack of spiritual expression or dreams; and
- genetic makeup, abilities, and disabilities. (Carter and McGoldrick 1999, 6)

> ➤ *Assessment content addresses family and other social systems connections.*

Table 2.3.
The ecological perspective and stress

1. Stress is brought about when people believe they have inadequate internal and external resources to meet environmental demands.
2. When people perceive stress, they try to adapt.
3. Stress can be reduced by improving the level of person–environment fit; this involves a change in people's behaviors, perceptions, and environmental responses.
4. Social systems also play an important role in enhancing person–environment fit.
5. The practitioner can help clients manage stressors by reinforcing their natural problem-solving skills, optimism, and resilience.

Note. From Greene (2007).

Figure 2.2.
The flow of stress through the family. (From Carter and McGoldrick 1999).

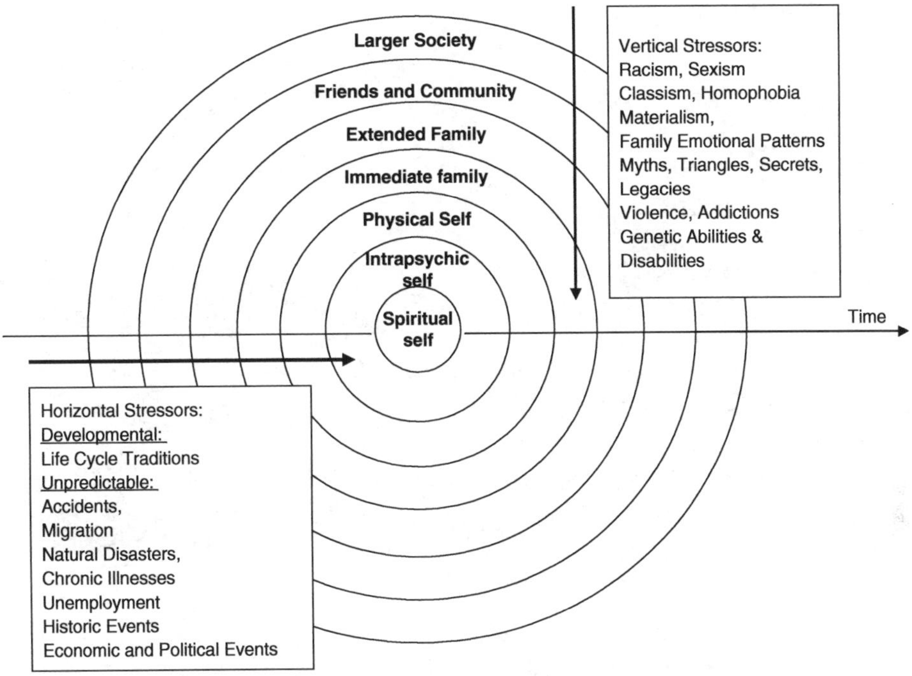

Another graphic device to illustrate connected case elements is an *Ecomap,* or a depiction of a family over time (Hartman 1978; see Chapter 6). Mattaini and Meyer (1988) suggested that by placing case elements within a boundary, the practitioner can further clarify the focus of mutual work (Figure 2.3). In this way, the practitioner is able to delineate the *focal system,* or the system that will receive primary attention (Longres 2000). Practitioners should make this decision with clients based on their mutual perception of the major source(s) of stress (CSWE 2015; see Table 2.4). In short, the social worker should be prepared to direct his or her assessment to stress-related problems in living that can occur anywhere in the person-in-environment constellation.

> ➤ Julia is a thirteen-year-old girl in middle school. She lives with her mother Charlotte and younger brother Alex in a neighborhood that is prone to violence. Drug dealers live in her rundown housing complex. Charlotte does not let her children play outside in the neighborhood and expects Julia and Alex to be home before dark. Although their apartment is threadbare, Charlotte gives each child a chore and keeps their home clean when she comes home

(Continued)

from work. Charlotte is also active with the school's parent–teacher association.

➤ Julia was an A student until she began middle school. She then became withdrawn. Her grades went down and, according to one of her teachers, she seemed to disappear in the back of the room. The teacher decided to talk to the school social worker about what could be done.

➤ *If you were the social worker, with whom would you talk about the various source(s) of stress in Julia's life? How would you delineate the focal system? Are you most interested in Julia's mental state? Have you considered institutional, legal, health, educational, social, media, and technological resources? Are you less likely to include organizational and programmatic structures in your assessment or to explore the large-scale or macrosystem societal context?*

Figure 2.3.
An ecomap. Adapted from Mattaini and Meyer 1988.

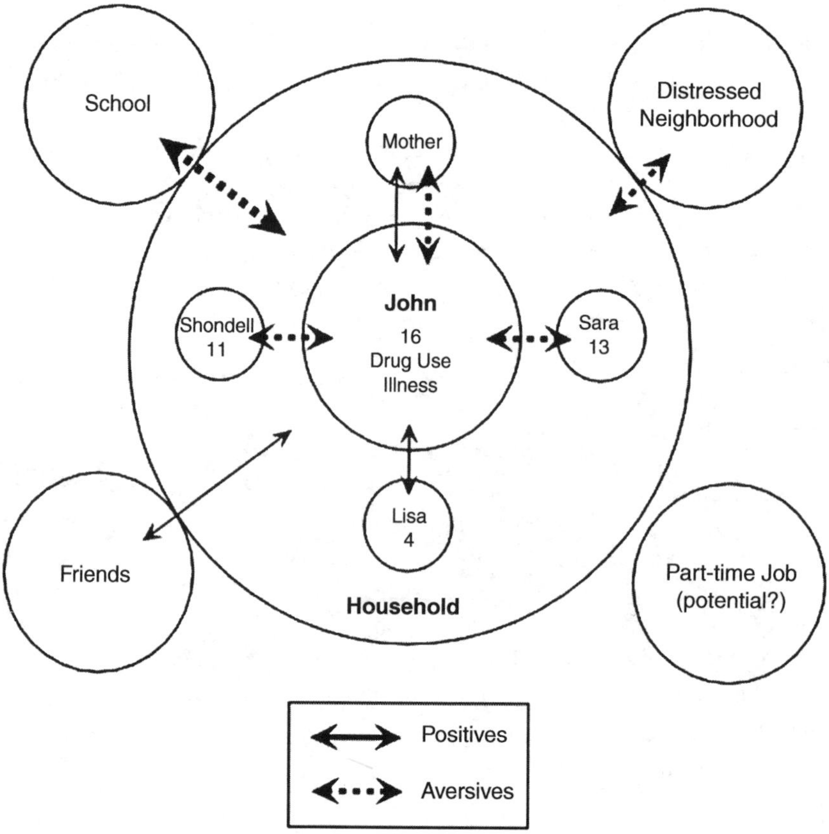

Table 2.4.
Principles of an ecological assessment

- Assessment requires the identification of a focal system to receive primary attention—the person, housing complex, or neighborhood.
- Practitioners need to comprehend clients' stress levels and ability to cope with stress and the imbalance between demands and the use of resources.
- Social workers need to assess client efficacy or confidence to act on the environment.
- Assessment encompasses how clients engage with people and their natural environment (i.e., the extent and quality of their relationships, and social and emotional ties).
- Key to the assessment process is determining the goodness of fit between the client and surrounding social systems.
- Assessment at the macrolevel should explore the large-scale societal context and how the client is affected by legal regulations or policies.

Note. Adapted from Greene and Barnes (1998).

Figure 2.4.
A timeline. (From Frank, Kurland, and Goldman, 1978.)

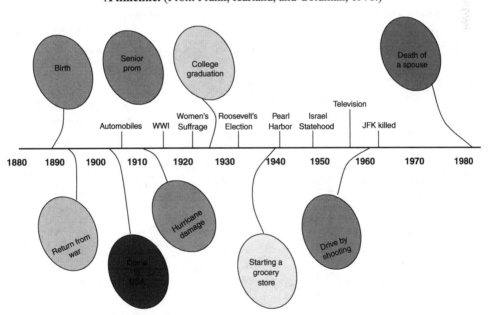

Person–Environment Life Course

In addition to a multisystem review, an ecologically based assessment may include an exploration of a person's or family's *life course,* or the timing of life events across the life span (Elder 1998; Hareven 1996). This helps the social worker learn about clients' or constituencies' development as well as the changing social conditions that surround them. The life course is best "understood within the context of physical, emotional, familial, organizational, political, historical, and economic factors" (Greene 2008, 210). The social worker can gain this information by asking clients and constituencies to tell a narrative or story about the most important events that occurred during their lifetime, as portrayed in Figure 2.4. This is in contrast to many life span developmental theories (see Chapter 40).

Even when working with an individual, the practitioner needs as much person-in-environment information as possible in the assessment. In this way, the social worker can come to an understanding of the client's *competence,* or ability to act on the environment. When working with families, groups, and larger-scale systems, their functional capacity and collective contribution to one another is of interest. Whether one is working with an individual, family, group, organization, or community, the next skill in the practice process is to "select appropriate intervention strategies based on the assessment, research knowledge, and values and preferences of clients and constituencies" (CSWE 2015, 7).

Intervene With Individuals, Families, Groups, Organizations, and Communities

It can be said that "all social work method is grounded in a common paradigm—to intervene effectively in the person-in-environment configuration" (Bartlett 1970, 23). Some social workers have historically referred to themselves by their area of practice, such as group worker or community planner. We will see throughout the *Handbook* that various theories are compatible with and rooted in the ecological perspective. They may be seen as extensions of the principle to provide intervention at specific systems levels. For example, family-centered social work emphasizes the "family–environment interface" (Hartman and Laird 1987, 582), social group work practice focuses on an interactionist approach to group and individual change (Schwartz 1977), whereas practice at the community level is concerned with structural problems and how to achieve collective or community efficacy (Sampson, Raudenbush, and Earls 1997).

When paying attention to community-level processes, social workers are drawn to

- *natural capital,* encompassing natural resources (e.g., water, energy);
- *ecosystem services,* dealing with human-made resources (e.g., water filtration, fisheries); and
- *human and social capital,* including the skills, abilities, and resources of people (e.g., carpentry).

These multilevel interventions offer the practitioner a choice of multiple service modalities and their social connections (e.g., families, neighbors, businesses, and organizations; Gamble and Weil 2010; Kropf and Jones 2014).

Multilevel Ethical Concerns

At the same time, ethical concerns can arise during intervention. The ecological perspective offers a means of visualizing ethical dilemmas at multiple system levels (Greene 1989; Figure 2.5). The schema allows the social worker to contemplate and hopefully resolve multiple layers of influence on ethical decision making from the client–worker encounter to the societal context. Therefore, as "social workers, (we) practice with an understanding of "the value base of the profession and its ethical standards, as well as relevant laws and regulations that may impact practice at the micro-, mezzo-, and macrolevels" (CSWE 2015, 3).

Figure 2.5.
Multiple-layers of influences on ethical decision making.
Adapted from Greene 1988.

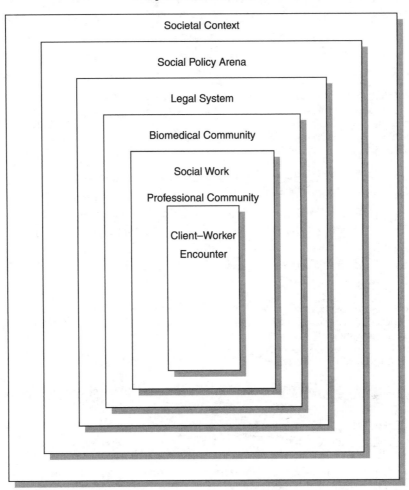

Prevention of Selection Bias

In 1987, Germain and Gitterman underscored the point that the social worker should be competent enough to use theory to intervene in any part of the person–group–environment gestalt. This idea was underscored in the 2015 CSWE Educational Policy and Accreditation Standards which requires social workers to use the person–environment construct as a lens for practice with individuals, families, groups, organizations, and communities (p. 1).

> ➤ *Choose change strategies from a wide range of alternatives that could improve person and environment fit.*

According to Germain and Gitterman (1996), intervention from an ecological perspective draws on an extensive repertoire of skill and techniques to improve problem-solving and coping skills. Whenever possible, clients' natural resources are used. In addition, interventions are based on clients' strengths and seek empowering solutions (Greene and Barnes 1998). Strengthening social support networks composed of households, relatives, friends, or neighbors—a hallmark of the ecological approach—is one such solution.

> Even if the social worker is helping an individual client, the assumption is made that the client cannot be understood without taking into account the quality of life within and among the community of systems of which the client is a part. . . . Social networks are of particular interest to social workers because they are a channel of support and nurturance, and may be instrumental in providing mutual aid. (Greene 2008, 218–19)

Social workers should become aware of whether they are biased in their selection of an approach to solving client situations. Do they see the problem as resting within a client or as located in the external environment? Research has shown that because the environment is often seen as so intractable and so difficult to affect, there is a tendency for practitioners to avoid environmental interventions in favor of changing people in isolation from their life situations (Kemp, Whittaker, and Tracy 1997; Saleebey 2004).

According to Meyer (1973),

> The case may be defined as a person, a family, a hospital ward, a housing complex, a particular neighborhood, a school population, a group with particular problems and needs, or a community with common concerns. . . . The drawing of a systemic boundary rather than a linear one provides for the true psychosocial perception of a case, because it includes the significant inputs into the lives of the individuals involved. (p. 269)

From this point of view, after making an assessment, the social worker needs to make the important decision about the *point of entry* of the case.

Whittaker (1983) summarized the ecological perspective as an inclusive view of human service practice that

- recognizes the complementarity of person-in-environment and seeks to strengthen each component;
- accepts the fact that an exclusive focus on *either* the individual *or* his or her immediate environment will generally not produce effective helping;
- acknowledges that interpersonal help may take many forms, as long as its goal is to teach skills for effectively coping with the environment;
- views social support not simply as a desirable concomitant to professional help but as an inextricable component of an overall helping strategy;
- recognizes the distinct and salutary features of both professional and lay helping efforts in an overall framework for service (pp. 36–37).

Critique of Diversity Issues in Social Work Practice

➤ *Universality is realized through attention to diversity as well as ecological, global, and cultural contexts.*

The ability to carry out social work practice that attends to difference requires that social workers

- use HBSE theories that relate to how to present themselves as learners and engage client systems as experts of their own experiences.
- apply HBSE theories that relate to self-awareness and self-regulation to manage the influence of personal biases and values in working with diverse client systems (CSWE 2015, 4; see Chapter 3).

Because social workers cannot possibly be competent enough to know and learn about all cultures, they must keep in tune with a client's or constituencies' specific culture. This concept is called *cultural humility* (Hook et al. 2013). Engaging with diverse clients and constituencies means the social worker must get to know the specific ecosystem or habitat in which a client lives. *Habitat* is the individual's physical and social setting within a cultural context (Germain and Gitterman 1987), whereas *niche* refers to the more immediate environment. For example, whatever the strategy of intervention, the social worker would want to know the socioeconomic status of a family with a low-birth-weight baby. (See Chapter 3 for a detailed discussion of client difference.)

The assumptions of the ecological perspective are useful in helping social workers understand strategies designed to eliminate oppressive structural barriers and to ensure that social goods and responsibilities are distributed equitably (CSWE 2015, 5). When a client's life space is examined, the practitioner is better able to identify societal conditions such as unemployment, homelessness, poverty, and discrimination that may act as debilitating sources of stress. For example, the social worker may want to become familiar with the multidisciplinary (health and economics) process of identifying *health disparities* or "differences in the incidence, prevalence, mortality, and burden of diseases and other adverse health conditions that exist among specific population groups in the United States" (National Institutes of Health 2002, 4).

Another area for multidisciplinary cooperation has to do with global concern for the reduction of greenhouse gas emissions and ongoing climate change. These of course also affect the basic elements of life: access to water, food production, and health. Development economists have come to similar conclusions that environmental crises are experienced by whole communities and should be planned for according to a particular geographical, social, and cultural habitat (Greene and Greene 2010).

Glossary

Adaptive. Indicative of a goodness of fit between person–environment exchanges. Goodness of fit is more likely when the environment supports people's general well-being and people act with a greater degree of competence.

Attachment. The mother–child bond.

Competence. A history of successful transactions with the environment. The ability to make confident decisions, to trust one's judgment, to achieve self-confidence, and to produce one's desired effects on the environment.

Coping skills. Behaviors that effectively ameliorate, eliminate, or master stress.

Ecology. A science that studies the relationships of living organisms and their environments. How organisms adapt or achieve goodness of fit with their environment is the focus.

Environment. Situational forces that work to shape the behavior and development of the individual in a particular setting.

Exosystem. A system comprising the linkages and processes occurring between two or more settings, at least one that does not ordinarily contain the developing person.

Field. The totality of coexisting facts that are viewed as mutually interdependent.

Goodness of fit. The extent to which there is a match between the individual's adaptive needs and the qualities of the environment.

Habitat. Specific places or locations where individuals are found, including their culture.

Life course. The timing of life events in relation to the social structures and historical changes affecting them.

Life space. The total psychological field, including the interdependent person and his or her environment.

Macrosystem. A system consisting of the overarching patterns of a given culture or broader social context.

Mesosystem. The interaction of two microlevel systems; considered mid-level systems.

Microsystem. A system comprising a pattern of activities and roles and interpersonal face-to-face relations in the immediate setting.

Niche. A status that is occupied by members of the community.

Paradigm. A distinctive concept or thought pattern stemming from a particular philosophical point of view.

Positivist. A person who adopts the philosophy of science that information derived from logical and sensory experience is the sole source of all authoritative knowledge.

Postmodernism. A philosophical movement claiming that reality is not simply mirrored in human understanding but rather constructed as the mind tries to understand its own personal reality. Meaning is created through human interaction.

Relatedness. Emotional and social exchanges among people. An individual's relationship with the natural environment.

Space. Physical settings, the built world, and psychological or personal ideas. Active, coping use of the environment.

Stress. An imbalance between a person's perceived demands and his or her perceived capability to use resources to meet those demands.

Theories. Assumptions used as a means of assessment, intervention, and evaluation. Theories provide order in collecting, organizing, and give meaning to case information. They may also be an interpretive device.

Time. The pacing, duration, and rhythm of the person–environment unit across evolutionary time and life course, encompassing biopsychosocial dimensions.

Transactions. Reciprocal people–environment exchanges.

References

Bartlett, H. M. 1970. *The Common Base of Social Work Practice*. New York: Putnam.

Bertalanffy, L. 1968. *General Systems Theory, Human Relations*. New York: Braziller.

Bloom, M. 1984. *Configurations of Human Behavior*. New York: Macmillan.

Boehm, W. W. 1958. "The Nature of Social Work." *Social Work* 12 (1): 10–8.

Boehm, W. W. 1959. *Objectives for the Social Work Curriculum of the Future: Social Work Curriculum Study*. New York: Council on Social Work Education.

Bronfenbrenner, U. 1979. *The Ecology of Human Development*. Cambridge, MA: Harvard University Press.

Buckley, W. 1968. "Society as a Complex Adaptive System." In *Modern Systems Research for the Behavioral Scientist*, edited by W. Buckley, 490–511. Chicago, IL: Aldine.

Carter, B., and McGoldrick, M. 1999. *The Expanded Family Life cycle: Individual, Family, and Social Perspectives*. 3rd ed. Boston, MA: Allyn & Bacon.

Compton, B., Gallaway, B., and Cournoyer, B. 2005. *Social Work Process*. Monterey, CA: Brooks/Cole.

Council on Social Work Education. 2015. *Educational Policy and Accreditation Standards*. Alexandria, VA: Council on Social Work Education.

Cowley, A. 1996. "Transpersonal Social Work." In *Social Work Treatment*, edited by F. Turner, 663–98. New York: Free Press.

Darwin, C. 2009. *Darwin's Shorter Works*. Cambridge: Cambridge University Press. (originally published 1829)

Elder, G. 1998. "The Life Course as Developmental Theory." *Child Development* 69 (1): 1–12.

Frank, C., Kurland, J., and Goldman, B. 1978. *Tips for Getting the Best from the Rest*. Baltimore, MD: Jewish Family & Children's Service Baltimore.

Gamble, D. N., and Weil, M. 2010. *Community Practice Skills: Local to Global Perspectives*. New York: Columbia University Press.

Garbarino, J. 1983. "Social Support Networks: Rx for the Helping Professions." In *Social Support Networks: Informal Helping in the Human Services*, edited by J. J. Whittaker, J. Garbarino, and Associates, 3–28. Hawthorne, NY: Aldine de Gruyter.

Germain, C. B., ed. 1979. *Social Work Practice: People and Environments*. New York: Columbia University Press.

Germain, C., and A. Gitterman. 1987. "Ecological Perspective." In *Encyclopedia of Social Work*, edited by A. Minahan (Ed.-in-Chief), vol. 1, 18th ed., 488–99. Silver Spring, MD: NASW Press.

Germain, C. B., and Gitterman, A. 1980. *The Life Model of Social Work Practice*. New York: Columbia University Press.

Germain, C., & Gitterman, A. 1996. *Life Model of Social Work: Advances in Theory and Practice*. New York: Columbia University Press.

Goldstein, E. G. 1995. *Ego Psychology and Social Work Practice*. 2nd ed. New York: Free Press.

Greene, R. 1988. *Continuing Education for Gerontological Careers*. Washington, DC: Council on Social Work Education.

Greene, R. R. 2005. "Redefining Social Work for the New Millennium: Setting a Context." *Journal of Human Behavior and the Social Environment* 10 (4): 37–54.

Greene, R. R. 2007. *Social Work Practice: A Risk and Resilience Perspective*. Monterey, CA: Brooks/Cole.

Greene, R. R. 2008. *Human Behavior Theory and Social Work Practice*. New Brunswick, NJ: Aldine Transaction.

Greene, R. R., and Barnes, G. 1998. "The Ecological Perspective and Social Work Practice." In *Serving Diverse Constituencies: Applying the Ecological Perspective*, edited by R. R. Greene and M. Watkins, 1–28. Hawthorne, NY: Aldine de Gruyter.

Greene, R. R., and Greene, D. G. 2010. "Resilience in the Face of Disasters: Bridging Micro and Macro-perspectives." *Journal of Human Behavior and the Social Environment* 19:1010–24.

Greene, R. R., and Watkins, M., eds. 1998. *Serving Diverse Constituencies: Applying the Ecological Perspective.* Hawthorne, NY: Aldine de Gruyter.

Hareven, T. K. 1996. *Aging and Generational Relations Over the Life Course: A Historical and Cross-cultural Perspective.* Hawthorne, NY: Aldine de Gruyter.

Hartman, A. 1978. Diagrammatic Assessment of Family Relationships. *Social Casework* 59:465–76.

Hartman, A., and Laird, J. 1987. "Family Practice." In *Encyclopedia of Social Work*, edited by A. Minahan (Ed.-in-Chief), Vol. 1, 18th ed., pp. 575–89. Silver Spring, MD: NASW Press.

Hook, J. N., Davis, D. E., Owen, J., and Utsey, S. 2013. "Cultural Humility: Measuring Opens to Culturally Diverse Clients." *Journal of Counseling Psychology* 60 (3): 353–66.

Kemp, S. P., Whittaker, J. K., and Tracy, E. M. 1997. *Person-Environment Practice.* Hawthorne, NY: Aldine de Gruyter.

Kropf, N. P., and Jones, B. 2014. "When Public Tragedies Happen: Community Practice Approaches in Grief, Loss, and Recovery." *Journal of Community Practice* 22:281–98.

Laird, J. 1993. "Introduction." In *Revisioning Social Work Education: A Social Constructionist Approach*, edited by J. Laird, 1–10. New York: Haworth Press.

Lazarus, R. S., and Folkman, S. 1984. *Stress, Appraisal, and Coping.* New York: Springer.

Longres, J. F. 2000. *Human Behavior in the Social Environment.* Monterey, CA: Thomson Wadsworth.

Maslow, A. H. 1959. "Cognition of Being in the Peak Experiences." *The Journal of Genetic Psychology* 94:43 –66.

Maslow, A. H. 1970. *Motivation and Personality.* 2nd ed. New York: Harper & Row.

Mattaini, M., and Meyer, C. 1988. "The Ecosystems Perspective: Implications for Practice." In *The Foundation of Social Work Practice*, edited by M. Mattaini and C. Meyer, 16 –27. Washington, DC: NASW Press.

Meyer, C. 1987. "Direct Practice in Social Work: Overview." In *Encyclopedia of Social Work*, edited by A. Minahan (Ed.-in-Chief), Vol. 1, 18th ed., pp. 409–22. Silver Spring, MD: NASW Press.

Meyer, C. H. 1973. "Purpose and Boundaries Casework Fifty Years Later." *Social Casework* 54:269–75.

Mondros, J. and Staples, L. 2008. "Community Organization." In *Encyclopedia of Social Work*, edited by T. Mizrahi and L. Davis, Vol. 1, 28th ed., pp. 383– 87. Washington, DC: NASW Press & Oxford University Press.

National Institutes of Health. 2002. NIH Strategic Research Plan to Reduce and Ultimately Eliminate Health Disparities Fiscal Years 2002–2006. Washington, DC: U.S. Department of Health and Human Services.

Newman, B., and Newman, P. R. 2005. *Development Through Life: A Psychosocial Approach.* Monterey, CA: Thomson Brooks/Cole.

Richmond, M. 1917. *Social Diagnosis.* New York: Russell Sage Foundation.

Robbins, S., Chatterjee, P., and Canda, E. 2006. *Contemporary Human Behavior Theory: A Critical Perspective for Social Work.* Boston, MA: Allyn & Bacon.

Saleebey, D. 1993. "Notes on Interpreting the Human Condition: A Constructed HBSE Curriculum." In *Revisioning Social Work Education: A Social Constructionist Approach*, edited by J. Laird, 197–217. New York: Haworth Press.

Saleebey, D. 2004. "'The Power of Place': Another Look at the Environment." *Families in Society* 85 (1): 7–16.

Sampson, R. J., Raudenbush, S. W., and Earls, F. August 15, 1997. "Neighborhoods and Violent Crime: A Multilevel Study of Collective Efficacy." *Science* 277:918–24.

Schriver, J. M. 2015. *Human Behavior and the Social Environment: Shifting Paradigms in Essential Knowledge for Social Work Practice.* 6th ed. New York: Pearson.

Schwartz, N. 1977. "Social Group Work: The Interactionist Approach." In *Encyclopedia of Social Work*, edited by J. B. Turner, Vol. 2, 17th ed., pp. 1328–38. New York: NASW Press.

Turner, F. J. 1995. "Social Work Practice: Theoretical Base." In *Encyclopedia of Social Work*, edited by R. L. Edwards (Ed.-in-Chief), Vol. 3, 19th ed., pp. 2258–65. Washington, DC: NASW Press.

White, R. W. 1959. "Motivation Reconsidered: The Concept of Competence." *Psychological Review* 66:297–331.

Whittaker, J. 1983. "Mutual Helping in Human Services." In *Social Support Networks*, edited by J. K. Whittaker, J. Garbarino, and Associates, pp. 29–70. Hawthorne, NY: Aldine de Gruyter.

Yalom, I. D. 1980. *Existential Psychotherapy.* New York: Basic Books.

Yalom, I. D., and Leszcz, M. 1995. *The Theory and Practice of Group Psychotherapy.* 4th ed. New York: Basic Books.

Zastrow, C., and Kirst-Ahman, K. 2009. *Understanding Human Behavior and the Social Environment.* Boston, MA: Cengage.

3

Human Behavior and the Social Environment:
Engaging Diversity and Difference in Practice

> ➤ *This chapter describes the use of human behavior and the social environment theory to support social workers in engaging diversity and difference in practice. The theory and models presented are guided by the ecological systems perspective and symbolic interaction theory. These are contrasted with Africentric concepts intended to inform micro- and macropractice with individuals, families, groups, organizations, and communities. Major concepts include power, oppression, and identity formation. Strategies to try and eliminate personal bias and to promote human rights are discussed.*

Chapter 2 described the reciprocal influence of the person and environment—"the nested context of social competence" (Walsh 1998, 12). This chapter expands the discussion by turning attention to how culture and diversity "characterize and shape the human experience" (Council on Social Work Education [CSWE] 2015, 4).

The chapter is divided into two sections. It first explores how larger-scale systems—political, economic, educational, and legal—may either be supportive influences in people's lives or oppress and marginalize people by limiting access to services and human rights. It then discusses how exclusionary policies and hostile environments affect identity formation, sometimes contributing to feelings of alienation. At the same time, it contrasts ways in which people's cultural heritage can positively influence well-being.

Models that help social workers conduct cross-cultural practice and combat bigotry and prejudice are also provided. These models stem from a theoretical base that incorporates the values of people of color (Schiele 1996). The purpose is to provide human behavior and the social environment theory for social work practice with diverse constituencies, "recognizing, supporting, and building on the strengths and resiliency of all human beings" (CSWE 2015, 10).

> ➤ *Well-being is limited or enhanced by the nature of political, economic, educational, and legal systems.*

Professional Purpose and Well-Being

Cultural diversity in social work practice *has* gradually come to embrace the multiple dimensions of human identity, biculturalism, and culturally defined social behaviors. This has not always been the case. The primary shift to a more inclusive social work practice came about because

> the civil rights and women's liberation movements, with the accompanied acceleration in social change, required that the social work profession reassess its direction and priorities. These social and political forces gave impetus to an advocacy approach to social work and its curriculum. (Greene and Kropf 2009, 33)

Students, faculty, and CSWE promoted the idea that groups less visible in the curriculum be given more attention (Tully 1994).

Organizational Support

The efforts of the National Association of Social Workers (NASW) and CSWE have contributed to "ever-expanding parameters related to cultural diversity" and client and constituency well-being (Tully 1994, 235). In 2001, the NASW National Committee on Racial and Ethnic Diversity developed the *NASW Standards for Cultural Competence in Social Work Practice* (Table 3.1). The committee was concerned with furthering *cultural competence,* or the ability to "provide services, conduct assessments, and implement interventions that are reflective of the clients' cultural values and norms, congruent with their natural help-seeking behaviors, and inclusive of existing indigenous solutions" (Fong and Furuto 2001, 1).

Table 3.1.
NASW standards for cultural competence in social work practice

Standard 1. Ethics and values

Social workers shall function in accordance with the values, ethics, and standards of the profession, recognizing how personal and professional values may conflict with or accommodate the needs of diverse clients.

Standard 2. Self-awareness

Social workers shall seek to develop an understanding of their own personal and cultural values and beliefs as one way of appreciating the importance of multicultural identities in the lives of people.

Standard 3. Cross-cultural knowledge

Social workers shall have and continue to develop specialized knowledge and understanding about the history, traditions, values, family systems, and artistic expressions of major client groups they serve.

Standard 4. Cross-cultural skills

Social workers shall use appropriate methodological approaches, skills, and techniques that reflect the workers' understanding of the role of culture in the helping process.

(Continued)

Table 3.1. (Continued)

Standard 5. Service delivery

Social workers shall be knowledgeable about and skillful in the use of services available in the community and broader society and be able to make appropriate referrals for their diverse clients.

Standard 6. Empowerment and advocacy

Social workers shall be aware of the effect of social policies and programs on diverse client populations, advocating for and with clients whenever appropriate.

Standard 7. Diverse workforce

Social workers shall support and advocate for recruitment, admissions and hiring, and retention efforts in social work programs and agencies that ensure diversity within the profession.

Standard 8. Professional education

Social workers shall advocate for and participate in educational and training programs that help advance cultural competence within the profession.

Standard 9. Language diversity

Social workers shall seek to provide or advocate for the provision of information, referrals, and services in the language appropriate to the client, which may include use of interpreters.

Standard 10. Cross-cultural leadership

Social workers shall be able to communicate information about diverse client groups to other professionals.

Note. The standards proposed by the National Association of Social Workers (NASW) National Committee on Racial and Ethnic Diversity were approved by the NASW Board of Directors on June 23, 2001. From NASW (2001).

In 2008 and 2015, the CSWE Commission on Educational Policy mandated a more inclusive educational competency to ensure that students could engage diversity and difference in practice. They proposed that

> the dimensions of diversity are understood as the intersectionality of multiple factors including, but not limited to, age, class, color, culture, disability and ability, ethnicity, gender, gender identity and expression, immigration status, political ideology, race, religion/spirituality, sex, sexual orientation, and tribal sovereign status. (CSWE 2015, 4; Table 3.2)

The concept of intersectionality has resulted in an overarching approach to curriculum that casts the social worker in the role of learner and the client as cultural guide (CSWE 2008, 2015). In the broadest sense, intersectionality encompasses a host of disenfranchised groups (Fong and Furuto 2001) as well as an array of diversity principles (Greene and Watkins 1998; Table 3.3).

> ➤ *Universality is realized at the intersection of our multiple identities.*

Section I.
Power Relationships

Diversity Theory: Applying Terms and Macroassumptions in Social Work Practice

The human behavior and the social environment theory base has been criticized for its Eurocentric perspective. For this reason, these theories are critiqued throughout the *Handbook*. However, the diversity in literature has produced a number of

Table 3.2.
The intersectionality of diversity and difference

Group	Description and legal protection
Age:	People may be devalued and discriminated against because of their age. Such *ageism* is an attitude that can result in actions that subordinate a person or the group because of age, bringing about unequal treatment. The Age Discrimination in Employment Act of 1967 protects individuals who are 40 years of age or older.
Class:	People who are seen as being in a certain class are affected by economic and educational (dis)advantage, especially those living in poverty. Class encompasses a misdistribution of wealth and variation in educational attainment, occupations, and patterns of deference accorded certain groups (Devore and Schlesinger 1998). The U.S. Department of Health and Human Services sets poverty guidelines for benefits and services every year.
Color:	*People of color* is a term sometimes preferred instead of *minority.* It generally refers to people who are not White and who face prejudice and discrimination. Title VII of the Civil Rights Act of 1964 prohibits employment discrimination based on race, color, religion, sex, or national origin.
Culture:	Culture is a people's way of life. Characteristics may include arts, music, cuisine, language, religion, and social habits. Culture is more broadly seen as a worldview or belief system.
Disability:	People with disabilities are perceived as being limited in lifestyle and activities. According to the Americans with Disabilities Act, a law that protects people with disabilities from discrimination, an individual with a disability (a) has a physical or mental impairment that substantially limits one or more major life activities, or (b) has a record of such an impairment, or (c) is regarded as having such an impairment.
Ethnicity:	Members of an ethnic group think of themselves as being a people or as having a common culture, history, and origin. An ethnic group may maintain a distinction between its members and perceived outsiders.
Gender:	Gender is the sex, male or female, to which one is born. Gender can be distinguished by roles and power issues. The Equal Pay Act of 1963 protects men and women who perform substantially equal work in the same establishment from sex-based wage discrimination.
Gender identity and expression:	Gender identity is an individual's personal sense of being male or female. Gender expression refers to manifested behaviors and mannerisms. These expressions exist on a continuum and may differ from culture to culture. Employers may apply the Equal Employment Opportunity (EEO) law—29 Code of Federal regulations (C.F. R.) Part 1614— to gender identity and expression if they so choose.
Immigration status:	Immigrants seeking economic opportunity in the United States must meet several conditions before they can immigrate. They must apply for an immigration visa and be sponsored by either a relative or employer who requires their work skills. They must also acquire a green card, which allows them to live legally in the United States as long as they retain their work status. Refugees are people who have been displaced and are given special permission to come to the United States. Their lives may be disrupted by famine, war, civil conflict, and/or persecution. Title VII of the Civil Rights Act of 1964 prohibits employment discrimination based on race, color, religion, sex, or national origin.
Political ideology:	A person's or group's beliefs about the social order and what constitutes well-being and fairness. Most employees in America working for private employers do not have any legal protection against discrimination on the basis of political affiliation or activity. (A *public* employer can, under certain circumstances, be prevented from firing someone based on political speech because that would constitute the government itself suppressing free speech.)
Race:	Race is a social category usually based on color. Title VII of the Civil Rights Act of 1964 prohibits employment discrimination based on race, color, religion, sex, or national origin.
Religion/spirituality:	Religion is the outward organized expression of one's faith system. Faith is an inner system of beliefs about the meaning of life and one's relationship with the transcendent. Title VII of the Civil Rights Act of 1964 prohibits employment discrimination based on race, color, religion, sex, or national origin.

(*Continued*)

Table 3.2. (Continued)

Sex: Sex is synonymous with gender. Title VII of the Civil Rights Act of 1964 prohibits employment discrimination based on race, color, religion, sex, or national origin.

Sexual orientation: There is no consensus among scientists about the exact reasons why an individual develops a heterosexual, bisexual, gay, or lesbian orientation (American Psychological Association 2008, 2). Several decades of research and clinical experience have led mainstream medical and mental health organizations to conclude that differences in sexual orientation represent normal forms of human expression (American Psychological Association 2009). The Supreme Court ruled same-sex marriage legal in all 50 states on June 25, 2015 (Obergellfell v Hodges). Other rights for the LGBT community vary and are in a state of flux.

Tribal sovereign status: There are 562 federally recognized Indian Nations. Tribal status recognizes the right of tribes to govern themselves and act as government entities. Actions are related to treaties or contracts between the U.S. government and indigenous tribes.

Table 3.3.
Self-examination: diversity principles

What is your agreement with the following diversity principles discussed in the *Handbook?* Rate yourself from 1 (lowest) to 5 (highest) on the following diversity principles.

Self-awareness and Self-reflection
- Diversity practice requires an appreciation for attitudinal differences between clients and social workers regarding autonomy or self-determination.
  1   2   3   4   5
- Social workers who are culturally sensitive appreciate differences.
  1   2   3   4   5
- Diversity practice requires that social workers understand that their decisions may be culture bound or ethnocentric.
  1   2   3   4   5
- Diversity practice requires social workers to be self-aware, open to cultural differences, and aware of their own preconceived assumptions of diverse groups' values and biases.
  1   2   3   4   5
- Diversity practice requires social workers to understand their own and the client's belief systems, customs, norms, ideologies, rituals, traditions, and so forth.
  1   2   3   4   5

Diversity and curriculum
- Diversity practice requires a model.
  1   2   3   4   5
- Diversity practice requires the ability to think critically.
  1   2   3   4   5
- Diversity practice requires that social workers be learners.
  1   2   3   4   5
- Diversity content encompasses practice methods, field education, ethics, research, social policy, and human behavior in the social environment.
  1   2   3   4   5
- Diversity content encompasses the selective and differential use of knowledge, skills, and attitudes pertaining to all areas of social work practice.
  1   2   3   4   5
- The most effective social workers in diversity practice differentially use assessment and intervention strategies.
  1   2   3   4   5

(Continued)

Table 3.3. (Continued)

- The most effective social workers in diversity practice use a blend of formal and informal resources.

  1   2   3   4   5

- Diversity practice requires an understanding of multiple theories, such as symbolic interaction and systems theory.

  1   2   3   4   5

Social and economic justice

- Diversity practice requires social workers to uphold the profession's commitment to social justice.

  1   2   3   4   5

- Diversity practice requires that social workers understand the processes of inclusion and exclusion.

  1   2   3   4   5

- Diversity practice requires social workers to understand that individuals and groups may have limited access to resources, live in unsafe environments damaging to self-esteem, and experience their environments as hostile.

  1   2   3   4   5

- The scope of diversity practice encompasses all populations at risk affected by social, economic, and legal biases; the distribution of rights and resources; and oppression.

  1   2   3   4   5

- Diversity practice requires an understanding of the effects of institutional racism, ageism, homophobia, and sexism.

  1   2   3   4   5

Development

- Theory building for social work practice with diverse constituencies should reevaluate concepts such as normalcy and deviance.

  1   2   3   4   5

- Diversity practice involves the use of knowledge or research conducted in a manner culturally congruent to the people involved in the study.

  1   2   3   4   5

- Diversity practice involves the integration of skills and theory grounded in the client's reality.

  1   2   3   4   5

- Diversity practice promotes a client's sense of self-efficacy and mastery of his or her environment.

  1   2   3   4   5

- Diversity practice recognizes differences in help-seeking patterns, the definition of the problem, the selection of solutions, and interventions.

  1   2   3   4   5

Cultural adaptation

- Using a diversity framework, one views culture as a source of cohesion, identity, and strength as well as strain and discordance.

  1   2   3   4   5

- A diversity framework needs to provide an understanding of a culture's adaptive strategies.

  1   2   3   4   5

- Diversity practice requires an understanding of bicultural status.

  1   2   3   4   5

- Diversity practice requires an understanding of a person's behavior as a member of his or her family, various groups and organizations, and community.

  1   2   3   4   5

Note. Adapted from Greene et al. (2003).

models that further elaborate the knowledge base on difference (Asante 1988; Devore and Schlesinger 1980; Lum 1992). For example, Molefi Asante (1988), a professor of Black studies, has written principles for an Afrocentric curriculum; Doman Lum (1992), a professor of social work, constructed a five-stage process model for clients of color; and Wynette Devore and Elfriede Schlesinger (2012), professors of social work, authored an ethnic sensitive practice model. Such researchers have enhanced understanding of culture, ethnosystems, and power.

Culture

Cross-cultural social work practice is based on an understanding of client culture. *Culture* is the way of life of a group of people, encompassing values, attitudes, mores, religion, and even food and music. Culture binds the group together through its worldview or belief system.

Anthropologist James Green (1978/1998) suggested that practitioners take a broader view of culture, thinking of it as a *community of interest*. He contended that communities of interest are not necessarily explicitly racial or ethnic but may encompass a school for deaf people, a drug house, or street people. He went on to offer an expansive definition: "Culture is not a specific value, physical appearance, or something that people have; rather, it is people's shared cognitive map, their discourse, and how they go about their lives—their life perspective" (p. 3).

Ethnosystems

Just as the United States can be pictured as being made up of social systems of various sizes, it may also be thought of as comprising ethnosystems of varying cultural makeup. Bush et al. (1983) defined an *ethnosystem* as "a collective of interdependent ethnic groups sharing unique historical and or ties and bound together by a single political system" (p. 99).

> ➤ *Assessment content addressed should encompass differences in ethnic group history, language, communication, and so forth.*

Language sometimes differs among ethnosystems, interfering with client access to social and health services (Gonzalez 2006). The literature historically treated language as a problem rather than seeing it as an expression of the client's culture (O'Hagan 2001). Practitioners tended to place the problem on the client (blame the victim) for not communicating in a language that the provider could understand. It is now increasingly accepted that understanding the client's language is a necessary factor in the helping process (Carrillo 2001).

Power Defined

Ethnosystems may differ not only in historical, cultural, and organizational patterns and language and communication but in the degree of power over material resources and in political decisions (Pinderhughes 1989). Therefore, cross-cultural practice necessitates an understanding of power differentials.

Table 3.4.
Power issues in social work practice: theoretical positions

General systems theory

- All social systems have an organizational structure and therefore have a status or power hierarchy.
- Personal and positional resource differentials are associated with differences in power. Resources are an interpersonal factor influenced by diversity.
- As a social system, the client–social worker relationship has inherent power issues that may mirror those found in the general society. Societal beliefs and practices tend to view professionals as authorities or experts over the lay public.

Ecological theory

- Power is related to the reciprocal process of goodness of fit between the person and the environment.
- A goodness-of-fit metaphor construct suggests that nutritive environments offer the necessary resources, security, and support at the appropriate times and in the appropriate ways. Such environments enhance the cognitive, social, and emotional development of communities and their members.
- When environments are not nutritive, the match tends to be poor. Hostile environments, in which there is a lack or a distortion of environmental supports, inhibit development and the ability to cope.
- The goal of the client–social worker relationship is empowerment, or a process of increasing personal, interpersonal, or political power to improve the client's life situation, knowledge, skills, or material resources.

Feminist theory

- Power is unlimited and can be widely distributed through empowerment strategies. Empowerment is a political act in which people take control over their own lives and make their own decisions.
- Power is a process in which people personally and collectively transform themselves. Power is derived from a person's internal energy and strength and requires openness and a connection with others.
- Whenever possible, the personal power between the therapist and the client approaches equality.

Note. Summarized from Greene (2006).

Power definitions vary from theory to theory. Ecological theory proposes that power is related to the person and environment fit, systems theory suggests that power is related to people's status and hierarchy within various systems, and feminist theory espouses the idea that power is unlimited and can be shared (Table 3.4). In addition, social constructionists believe that societal power issues should be infused in treatment (Gergen and Gergen 1983; McNamee and Gergen 1992; see Chapter 5). For example, a client who is a battered woman could directly discuss her experience with power abuse with the social worker. The social worker should also be cautious about how his or her power is perceived by the client.

Power Levels

According to Foucault (1980), "Power is everywhere . . . because it comes from everywhere" (p. 86). Power may be expressed at the *personal level,* referring to a person's sense of personal control; the *interpersonal level,* relating to one's influence over others; and the *institutional/structural level,* encompassing the extent to which discrimination is embedded in organizations and societal institutions (Cohen and Greene 2005). Social workers need to keep these levels of power in mind during the assessment and intervention process.

> ➤ *Social workers' change strategies can be intended to increase client power.*

Engage With Individuals, Families, Groups, Organizations, and Communities

Macrolevel Power Factors

Before they engage with health and social services, far too many people will have had to overcome structural barriers involving power and privilege. Power and privilege can first be understood as a macrolevel phenomenon that requires that "social workers recognize the extent to which [U.S.] culture's structures and values may oppress, marginalize, alienate, or create or enhance privilege and power" (CSWE 2015, 4).

This idea has been called *institutional racism,* or a system of White supremacy that permeates the U.S. social fabric, including its history, culture, politics, and economics (McIntosh, 1988). Institutional racism may also be understood as a normalized and legitimized hierarchy of power that negatively affects multiple institutions and people's normative values (NASW 2007).

White privilege. The idea that prejudice is embedded in institutions and social norms is known as *White privilege.* The concept has been applied in the circumstances of ageism, ableism, homophobia, sexism, and other forms of discrimination based on stereotypes. Privilege can be invisible unless social workers make a particular effort to ask, "What are some of the advantages of being white, male, middle-class, and so forth?" (Swigonski 1996, 154). Table 3.5 illustrates how White privilege may influence daily behaviors.

> ➤ *Change strategies selected should address structural barriers to service that often are shaped by policy decisions.*

Structural barriers. Most important is that structural barriers at the societal level may keep potential clients from using services. For example, older Latinos have limited access to health care because of economic, administrative, cultural, and linguistic barriers (Angel, Angel, and Markides 2002), which negatively influences their decisions to seek help, particularly mental health treatment (Choi and Gonzalez 2005). Another structural barrier that was overcome on July 25, 2015 was the Supreme Court ruling on Obergellfell v Hodges, making same-sex marriage legal in all fifty states (www.cnn.com/2015.06/25.../Supreme-court-ruling-same-sex-marriage...).

Table 3.5.
Types of privilege reflected in statements

Type of privilege	Sample statement
The freedom to associate exclusively or primarily with members of your own group	"I can, if I wish, arrange to be in the company of people of my race most of the time" (p. 5)
The level of social acceptance you can presume across varying contexts	"If I should need to move, I can be pretty sure of renting or purchasing housing in an area in which I want to live" (p. 5)
	"Whether I use checks, credit cards, or cash, I can count on my skin color not to work against the appearance of financial reliability" (p. 6)
	"I do not have to educate my children to be aware of systemic racism for their own daily protection" (p. 6)
The ability to see members of your group in a positive light in history records, in texts, in media, and as role models	"When I am told about our national heritage or about civilization, I am shown that people of my color made it what it is" (p. 6)
	"I can be pretty sure that if I ask to speak to the person in charge, I will be facing a person of my own race" (p. 7)
Freedom from stereotyping	"I can swear, dress in second-hand clothes, or not answer letters, without having people attribute these choices to the bad morale, poverty, or illiteracy of my race" (p. 7)
	"I can do well in a challenging situation without being called a credit to my race" (p. 7)
	"I can be late to a meeting without having the lateness reflect on my race" (p. 8)
The ability to be oblivious to other groups in your culture	"I can remain oblivious to the language and customs of people of color who constitute the world's majority without feeling any penalty for such obliviousness" (p. 7)

Note. Adapted from McIntosh (1995).

> ➤ Maria is a seventy-five-year-old woman originally from Mexico. She came to the United States forty-five years ago and became a U.S. citizen. She is married and has four children and ten grandchildren. She has recently become forgetful and confused and no longer is capable of babysitting the younger grandchildren. She told her curandera, or herbalist, that she misses her grandkids and feels very sad.

Assessing Power Characteristics

Power is a marked feature in all complex societies that can create inequalities in social position (Anderson, Carter, and Lowe 1999). Such inequalities have seven common characteristics. Each power characteristic is accompanied here by a question or statement that may help social workers explore what inequality clients may be facing.

1. Inequality in social resources, social position, and political and cultural influences
   The social worker can ask questions related to the clients' (system) sense that they have the ability to control their environment (e.g., "Do you sometimes feel that life is out of your control?").
2. Inequality in opportunities to make use of existing resources
   The social worker can make inquiries about the availability of "fundamental human rights such as freedom, safety, privacy, [and] an adequate standard of living, health care, and education" (CSWE 2015, 5) for clients and constituencies (e.g., "Do you sense that you are living from paycheck to paycheck?" "How would you say you manage with your budget?" "Does your community have resources for your children—nice parks and libraries?").
3. Inequality in the division of rights and duties
   The social worker could ask questions related to reciprocal obligations and hierarchy within the various social systems in which clients interact (e.g., "How are the major decisions made in your household?" "Are raises and promotions handled fairly at your workplace?").
4. Inequality in implicit or explicit standards of judgment, often leading to differential treatment (in laws, the labor market, educational practices, etc.)
   The practitioner wants to know whether clients believe they have adequate access to jobs and education, especially those protected by law (e.g., "What are the schools like in your neighborhood?" "How did your job interview go?" "Do you think you will get that promotion?").
5. Inequality in cultural representations—devaluation of the powerless group, stereotyping, references to the "nature" or (biological) "essence" of the less powerful
   The social worker wants to know how clients' self-identity is influenced by their group's portrayal in the media, music, and arts, especially for developing teenagers (e.g., "I wonder, what is the route to success in your peer group—sports, education?").
6. Inequality in psychological consequences—a "psychology of inferiority" (insecurity, "double-bind" experiences, and sometimes identification with the dominant group) versus a "psychology of superiority" (arrogance, inability to abandon the dominant perspective)
   The social worker can explore whether clients express seemingly negative psychological outcomes due to prejudice (e.g., "Do you sometimes think you will never be treated as an equal?" "What success have you had in overcoming poor treatment?").
7. A social and cultural tendency to minimize or deny power inequality—(potential) conflict often represented as consensus, power inequality as "normal"
   The social worker can ask questions related to the client's acceptance of powerlessness (e.g., "Do you think we will ever see progress in getting a safer neighborhood?" "Are there organizations to advocate for you?" "What do you think we can do to get organized?" based on Davis, Leijenaar, and Oldersma 1991, 52).

> ➤ *Change strategies selected should address individual and community marginalization and work toward empowerment.*

Marginalized Groups

Oppression by the mainstream society at the structural level of society shapes discrimination against people of color and all disenfranchised groups throughout their daily lives. Those who are *marginalized* have less control or influence over goods and services or have less access to social, economic, and political resources (Garcia and Van Soest 2006; Pinderhughes 1978; Wilson 1973, 1985). People and communities, especially those living in poverty, may feel "expendable, hopeless, and helpless" (Goldenberg 1978, 2).

The process of discrimination can be seen as a cycle of powerlessness in which the failure of the larger social system to provide needed resources operates in a circular manner. . . . The more powerless a community is, the more the families within it are hindered from meeting the needs of their members and from organizing the community so that it can provide them with more support. (Pinderhughes 1983, 332)

Economist, sociologists, and a handful of social workers at the World Bank are tackling this problem, attempting to build human capital and addressing the quantity and quality of societal interactions that lead to well-being (econ.worldbank.org/indicators]. These community development projects focus first on building trust in communities and their respective relationship networks. Civic involvement is encouraged through collaboration and coalitions. The goal is to improve physical and social environments and to increase collective capacity.

Social Stratification

In a similar vein, the cycle of powerlessness, among other factors, has created a social stratification system in the United States based on social and economic status (Parsons 1951, 1964). A well-known six-part hierarchy categorizes members as follows:

1. Upper-upper class: the most wealthy (often old wealth)
2. Lower-upper class: the newly wealthy
3. Upper-middle class: successful professionals and business people
4. Lower-middle class: white-collar workers
5. Upper-lower class: blue-collar workers
6. Lower-lower class: unemployed persons and recipients of public assistance (Hollingshead and Redlich 1958a, 1958b)

Movement up the status ladder can be difficult and is often limited by systemic constraints, inequities in education and power, the presence of job ceilings, and the extent to which an individual develops a strong cultural frame of reference that allows him or her to feel accepted (rather than rejected) by society (Ogbu 1985).

Section II.
Theories of Identity

> ➤ *Critique theories for whether they are culturally sound.*

Diversity Theory: Applying Terms and Microassumptions
in Social Work Practice

As described previously, assessment, particularly of minority clients, involves an evaluation of clients' power position within U.S. society. This can explain the disproportional use of services and why some people have lost hope in the system. Theories of identity are used in assessment to better comprehend people's relative ability to overcome the effects of discrimination and become resilient (Greene et al. 2009). This area of inquiry is critical because "the consequences of negative valuations directed toward members of stigmatized groups . . . and the relationship between power, powerlessness, [negatively affect] the processes of human growth and development" (Solomon 1976, 13–17). This section outlines selected theories of personal identity and their application in social work practice (Table 3.6).

Table 3.6.
Selected theoretical foundations of cross-cultural practice:
a systems-ecological perspective

Time adopted	Major theorist(s)	Theme	Concept for Practice
1934	G. H. Mead: Generalized other	People take on social roles as they interact in everyday life	Role conflict and strain
	Social interactionism	The self is socially constructed	The "I" and the "me"
1949	Mead: Cultural environments	Personality development is understood by understanding ethnographic information and the cultural environment	Cross-cultural social work
1983–1989	Pinderhughes: Empowerment	Empowerment occurs when people can affect their own space beneficially	Cycle of powerlessness; power sharing
1976	Solomon: Power differentials	There is a hierarchy of power in society	Social and economic justice
1972	Chestang: Hostile environments	Oppressive societies are characterized by social injustice, societal inconsistency, and personal impotence	Negative quality of oppressive environments

Erikson's Theory of Psychosocial Development

One of the most well-known theorists to address identity formation within a cultural milieu was Erik Erikson (1959). Erikson's fifth stage of psychosocial development, *Identity vs. Identity Confusion,* occurs between ages twelve and twenty-two. The task of this stage requires a youth to "formulate successive and tentative identifications, culminating in an overt identity crisis in adolescence" (Greene 2008, 97). Although Erikson took social forces into consideration, he saw identity primarily as a psychosocial process that takes place in the context of one's peer group (see Chapter 4).

Symbolic Interactionism

Symbolic interactionism is another theory that explains how the self emerges through social interaction. The school's two basic assumptions are that (a) people develop their personalities through reflection and social engagement, and (b) societal institutions derive their meaning through the social interaction of their members (Ephross and Greene 1991). In this way, both individual and community development is accounted for.

Social psychologist George Herbert Mead, one of the founding members of the school of symbolic interactionism, studied how people understand themselves as well as others. He proposed that once children master the use of symbols, expectations for behavior solidify into what is known as the *generalized other:* "the internalized organized community or social group which gives the individual his unity of self" (Mead 1934, 154; Table 3.6).

Mead suggested that the self consists of two parts: (a) the "I," which are the impulsive, spontaneous aspects of the self unique to the individual; and (b) the "me," which refers to the organized expectations of others, social norms, and values. Therefore, the concept of the "me" suggests that the social worker must examine the collective nature of behavior and its social context.

Relational Worldviews

Erikson and Mead have been criticized for their limited, perhaps Eurocentric, view of self-development. According to Sue (2006), because "social work theories, concepts, and practices are often rooted in and reflect the dominant values of the larger society . . . forms of treatment may represent cultural oppression and may reflect primarily a Eurocentric worldview" (p. xvii).

In contrast, relational worldview models present an alternative approach to the development of the self and well-being. For example, Cross's (1998) schema was originated to explain how members of a tribal nation (or other diverse clients) may view "disease" and health (p. 144; Figure 3.1). The model depicts culture as a circle resembling a medicine wheel consisting of four factors: (a) *context,* involving family, culture, and history; (b) *mind,* including intellect, emotion, and memory; (c) *spirit,* referring to dreams, symbols, and stories; and (d) *body,* encompassing genetics, condition, and age. (Cross saw the items listed in the circle as examples only.) When a tribal member keeps all four parts in balance, he or she experiences

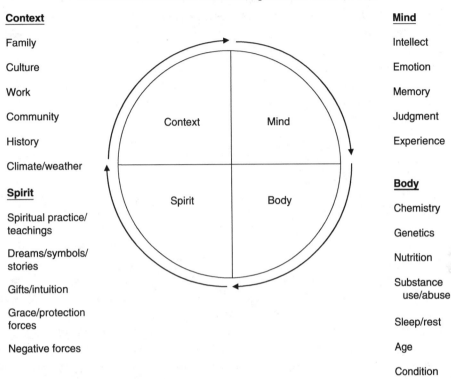

Figure 3.1.
A relational worldview model. Adapted from Cross (1998).

Context

Family

Culture

Work

Community

History

Climate/weather

Spirit

Spiritual practice/
teachings

Dreams/symbols/
stories

Gifts/intuition

Grace/protection
forces

Negative forces

Mind

Intellect

Emotion

Memory

Judgment

Experience

Body

Chemistry

Genetics

Nutrition

Substance
use/abuse

Sleep/rest

Age

Condition

harmony or health. But when a person has a sense of imbalance, then he or she feels disharmony or disease.

> ➤ *Change strategies selected can address universality.*

From this point of view, healing may come from any or all of the four parts of the circle. Nothing in the circle changes without every other thing in the circle changing as well. The circle is constantly evolving because of the passage of days, weeks, and seasons and because of development and different experiences.

Similarly, Schiele's (1996) Africentric theory explores the ethos and values of Africans and African Americans. He felt that African cultural forms are transmitted from one generation to another in the United States, and people also engage with the mainstream culture. Whereas the Euro-American perspective is more individually oriented, the African perspective focuses on cooperation and harmony. The theory recognizes African history, culture, and worldview as a holistic context for understanding the interconnectedness of mind, body, and spirit and the development of collective identity (Swigonski 1996). Learning about such cultural meanings related to self-identity is central to the helping process. These theories build on an empowerment philosophy in which people define their own worldviews and pathways, hoping to move from feelings of powerlessness to empowerment (Goldenberg 1978).

Jean Baker Miller and colleagues developed another example of the relational self in their relational–cultural theory. Collaborating as theorists at the Stone Center at Wellesley College, they first studied empathy among women (Jordan 1997; Miller and Stiver 1991). They contended that although women tend to hope for connections with others, they generally keep a large part of themselves private. Therefore, for trust and growth to take place in the helping relationship, empathy and mutuality in goal setting must occur (CSWE 2015). This viewpoint has since been extended to clinical work with men as well as other population groups (Brown and Ballou 2002).

The Social Construction of Race and other Social Groups

The idea of the social creation of the self has been applied to the social construction of race (Ore 2014). Race is considered by most social scientists to be a social concept with no standing as a scientific or analytic category (Green 1978/1998). The disuse of the term *race* as a scientific category relates to the understanding that there are only superficial physical differences between people, such as skin color, and that people differ more within a race than between races.

Nonetheless, race may be thought of as a social construct that can result in discrimination, leading to social injustice or the denial of legal rights. According to Leon Chestang (1972), the double standard for Blacks and Whites and the disparity between societal ideals and actions can lead to a feeling of *personal impotence*. Children who are not protected from hostile environments may develop a diminished sense of self characterized by suspicion and mistrust.

Nigerian American anthropologist John Ogbu's (1985) international research culminated in a *cultural-ecological* framework explaining why minority immigrant youth may develop an oppositional culture toward educational achievement. He contended that when youth face systemic barriers to job opportunities, they can come to believe that education is not for them. That is, they feel that they are precluded from meaningful roles in society. However, children who are proactively socialized to ward off such discrimination can become more resilient (Greene 2012).

> ➤ Change strategies selected can foster positive societal roles played by clients and constituencies.

Similarly, people with disabilities have historically been thought of as deficient and expected to fill roles forced on them by the larger society. For example, persons with mental health disabilities have routinely been institutionalized. When their behavior has exhibited signs of institutionalization, it has reinforced stereotypes and falsely vindicated the idea that they need to be institutionalized (Mackelsprang and Salsgiver 2014).

During the deinstitutionalization movement beginning in the 1960s, patients with intellectual or developmental disabilities needed to learn about living in a new world. Social workers often assisted them in entering life in the community.

For example, consider James, a fifteen-year old released from a New England institution in 1962 when he was fifteen: What new cultural forms would such a teenager have to master? How would you teach him about dress and hair styles? Music? Rules of dating?

Imagine the "remaking identities" of immigrant children and what it takes for them to adapt. According to Suarez-Orozco and Suarez-Orozco (2001), they must

> find suitable behaviors for different settings such as home, schools, the world of peers, and the world of work. They may have their breakfast conversation in Farsi, listen to African American rap with their peers on the way to school, and learn about the New Deal from their social studies teacher in mainstream English. (p. 92)

Questioning youth, or those who question their sexual orientation, is another group that can face stigma due to their personal identity. *Stigma* is a negative social construct or meaning placed on a given group based on stereotypes (Goffman 1963). Recent research underscores the fact that teens who self-identify as gay or lesbian have relatively insufficient support resources specifically designed to meet their needs. A study conducted by CSWE and Lambda Legal (Lambda, n.d.) found that the problem of the invisibility of this population is intensified when social workers have insufficient knowledge to practice effectively with the lesbian, gay, bisexual, transgender, and questioning (LGBTQ) population (Martin et al. 2009). Helping professionals can benefit from using online resources to enhance their own knowledge as well as that of their clients.

Engage With Individuals, Families, Groups, Organizations, and Communities

Self-Awareness and Self-Regulation

Before beginning the assessment and intervention process, social workers should become more self-aware about what inequalities are affecting their clients. For example, people with developmental disabilities may be prevented from realizing their potential unless an empowering approach is taken. As Mackelsprang and Salsgiver (2014) have suggested,

> One of the most important tools for effective human service practitioners is an understanding of our personal values. This particularly holds true for those who work with persons with disabilities. Our internalized values and beliefs come from a variety of sources, including the aggregate culture, various subcultures, family teaching, life journeys, and educational experiences. Values and beliefs concerning disability affect the work that you will be doing with one of the largest minority groups in the world—persons with disabilities. (p. 20)

➤ *Client–social worker relationships are based on trust and cultural sensitivity.*

Social workers need to come to terms with the incongruities between values, norms, and worldviews they do *not* share with clients. Unless overcome, these incongruities can serve as barriers to forming a helping relationship and expressing appropriate empathy. Moreover, the social worker can turn to theories that use intervention strategies to reframe identity based on negative self-perceptions (see Chapter 5).

Trust Building

Diverse clients may be on guard when seeking social work services. They may wish for empathy but believe that their meaning of events may not be understood (Kadushin and Kadushin 1997). Obtaining feedback from clients and constituencies builds trust and a positive helping relationship.

Helping Pathways

Lewis (1980) recommended that social workers recognize that there may be an extended path to seeking professional help. He depicted a help-seeking path in which a tribal member goes first to family and extended family (cousins, aunts, uncles, etc.); then to his or her social network, religious leader, or tribal council; and finally to the formalized healthcare delivery system (Figure 3.2). Social workers should ask specific questions to understand a client's path to treatment, such as what other help or solutions he or she has already sought. This can help social workers foster access and retention in care.

Figure 3.2.
Help-seeking pathways. (From Lewis 1980).

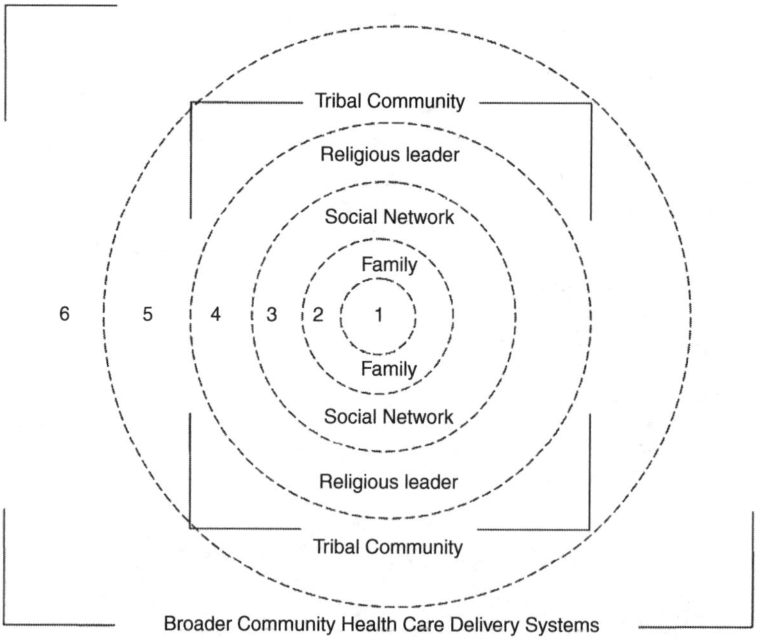

1. Individual
2. Goes to family first
3. Then to extended family (cousins, aunts, uncles, etc.)—social network
4. Religious leader
5. Tribal council
6. Finally formalized healthcare delivery system

Structural Domains of Care

In a similar vein, the social context of the healthcare culture may be thought of as consisting of three structural domains: (a) The *professional domain* refers to doctors and nurses or other licensed practitioners; (b) the *popular domain* comprises family, the social network, and the community; and (c) the *folk domain* consists of nonprofessional healers, such as herbalists. Each domain has its own explanatory systems, social roles, interaction settings, and institutions. Therefore, social work practice that engages difference is a cross-cultural process.

Crossing Cultural Boundaries

With the concepts of helping pathways and structural domains in mind, the assumption can be made that cross-cultural practice occurs in many helping situations. Therefore, social workers need to first recognize that their culture is different from that of their clients. They will have to gain culturally specific information to infuse throughout the helping process (Greene and Kropf 2009). This is best accomplished when "social workers view themselves as learners and engage clients and constituencies as experts on their own experiences" (CSWE 2015, 4). You may want to think of the social worker and client having "two stocks of knowledge": (a) what the client knows from daily experiences and (b) what the practitioner knows from formal education and training (Green 1978/1998, 57).

Help-seeking model. Another way of visualizing the client–social worker relationship as a cross-cultural experience can be seen in Figure 3.3. This help-seeking explanatory model is composed of the *client culture* and the *professional subculture*. Each of these systems has its own belief system(s), means of recognizing problems, and ways of making healthcare decisions (Green 1978/1998; Kleinman 1980). For example, clients from minority cultures may prefer feedback from their social network, such as their families, friends, and community members.

Indigenous help providers, such as natural healers, may also be sought. Although the professional subculture may see referral to a specialist as a way to resolve a (health) concern, Bhui and Bhugra (2002) suggested that, in addition to their usual assessment questions, practitioners use a mini-ethnographic approach to explore client concerns. These everyday questions may include "Why me? Why now? What is wrong? How long will it last? How serious is it? Who can intervene or treat the condition?" (p. 6).

> ➤ People who experience two environments live in a dual perspective.

Dual Perspective

DuBois (1903), a freed slave, first described the dual perspective. He said, "One ever feels his twoness—an American; a Negro; two souls, two thoughts, two unreconciled strivings; two warring ideals in one dark body, whose dogged

Figure 3.3.
Green's explanatory model. Adapted from Green (1998).

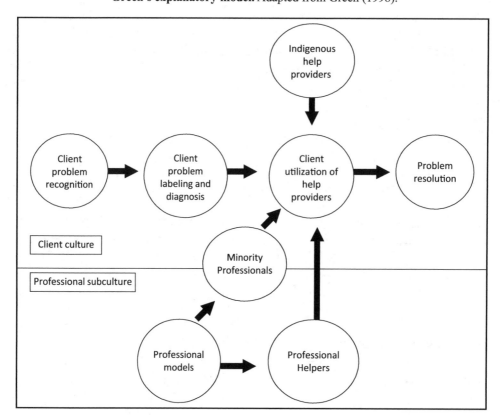

strength alone keeps it from being torn asunder" (p. 17). The dual perspective provides another way of thinking about people's participation in a multicultural society and can be used as a framework for engaging and assessing difference. It is also a way of examining the socialization of children who are not members of the mainstream.

The *dual perspective* is a process of consciously and systematically understanding the values, attitudes, and behaviors of both the minority and mainstream cultures (Chestang 1972; Miller 1980; Norton 1978). The perspective suggests that people first learn from their *nurturing, immediate culture* in the family system. They later encounter the majority, *sustaining culture* when they interact with the institutions that control the provision of goods and services, such as schools and health and human services agencies (Figure 3.4).

> ➤ Assessment content addressed from a dual perspective examines the extent to which a particular culture is nourishing or hostile. Is there congruence between social systems, or is their stress/conflict?

Figure 3.4.
The dual perspective. Adapted from Norton (1978).

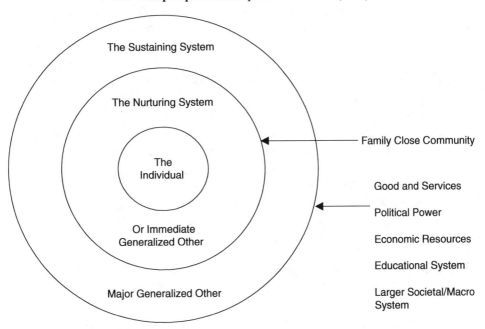

When people grow up being socialized within a dual perspective, they are relatively *bicultural;* that is, their two cultures exist side by side. According to Greene (2012),

> Biculturalism allows a child to learn about and take advantage of mainstream culture without compromising ethnic pride. For the child to develop knowledge of and a positive attitude toward both cultures, the family needs to validate that it is acceptable to live in two communities. A child who is bicultural can communicate effectively across cultures, and feels effective and well-grounded in both ethnic and mainstream cultures. (p. 262)

This suggests that over time, people may become more familiar with the mainstream culture. This process is known as *acculturation,* or a change in one's culture resulting from contact between cultures. Some people, however, become *assimilated,* or take on most of the beliefs and behaviors of the mainstream culture. Still others experience a disconnect or incongruence between cultures.

A client's relative capacity to function in two cultures falls along a continuum, from most (ethnically) traditional to taking on many aspects of the mainstream culture (Pedersen 1997). *Bicultural competence* is a person's ability to alternate between and integrate cultural forms. The social worker's assessment from the dual perspective involves an evaluation of the incongruence "of these disparate systems and determines where the major stress lies" (Norton 1978, 7). If desired, intervention strategies can then be mutually agreed on.

Empowerment and Resilience

Social workers who embrace an empowerment philosophy of practice seek ways to tap into clients' strengths and natural healing processes, moving them from the margins to the center of society (Simon 1994). This entails learning which social networks contribute to client well-being. For example, research has documented that religion and religious institutions, including the provision of social integration and support, have had an empowering impact on African American individuals and communities (Taylor, Chatters, and Levin 2004). Taylor, Chatters, and Levin (2004) research indicated that religion could serve as a *protective* or preventive factor against the recurrence of mental illness and as a *moderating* factor to ease the influence of life stress.

Assess Individuals, Families, Groups, Organizations, and Communities

The following assessment questions summarize the diversity issues discussed throughout the chapter and should be adjusted and applied differentially depending on the client system size and culture:

1. What are your professional self-expectations for working with difference?
2. What solutions has the client or constituency already tried?
3. What does the client expect of you?
4. What is the effect of cultural structures and values on your client system? (see additional questions on power dynamics in Assessing Power Characteristics)
5. Is the client(s) a member of an identifiable ethnosystem or marginalized group? What have you learned about the client's cultural patterns or belief systems?
6. Does the client or constituency think it has been marginalized, stereotyped, or denied access to resources?
7. In what general economic circumstances is your client? Are opportunities limited?
8. How does the client think about his or her dual perspective? What is the level of person and environment fit? Is he or she relatively bicultural, or is there acculturation stress?
9. Does your client live in a competitive or collaborative culture?
10. What is your client's self-construct? What does he or she hope for in the future?

> ➤ *Change strategies selected for marginalized or disempowered*
> *clients should involve person and environment solutions.*

Intervene With Individuals, Families, Groups, Organizations, and Communities: Policy Practice

Intervention with individuals, groups, organizations, and communities varies depending on the client system size and culture and the client assessment. Most interventions fall in the realm of advancing social, economic, and environmental justice (CSWE 2015). Intervention approaches may be thought of as a strategic use of power (Cummins, Byers, and Pedrick 2011). Examples can include eliminating health disparities and raising the minimum wage. Consequently, questions to guide interventions primarily come under the umbrella of policy practice (Cummins Byers, and Pedrick 2011). They include the following:

1. Are your agency's institutional history and policy directives congruent with the needs of diverse client groups? If not, what action needs to be taken?
2. Can you change social systems or institutions oppressing the client through your intervention? Will there be change in laws, budgets, and/or policy?
3. Who are the stakeholders? With whom will you collaborate or build coalitions?
4. Are coalitions addressing inequities in your area?
5. How can the social capital of the community be enhanced?
6. Do your strategies build physical and social environments?

Critique of Diversity Issues in Social Work Practice

The *NASW Standards for Cultural Competence in Social Work Practice* have been revised and now encompass *cultural humility* in which diversity practice is seen as never realized, achieved, or completed, but rather a lifelong process of learning and introspection.

Finally, as you continue through the *Handbook,* this chapter should help you critique each theory to see how difference is addressed.

Glossary

Belief systems. Sets of precepts from which one lives one's daily life; those that govern one's thoughts, words, and action.

Biculturalism. Living in one's [ethnic] immediate environment and the larger distal environment.

Cultural competence. The ability to provide services, conduct assessments, and implement interventions that are reflective of clients' cultural values and norms, congruent with their natural help-seeking behaviors, and inclusive of existing indigenous solutions.

Culture. The way of life of a group.

Dual perspective. A process of consciously and systematically understanding the values, attitudes, and behaviors of both the minority and mainstream cultures.

Empowerment. A process whereby an individual gains power and increased interpersonal influence, often achieved by building support systems and reducing societal discrimination.

Ethnic group. Members of an ethnic group think of themselves as being a people or as having a common culture, history, and origin. An ethnic group may maintain a distinction between its members and perceived outsiders.

Ethnosystem. A collective of interdependent ethnic groups sharing unique historical ties and bound together by a single political system.

Helping pathways. Pathways and solutions clients use for help seeking.

Hostile environments. Environments in which there is social injustice, social inconsistency, and personal impotence.

Institutional racism. Reinforcing discrimination within institutions.

Marginalization. The process whereby someone is placed in a position of marginal importance, influence, or power.

Minority. A group of people who differ from the larger group of which it is a part. As U.S. society becomes increasingly diverse, the minority will become the majority, posing different power differentials.

Oppression. The withholding of power by the dominant group(s) in society.

Personal impotence. A diminished sense of self that is characterized by suspicion and mistrust.

Power differential. Differences generated because of the hierarchy of power in society.

Powerlessness. The perception of lack of control over a current situation or immediate happening.

Race. A socially constructed concept of classifying people based on skin color.

Racism. A form of prejudice that espouses that one group of people is superior to another and is therefore denied access to resources.

Relational self. The view that identity is formed through human interaction; a collective sense of self.

Self. The union of elements of body, emotions, and thoughts that constitute the individuality and identity of a person.

Social injustice. Unfairness or injustice in a society in which people do not realize their potential equally and do not have the same access to opportunities.

Socialization. A process of consciously and systematically understanding the values, attitudes, and behaviors of the society necessary for participating within the society.

Societal inconsistencies. Having a double standard for mainstream versus minority populations.

References

American Psychological Association. 2009. *Report of the Task Force on Appropriate Therapeutic Responses to Sexual Orientation.* Washington, DC: American Psychological Association.

Anderson, R. E., Carter, L., and Lowe, G. 1999. *Human Behavior in the Social Environment: A Social Systems Approach.* 5th ed. Hawthorne, NY: Aldine de Gruyter.

Angel, R. J., Angel, J., and Markides, K. S. 2002. "Stability and Change in Health Insurance Among Adult Hispanics." *The Gerontologist* 36:332–40.

Asante, M. K. 1988. *Afrocentricity.* Trenton, NJ: Africa World Press.

Bhui, K., and Bhugra, D. 2002. "Exploratory Models or Mental Distress: Implications for Clinical Practice and Research." *British Journal of Psychiatry* 181:6–7.

Brown, L., and Ballou, M. 2002. *Rethinking Mental Health and Disorder: A Feminist Perspective.* New York: Guilford Press.

Bush, J. A., Norton, D. G., Sanders, C. L., and Solomon, B. B. 1983. "An Integrative Approach for the Inclusion of Content on Blacks in Social Work Education." In *Mental Health and People of Color,* edited by J. C. Chunn, P. J. Dunston, and F. Ross-Sheriff, pp. 97–125. Washington, DC: Howard University Press.

Carrillo, E., ed. 2001. "Assessment and Treatment of the Latino Patient." In *The Latino Psychiatric Patient: Assessment and Treatment,* edited by A. G. Lopez and E. Carrillo, 47–67. Washington, DC: American Psychiatric Press.

Chestang, L. 1972. *Character Development in a Hostile Environment* (Occasional Paper No. 3). Chicago, IL: University of Chicago, School of Social Service Administration.

Choi, N. G., and Gonzalez, J. 2005. "Barriers and Contributions to Minority Older Adults' Access to Mental Health Treatment: Perceptions of Geriatric Mental Health Clinicians." *Journal of Gerontological Social Work* 44 (3/4): 115–35.

Cohen, H., and Greene, R. 2005. "Older Adults Who Overcame Oppression." *Families in Society* 87 (1): 1–8.

Council on Social Work Education. 2008. *Educational Policy and Accreditation Standards.* Alexandria, VA: Council on Social Work Education.

Council on Social Work Education. 2015. *Educational Policy and Accreditation Standards.* Alexandria, VA: Council on Social Work Education.

Cross, T. 1998. "Understanding Family Resiliency from a Relational World View." In *Resiliency in Native American and Immigrant Families,* edited by H. I. McCubbin, E. A. Thompson, A. I. Thompson, and J. E. Fromer, 143–58. Thousand Oaks, CA: Sage.

Cummins, L., Byers, L., and Pedrick, L. 2011. *Policy Practice for Social Workers: New Strategies for a New Era.* London: Pearson.

Davis, K., Leijenaar, M., and Oldersma, J., eds. 1991. *The Gender of Power.* Newbury Park, CA: Sage.

Devore, W., and Schlesinger, E. 1980. *Ethnic Sensitive Social Work Practice.* New York: Council on Social Work Education.

Devore, W., and Schlesinger, E. G. 1998. *Ethnic-Sensitive Social Work Practice.* Boston, MA: Allyn & Bacon.

Devore, W., and Schlesinger, E. G. 2012. *Ethnic-Sensitive Social Work Practice.* 5th ed. Boston: MA: Pearson.

DuBois, W. E. B. 1903. *Souls of Black folk.* Chicago, IL: McClurg.

Ephross, P., and Greene, R. R. 1991. "Symbolic Interaction." In *Human Behavior and Social Work Practice,* edited by R. R. Greene and P. Ephross, 203–26. Hawthorne, NY: Aldine de Gruyter.

Erikson, E. H. 1959. *Identity and the Life Cycle.* New York: W. W. Norton.

Fong, R., and Furuto, S., eds. 2001. *Culturally Competent Practice: Skills, Interventions, and Evaluations.* Boston, MA: Allyn & Bacon.

Foucault, M. 1980. *Power/Knowledge: Selected Interviews and Other Writings, 1972–1977.* New York: Pantheon.

Garcia, B., and Van Soest, D. 2006. *Social Work Practice for Social Justice: Cultural Competence in Action.* Alexandria, VA: Council on Social Work Education.

Gergen, K. J., and Gergen, M. J. 1983. "Narratives of the Self." In *Studies in Social Identity,* edited by T. R. Savin and K. E. Scheibe, 40–53. New York: Praeger.

Goffman, E. 1963. *Stigma: Notes on the Management of Spoiled Identity.* Englewood Cliffs, NJ: Prentice Hall.

Goldenberg, I. I. 1978. *Oppression and Social Intervention.* Chicago, IL: Nelson Hall.

Gonzalez, J. 2006. "Older Latinos and Mental Health." In *Contemporary Issues in Life Care,* edited by R. Greene, 73–94. New York: Haworth Press.

Green, J. 1998. *Cultural Awareness in the Human Services.* London: Pearson. (Original work published 1978)

Greene, R. R. 2006. *Contemporary Issues in Life Care.* New York: Haworth Press.

Greene, R. R. 2008. *Human Behavior Theory and Social Work Practice.* 3rd ed. New Brunswick, NJ: Aldine Transaction Press.

Greene, R. R., ed. 2012. *Resiliency: An Integrated Approach to Practice, Policy, and Research.* 2nd ed. Washington, DC: NASW Press.

Greene, R. R., Cohen, H., Gonzalez, J., and Lee, Y. 2009. *Narratives of Resilience and Social and Economic Justice.* Washington, DC: NASW Press.

Greene, R. R., and Kropf, N. 2009. *Human Behavior Theory: A Diversity Framework*. 2nd ed. New Brunswick, NJ: Aldine Transaction Press.

Greene, R. R., and Watkins, M. 1998. *Serving Diverse Constituencies: An Ecological Perspective*. Hawthorne, NY: Aldine de Gruyter.

Greene, R. R., Watkins, M., Evans, M., David, V., and Clark, E. J. 2003. "Defining Diversity: A Practitioner Survey." *Arête*, 27 (1): 51–71.

Hollingshead, A. B., and Redlich, F. C. 1958a. *Social Class And Mental Illness: A Community Study*. New York: Wiley.

Hollingshead, A. B., and Redlich, F. C. 1958b. "Social Stratification and Psychiatric Disorders." In *Social Perspectives on Behavior*, edited by H. D. Stein and R. A. Cloward, 449–55. New York: Free Press.

Jordan, J. V. 1997. *Women's Growth in Diversity: More Writings from the Stone Center*. New York: Guilford Press.

Kadushin, A., and Kadushin, G. 1997. *The Social Work Interview: A Guide for Human Service professionals*. 4th ed. New York: Columbia University Press.

Kleinman, A. 1980. *Patients and Healers in the Context of Culture*. Berkeley: University of California press.

Lambda. n.d. *Lesbigay Youth Facts*. Retrieved from http://www.lambda.org/youth.htm#youth facts.

Lewis, R. 1980. "Cultural Perspective on Treatment Modalities with Native Americans." In *Life Span Development*, edited by M. Bloom, 434–41. New York: Macmillan.

Lum, D. 1992. *Social Work Practice and People of Color: A Process-Stage Approach*. Pacific Grove, CA: Brooks/Cole.

Mackelsprang, R., and Salsgiver, R. 2014. *Disability: A Diversity Model Approach in Human Service Practice*. 2nd ed. Chicago, IL: Lyceum.

Martin, J. I., Messinger, L., Kull, R., Holmes, J., Bermudez, F., and Sommer, S. 2009. *Council on Social Work Education—Lambda Legal Study of LGBT Issues in Social Work*. Alexandria, VA: Council on Social Work Education.

McIntosh, P. 1988. *White Privilege and Male Privilege: A Personal Account of Coming to See Correspondences through Work in Women's Studies* (Working Paper No. 189). Wellesley, MA: Wellesley College Center for Research on Women.

McIntosh, P. 1995. "White Privilege and Male Privilege: A Personal Account of Coming to See Correspondence Through Work in Women's Studies." In *Race, Class, and Gender: An Anthropology*, edited by M. L. Andersen and P. H. Collins, 76–87. New York: Wadsworth.

McNamee, S., and Gergen, K. J., eds. 1992. *Therapy as Social Construction*. Newbury Park, CA: Sage.

Mead, G. H. 1934. *Mind, Self, and Society*. Chicago, IL: University of Chicago Press.

Miller, J. B., and Stiver, I. P. 1991. *A Relational Reframing of Therapy Work in Progress* (No. 52). Wellesley, MA: Stone Center at Wellesley College.

Miller, S. 1980. "Reflections on the Dual Perspective." In *Training for Service Delivery for Minority Clients*, edited by E. Mizio and J. Delany, 53–61. New York: Family Service of America.

National Association of Social Workers. 2001. *NASW Standards for Cultural Competence in Social Work Practice*. Retrieved from http://www.socialworkers.org/practice/standards/NASWculturalstandards.pdf.

National Association of Social Workers. 2007. *Institutional Racism and the Social Work Profession: A Call to Action*. Washington, DC: National Association of Social Workers .

Norton, D. G. 1978. *The Dual Perspective: Inclusion of Ethnic Minority Content in Social Work Curriculum*. New York: Council on Social Work Education.

O'Hagan, K. 2001. *Cultural Competence in the Caring Professions*. Philadelphia, PA: Jessica Kingsley.

Ogbu, J. U. 1985. "A Cultural Ecology of Competence Among Inner-City Blacks." In *The Beginnings: The Social and Affective Development of Black Children*, edited by M. Spenser, G. K. Brookings, and W. R. Allen, 45–66. Hillsdale, NJ: Erlbaum.

Ore, T. E. 2014. *Social Construction of Difference and Inequality: Race, Class, Gender, and Sexuality*. 6th ed. New York: McGraw-Hill.

Parsons, T. 1951. *The Social System*. New York: Free Press.

Parsons, T. 1964. "Age and Sex in the Social Structure." In *The Family: Its Structure and Functions*, edited by R. L. Coser, 251–66. New York: St. Martins Press.

Pedersen, P. B. 1997. *Culture-Centered Counseling Interventions: Striving for Accuracy*. Thousand Oaks, CA: Sage.

Pinderhughes, E. B. 1978. "Power, Powerlessness, and Empowerment in Community Mental Health." *Black Caucus Journal* 10–15.

Pinderhughes, E. B. 1983. "Empowerment for Our Clients and for Ourselves." *Social Casework* 64:331–38.

Pinderhughes, E. B. 1989. *Understanding Race, Ethnicity, and Power: The Key to Efficacy in Clinical Practice.* New York: Free Press.

Schiele, J. H. 1996. "Afrocentricity: An Emerging Paradigm in Social Work Practice." *Social Work* 41(3): 284–94.

Simon, B. L. 1994. *The Empowerment Tradition in American Social Work.* New York: Columbia University Press.

Solomon, B. B. 1976. *Black Empowerment: Social Work in Oppressed Communities.* New York: Columbia University Press.

Suarez-Orozco, C., and Suarez-Orozco, M. M. 2001. *Children of Immigrants.* Cambridge, MA: Harvard University Press.

Sue, D. W. 2006. *Multicultural Social Work Practice.* New York: Wiley.

Swigonski, M. E. 1996. "Challenging Privilege Through Africentric Social Work Practice." *Social Work* 41(2): 153–61.

Taylor, R. L., Chatters, L., and Levin, J. 2004. *Religion in the Lives of African Americans: Social, Psychological, and Health Perspectives.* Thousand Oaks, CA: Sage.

Tully, C. T. 1994. "Epilogue: Power and the Social Work Profession." In *Human Behavior Theory and Social Work Practice: A Diversity Framework,* edited by R. R. Greene, 235–43. Hawthorne, NY: Aldine de Gruyter.

Walsh, F. 1998. *Strengthening Family Resilience.* New York: Guilford Press.

Wilson, W. J. 1973. *Power, Racism, and Privilege.* New York: Free Press.

Wilson, W. J. 1985. "Cycles of Deprivation and the Underclass Debate." *Social Service Review* 59:541–59.

4

Developmental Theories

➤ This chapter presents selected developmental theories and reviews how they inform the social work practice processes of engagement, assessment, and intervention. The strengths and limitations of developmental theory in regard to difference are also discussed.

This chapter explores how developmental theory contributes to social work practice. Some developmental theories, such as Freud's theory of psychosexual development, suggest clinical interventions. And Erikson's psychosocial theory, also in the psychodynamic tradition, offers additional ideas to apply in social work practice. In contrast, Piaget's cognitive theory and Kohlberg's moral theory are explanatory theories, proposing which development tasks are to be accomplished at a particular life stage. Developmental theory, an area of *scientific inquiry*, focuses on specific aspects of individual growth, organizes life cycle events, and suggests the tasks a person must accomplish at each life stage (Table 4.1).

Table 4.1.
The value of developmental theory

Developmental theory can

- provide a means of organizing life cycle tasks and events
- outline how each life stage emerges from earlier stages
- explain how a person's successes and failures at each stage are shaped by the outcome of earlier stages
- describe a process that is both continuous and changing from conception to adulthood, and sometimes death
- address how a person experiences stability and change in the unfolding of life transitions
- account for contributing factors that may shape development at each specific life stage
- include a discussion of the biopsychosocial factors shaping development
- suggest the tasks a person must accomplish at each life stage
- identify personal differences in personal development

Note. Modified from Greene (2008).

You will see that stage theories suggest a prototype of well-functioning adult behavior. Depending on the theory he or she chooses, the practitioner listens for clues about the various proposed stage outcomes and makes a professional judgment about whether the client has accomplished an outcome successfully. For example, when applying Piaget's concept of assimilation in a child welfare situation, the practitioner might hear comments from the child that lead to the assessment supposition that the child seems to have a developmental delay. Further interview questions could clarify this and lead to the suggestion of parent–child exercises to improve cognitive function. However, to truly understand life span development, the social worker must draw multiple theories from many scientific disciplines, taking into account an individual's genetic endowment, physiology, psychology, family, home, community, culture, education, religion, ethnicity/race, gender, sexual orientation, economic status, and so forth (Rogers 1982).

Figure 4.1.
Erikson's positive stage outcomes.
Adapted from Erikson 1959/1980.

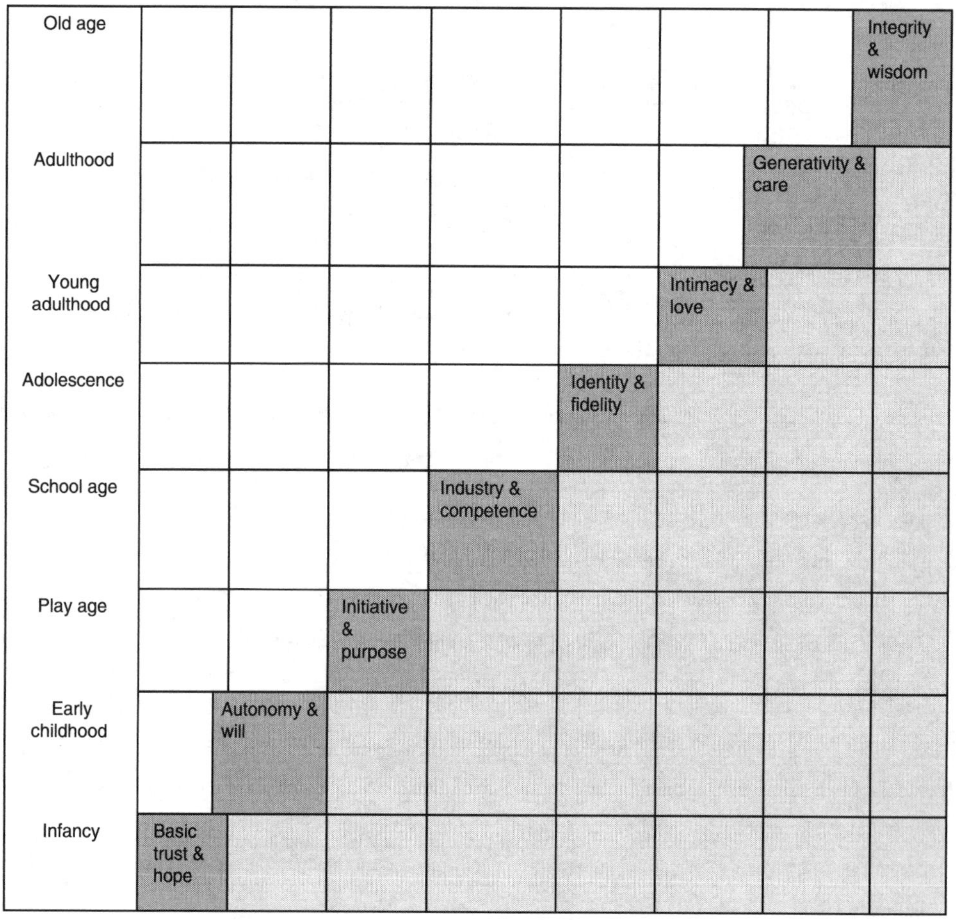

Old age								Integrity & wisdom
Adulthood							Generativity & care	
Young adulthood						Intimacy & love		
Adolescence					Identity & fidelity			
School age				Industry & competence				
Play age			Initiative & purpose					
Early childhood		Autonomy & will						
Infancy	Basic trust & hope							

Professional Purpose and Well-Being

Stage Theory Defined

Developmental theory, sometimes called *stage theory*, may be pictured as a predetermined stepwise progression of growth, with one developmental phase building on the next (see Figure 4.1, which shows Erikson's, 1968, stages of the healthy personality, as an example). Stage theory is usually presented as if each stage were *universal*, that is, could be applied to everyone at all times and in all places. Furthermore, life cycle events are seen as *normative*, or age-related developmental tasks everyone goes through at a given time, such as getting married or becoming a parent at a certain time of life.

Most stage theorists conduct research in a selected feature of human development. They may limit their explanation of that behavior to certain periods in the individual life cycle. Therefore, the scope of stage theory may be narrow because it can emphasize the individual without taking into consideration the many features of his or her environment, especially the cultural milieu (Ogbu 1999). For example, Piaget (1896–1980) outlined an approach to the cognitive maturation or reasoning of children, whereas Freud's stages of psychosexual development present the emergence of a person's personality from childhood until adulthood in relationship to his or her family of origin.

Given this about developmental theory, why can it be used to fulfill social work's purpose and inform well-being? Inherent in each approach to stage theory is the theorist's idea of what constitutes a positive outcome for each stage. This may be thought of as the theorist's ideal picture of human development, specifying which behavioral tasks people must achieve at a given time in their lives.

> ➤ *When well-being is considered in social work practice, the social worker uses clinical processes based on normative judgments.*

Therefore, social workers must make professional decisions about whether developmental tasks are being met successfully, inferring what might be useful clinical strategies to ameliorate difficulties. In other words, social workers need to critically evaluate how each developmental theory is helpful in their practice.

Biopsychosocial and Spiritual Well-Being

Another way of thinking about development is to assess and understand the client's biological, social, cultural, psychological, and spiritual development across the life cycle. An *assessment* of life cycle development involves an appreciation of the biopsychosocial-spiritual behaviors that affect a client's everyday function. *Functional assessments* include *biological factors*, encompassing health, physical capacity, or vital life-limiting organ systems; *psychological factors*, including an individual's affect state or mood, cognitive or mental health, and behavioral dimensions; and

Table 4.2.
Framework for spiritual assessment

Initial narrative framework

1. Describe the religious/spiritual tradition you grew up in. How did your family express its spiritual beliefs? How important was spirituality to your family? Extended family?

2. What sort of personal experiences (practices) stand out to you from your years at home? What made these experiences special? How have they informed your later life?

3. How have you changed or matured from those experiences? How would you describe your current spiritual or religious orientation? Is your spirituality a personal strength? If so, how?

Interpretive anthropological framework

1. Affect: What aspects of your spiritual life give you pleasure? What role does your spirituality play in handling life's sorrows? Embracing life's joys? Coping with life's pain? How does spirituality give you hope for the future? What do you wish to accomplish in the future?

2. Behavior: Are there particular spiritual rituals or practices that help you deal with life's obstacles? What is your level of involvement in faith-based communities? How are they supported? Are there spiritually encouraging individuals with whom you maintain contact?

3. Cognition: What are your current spiritual/religious beliefs? On what are they based? What beliefs do you find particularly meaningful? What does your faith say about personal trials? How does this belief help you overcome obstacles? How do your beliefs affect your health (mental health) practices?

4. Communion: Describe your relationship to the Ultimate. What has been your experience of the Ultimate? How does the Ultimate communicate with you? How have these experiences encouraged you? Have there been times of deep spiritual intimacy? How does your relationship help you face life challenges? How would the Ultimate describe you?

5. Conscience: How do you determine right or wrong? What are your key values? How does your spirituality help you deal with guilt (sin)? What role does forgiveness play in your life?

6. Intuition: To what extent do you experience intuitive hunches (flashes of creative insight, premonitions, spiritual insight)? Have these insights been strength in your life? If so, how?

Note. Adapted from Hodge (2001).

sociocultural aspects, involving the cultural, political, and economic aspects of life events (Greene 2008). *Spiritual factors* may include a client's relationship with his or her faith/religious community and/or an inner system of beliefs. Religion and spirituality are among the diverse areas that social workers should understand because they "shape the human experience and are critical to the formation of identity" (Council on Social Work Education [CSWE] 2015, 4; see Table 4.2 for questions about spiritual identity).

Section I.
Freud's Psychosexual Theory

Professional Purpose and Well-Being

> ➤ *A person who experiences well-being acts as a mature adult who is able to function effectively through work and love.*

Freud, the father of psychoanalysis, authored the most comprehensive and widely used theory of personality development (Corey 2005). Although some of his work is disputed, understanding his terminology is a prerequisite to becoming a mental health professional (Greene 2008), and many of his concepts remain infused in social work practice today (see below; Boyle et al. 2008; Sheafor and Horejsi 2011).

A well-known example of how Freud's stages of development relate to well-being concerns his explanation of what he called the *oral stage,* in which infants derive sexual pleasure from nursing during their first year of life. As infants emerge from this stage, they should be able to individuate or form viable attachments with others. Understanding this concept, commonly known as *object relations* (Bowlby 1969, 1973; Mahler 1968; Mahler, Pine, and Bergman 1975), helps psychodynamically oriented practitioners listen for interview content that implies issues of client independence or dependence.

Freud argued that to be mentally well, an individual must have completed each of his five stages somewhat effectively. (He believed that most people do not.) The summation of the positive outcome of each stage could result in what Freud considered to be the *mature adult,* a person who is able to work and love successfully—or what is referred to here as a person who exhibits a sense of *well-being.*

The Medical Model

Freud's idea of personality assessment and diagnosis set the stage for the medical model in social work. The *medical model* is a therapeutic perspective with an emphasis on diagnosis, treatment, and cure. It also places a heavy emphasis on intrapsychic factors. This perspective dominated social work theory until the 1970s, when practitioners sought out theories that gave more attention to people's social functioning and to their social environment. This marked the advent of general systems theory and postmodern helping strategies (see Chapters 5 and 6).

Applying Terms and Assumptions in Social Work Practice

> ➤ *Psychodynamic assessment content addressed and change strategies selected for social work practice refer to Freud's five developmental stages.*

Freud developed the psychodynamic approach to psychiatric treatment through his research with patients during his clinical practice. When Freud began his private psychoanalytic practice, psychology was just emerging as an independent discipline. His work reflected the scientific tradition of his day, when explanations of complex experiences were reduced to a number of seemingly elementary phenomena, an approach called *reductionism* (Schriver 2014). As a neurologist, Freud originally hoped to find biological causes for mental illness. Failing at this, his case-by-case research design led to his theory of developmental stages and the structural elements of the conscious mind.

Stages of Development

A major focus of Freud's theoretical work was to explain the way personality develops within the context of the parent–child triangle. Freud's theory of development consists of five stages:

- The first phase of personality development (birth to eighteen months) is the *oral stage,* in which children separate or individuate themselves from their maternal figure. When well individuated, they are able to form viable *object relationships* or relate well to others. Those who have not completed this stage well may be overly dependent as adults.
- The outcome of the *anal stage* of development (eighteen months to three years of age) is a person who can accept responsibility and control and negotiate with others in authority. Those who have not completed this stage well may exhibit compulsive or noncompliant adult behavior.
- During the *phallic stage* (three to six years of age) children adopt their gender orientation. Freud attributed gender identity to an adequate identification with the same-sex parent. Identification occurs when a boy rivals his father for the love of his mother. When this fails, he identifies with his father. This is known as the *Oedipus complex.* The analogous stage for girls is known as the *Electra complex.* At this stage, children are also expected to have incorporated the value orientation and ethics of their society.
- During the *latency stage* (six years of age to puberty), children use more advanced ego defenses (see below). Thus, sexual and aggressive drives are more repressed.
- Finally, in the *genital stage* (puberty until adulthood), youth may learn to work and love as successful adults. If not, they may lack self-confidence and self-esteem.

Freud concluded that poor experiences during childhood could result in neurotic adult behaviors. Therefore, he encouraged his patients to reveal, relive, and gain insight into these past experiences, considering this a curative feature of therapy (see below).

> ➤ Psychodynamic assessment content addressed and change strategies selected for social work practice deal with the functioning of the three parts of the personality.

Parts of the Personality

Freud's theory outlines three parts to the personality: the *id,* the original, inherent system of the personality that consists of everything present at birth, including instincts; the *ego,* or that part of the personality which has been modified by the direct influence of the external world (Freud 1923/1961, 25); and the *superego,* consisting of the values and ideals of society that children derive from their parents (Greene 2008). Freud viewed these three parts of the personality as a dynamic system that needed to be kept in balance.

Ego mastery. Freud espoused that ego mastery is a vital part of the mature personality. Ego mastery is exhibited when a person can deal effectively with the id, the superego, and the reality of the environment. Therefore, one of the goals of treatment is to enhance ego mastery. Ego-supportive therapy is still recognized as important in clinical social work practice today (Sheafor and Horejsi 2011; see below).

> ➤ *Psychodynamic assessment content addressed and change strategies selected for social work practice may refer to Sigmund and Anna Freud's ego defense mechanisms.*

Ego Defense Mechanisms

Modification of ego defense mechanisms is another aspect of psychodynamically based therapies. Freud and his daughter Anna proposed that people's conflictual feelings, such as anger, fear, or guilt, are guarded against through their use of *defense mechanisms,* or unconscious mental processes that distort reality. Common defense mechanisms are said to prevent the enactment of sexual and aggressive instinctual drives. When the practitioner interprets these and brings them to the client's conscious attention, they may be modified. Defense mechanisms include the following:

- *Regression.* Returning to earlier stages of behavior.
- *Repression.* Excluding painful or threatening thoughts and feelings from awareness.
- *Reaction formation.* Warding off negative impulses by expressing the opposite impulse.
- *Projection.* Attributing to others one's own unacceptable desires.
- *Rationalization.* Explaining away failures or losses.
- *Identification.* Seeing oneself as someone else.
- *Sublimation.* Diverting sexual energies to a higher channel or activity.
- *Denial.* Failing to acknowledge reality. (Greene 2008)

When people have extreme anxiety and a lack of impulse control, they may need professional help. By listening to clients recall past experiences, the practitioner learns whether excessive anxiety or conflicts need to be resolved. Interpretation of the client's negative use of defense mechanisms is sometimes addressed in clinical social work practice (Sheafor and Horejsi 2011).

Engage With Individuals, Families, Groups, Organizations, and Communities

> ➤ In psychodynamic therapies, the client–social worker relationship
> is defined as a microcosm of the client's parent–child relationship,
> with the practitioner as the expert.

The Relationship

Although a controversial figure now and in his time, Freud was respected by his patients as a medical authority. The use of his authoritative stance—the practitioner as expert—was based on the idea that uncovering the cause will reveal the cure. This notion was also expressed by social work pioneer Mary Richmond (1917, 10–13). As stated previously, this early influence led to the social work profession's strong interest in the medical model, diagnostic processes, and history taking. In the 1970s, this emphasis on the diagnosis of pathology gradually came under criticism (see the summary in Saleebey 1993). As the profession became more focused on self-determination and practitioner self-awareness, the notion of the social worker as expert also came into question (Weick 1993; see Chapter 5). There was particular concern about how the needs of diverse clients, particularly women and people of color, were being met. Today there is a mandate from CSWE (2015) for social workers to "present themselves as learners and engage client systems as experts of their own experiences" (p. 4).

Transference and Countertransference

Freud believed that the therapist–client relationship is the cornerstone of the helping process. Freud contended that to engage clients, the practitioner should encourage them to gradually recall their childhood experiences with parental figures, focusing on what is referred to as a *psychosexual history.*

The practitioner–client relationship becomes a microcosm of those past relationships. That is, patients transfer intense feelings of affection (or hostility) toward the therapist "which are justified neither by the [therapist's] behavior nor by the situation that has developed during treatment" (Freud 1916–1917/1963, 440–41). Rather, these intense feelings are based on the client's past child–parent interactions. This client response to the practitioner is known as *transference.*

To deal with transference reactions, the practitioner may interrupt the patient's train of thought to interpret relevant statements about formative past events, such as rivalry between siblings. Today's social work methods texts suggest that practitioners put the client's feelings into words, affirming that they understand them. This affirmation in turn can enhance the social worker–client relationship (Hepworth et al. 2010).

At the same time, Freud (1956) recognized that therapists could have irrational emotional reactions to the client as part of the helping process. He called this reaction *countertransference,* or the practitioner's response to the client based on the therapist's own past events. This involves feelings that can interfere with the therapeutic work. Today the term is generally used to refer to unrealistic perceptions and reactions held by the helping professional (Freud 1956). Therefore, there is the expectation that "social workers are to use reflection and self-regulation to manage personal values and maintain professionalism in practice situations" (CSWE 2015, 4).

Assess Individuals, Families, Groups, Organizations, and Communities

Freud (1933, 1916–1917/1963) assumed that all people hold deeply personal, hidden meanings stemming from negative, conflictual past events. These events produce anxiety and are *unconscious,* or out of one's mental awareness. To assess these meanings, social workers examine clients' psychosexual history, the extent of their ego mastery, and the effectiveness of their ego defense structure. Assessment also involves the practitioner uncovering past events that cause negative behaviors and helping the client to gain an understanding of these unconscious motivations.

Intervene With Individuals, Families, Groups, Organizations, and Communities

> ➤ *The major change strategy in psychodynamic therapies is insight.*

Freud's major assumption about the helping process was that the interpretation of hidden meanings results in patient *insight,* which is in itself curative. Therefore, the practitioner's role when using psychodynamic theory is to

- use the relationship as a microcosm of crucial experiences,
- examine and explain the symbolic nature of symptoms,
- uncover pertinent hidden and repressed feelings and bring them to consciousness,
- express emotional conflicts to free the individual from traumatic memories,
- reconstruct and understand difficult early life events, and
- develop and expand client self-awareness and self-control (Greene 2008).

Contemporary Interventions

When comparing contemporary applications of psychoanalytic theory in social work practice to more orthodox Freudian thought, the following contrast can be made. Contemporary theorists have

- placed a greater emphasis on ego mastery;
- examined the function of the ego across the life span;
- given more attention to the environment;
- focused on the rational and problem-solving capacities of the ego; and
- redirected their attention to *adaptation,* or person–environment fit (Goldstein 1984, xvii).

The ultimate goal of contemporary psychodynamic practitioners is to strengthen the ego.

Eda Goldstein (1995, 1996) combined several Freudian concepts to create such an approach to social work practice. She proposed that the social worker can be ego supportive or ego modifying: "Ego-supportive intervention aims at restoring, maintaining, or enhancing the individual's adaptive functioning as well as strengthening or building the ego where there are deficits or impairments. In contrast, ego-modifying intervention aims at changing basic personality patterns or structures" (Goldstein 1995, 166).

Ego-supportive treatment is short term, especially if one is under managed care. Techniques focus on the here and now and combine individual and environmental change. Ego-modifying treatment is more long term and may encompass interpretation of transference and past relationships. As seen in the case study below, a combination of intervention strategies may be needed.

Case Study

> ➤ Sheila has been referred by her workplace supervisor to the employee assistance counselor, Ms. Bell, because she is resistant to work regulations and does not take initiative. Yet she is a valued worker because she is creative and forward thinking.

> ➤ As she arrives in the social worker's office, Sheila appears shy and does not seem to know where to sit. She starts off by saying that she does not know why she has been referred. It is really a coworker who is the problem.

> ➤ During the third interview, Sheila yells at Ms. Bell, saying, "I really don't need to listen to you anyway! I will do what I want!"

Critique of Diversity Issues in Social Work Practice

How does Freud's theory meet the CSWE (2015) requirement that diversity "be understood as the intersectionality of multiple factors" (p. 4)? Freud wrote his theory in the historical context of Vienna in the late 1800s and early 1900s. He saw little diversity in his practice, treating mostly middle-class, middle-aged women. Although he did set the stage for a discussion of gender identity, even in his day he was criticized by Karen Horney (1939) and Alfred Jones (1955), both students of his and distinguished psychoanalysts in their own right. They saw Freud's views on women as both biased and inaccurate. In their opinions, Freud thought of women as a derivative of men and "disregarded the fact that femininity is not just the result of the frustration of women's attempts to be 'masculine'" (Gay 1988, 519–21).

Another area of controversy was that Freud thought that people are born bisexual (Drescher 2012). In a letter to an American mother requesting treatment for her son, he revealed his ambivalence about homosexuality as a natural variation of sexual behavior (Zijlstra 2014). He stated,

> Homosexuality is assuredly no advantage, but it is nothing to be ashamed of, no vice, no degradation; it cannot be classified as an illness; we consider it to be a variation of the sexual function, produced by a certain arrest of sexual development. (Freud 1935/1951, 786)

Freud's statement makes for an important contrast to today's research and clinical experience, which has led mainstream medical and mental health organizations to conclude that differences in sexual orientation represent normal forms of human expression (American Psychological Association 2009).

Section II.
Erikson's Psychosocial Theory

Professional Purpose and Well-Being

Eric Erikson (1964) made several important departures from Freudian theory. In contrast to Freud's psychosexual theory, Erikson's *psychosocial theory* explores the lifelong development and growth of the ego. Erikson (1964) also gave considerable attention to social as well as psychological forces, espousing the idea of a "nourishing exchange of community life" (p. 89) as key to mental health and well-being.

Erikson's theory of the healthy personality envisions a positive outcome at each stage and emphasizes that people can be socialized positively to become part of the historical and ethnic "intertwining of generations" (Erikson 1964, 93). Because of this strengths-based outlook, his theory is taught in many schools of social work.

Applying Terms and Assumptions in Social Work Practice

> ➤ *Eriksonian assessment content addressed includes person and environment factors.*

Erikson used several research methods to develop his theory. As a young man, he studied childrearing patterns of the South Dakota Sioux. He later had his own clinical practice, where he observed children playing in his waiting room (Erikson 1977). In addition, he wrote biographical case studies of famous men such as Martin Luther (Erikson 1962) and Mohandas Gandhi (Erikson 1969).

The Radius of Significant Relationships

Erikson proposed that at each stage of development—a precursor to the ecological perspective—caretakers and institutions shape the development of the healthy personality. He claimed that positive growth and development was shaped by a radius of significant relationships, an ever-widening social radius "beginning with the dim image of a mother and ending with mankind" (Erikson 1959/1980, 54; Figure 4.2).

Figure 4.2.
The radius of significant relationships. Modified from
Newman and Newman (2005).

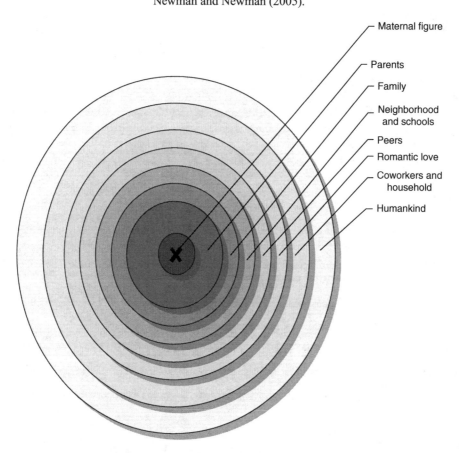

The Biological Ground Plan: Epigenesis

Erikson (1959/1980) suggested that people develop because of a biological ground plan, with each stage emerging at its special time. At each stage, the personality reconfigures itself to form a functioning whole. This principle is known as *epigenesis*. The ground plan consists of eight psychosocial crises.

Psychosocial Crises

According to Erikson (1963), a *psychosocial crisis* is precipitated within the person (interpsychically) and is resolved through interactions between the self and the nourishing outer world. Crises are not really a time of trouble. But they offer a person the opportunity for new experiences and demand a "radical change in perspective" (p. 212), or a new orientation toward one's identity and the world.

The poles of each crisis exist on a wellness continuum from positive to negative behaviors (e.g., Identity vs. Identity Confusion). Crisis outcomes generally consist of a blend of each polarity. The social worker's role in assessment is to evaluate the *healthy personality,* a culmination of relatively successful outcomes at each stage. Erikson did not see each stage outcome as fixed. Rather, new opportunities in future stages could enhance the personality. This is important for social workers to keep in mind during the helping process, as they can be central in furthering stage resolution.

Like other stage theories, Erikson's conceptualization of well-being can be understood by critically analyzing his eight stages.

1. In Stage 1 during infancy (birth to two years of age), children deal with the psychosocial crisis of *Trust versus Mistrust.* The mother is the significant relationship. Children who are relatively successful at this stage become trusting and *hopeful;* those who are less successful can be withdrawn, even as adults.

2. In Stage 2 during early childhood (two to four years of age), children face the crisis of *Autonomy versus Shame and Doubt.* Parents are the significant relationship. Those children with a more positive outcome have *will* and are not easily shamed. They grow up to be adults with less self-doubt and compulsion.

3. During the play age, the third stage (four to five years of age), children experience the crisis of *Initiative versus Guilt.* The family is the significant relationship. Those children who are more successful are creative, are expressive, and have a *sense of purpose.* Children with less success may be inhibited.

4. When children reach school age (five to twelve years of age), they deal with the crisis of *Industry versus Inferiority.* Neighbors and school personnel are the significant relationship. Productivity is a positive outcome of this stage, whereas inertia is the negative. When children are more productive, they develop a sense of *competence.*

5. In adolescence (thirteen to nineteen years of age), youth struggle with the crisis of *Identity versus Identity Confusion.* Peers and role models become the important social relationship. Those adolescents who are more successful at this stage exhibit *fidelity* or loyalty to family and peers.

6. Young adulthood (twenty to thirty-nine years of age) is when people experience the crisis of *Intimacy versus Isolation.* Romantic relationships become important. Those young adults who are more successful are better able to *love* another.

7. In adulthood (forty to sixty-four years of age), people deal with the crisis of *Generativity versus Stagnation.* The household and workplace colleagues are the important relationship. The more successful an adult is in resolving this crisis, the more able he or she is to *care* for and give to others. Erikson saw people's ability to nurture others as a means of institution building, an important aspect in the development of a healthy personality.

8. During old age (sixty-five and older), people attempt to resolve the crisis of *Integrity versus Despair.* Identification with all of humankind is the critical relationship. When older adults are able to feel that their life has been worthwhile, they impart *wisdom* to the next generation. Erikson believed that this form of intergenerational reciprocity contributes to societal well-being (Erikson 1978, 1982; Erikson, Erikson, and Kivnick 1986).

As Erikson aged, he clarified his theory through a further discussion of the diverse identity opportunities available in adolescence, adulthood, and old age (Hoare 2002).

Engage With Individuals, Families, Groups, Organizations, and Communities

> ➤ *Assessment content addressed is an evaluation of the outcome of Erikson's eight stages.*

Because Erikson emphasized social relationships and how people can make positive contributions to society, his theory can be useful in social work practice. He might contend that a client's ability to connect with significant relationships at each life stage is reflected in the helping process.

Assess Individuals, Families, Groups, Organizations, and Communities

Greene (2012) devised assessment questionnaires based on Erikson's eight stages of the healthy personality. Questions reflect the psychosocial crisis to be resolved at past or current stages and require the social worker to make a professional judgment about its relative resolution (Tables 4.3 and 4.4).

Table 4.3.
Social worker assessment questions: Erikson

Stage	Questions to Explore
Trust vs. Mistrust	How hopeful do you find the client?
	How socially attached does the client seem to be?
	How well does the client appear to trust you?
Autonomy vs. Shame and Doubt	Does the client appear to move ahead with a sense of determination?
	Does the client seem to have a strong or relatively weak sense of self-control?
	Does he or she appear to have self-confidence?
Initiative vs. Guilt	To what degree do you think the client has a sense of purpose?
	Does he or she take on new opportunities?
	Does he or she face new events with trepidation?
Industry vs. Inferiority	How competent do you think the client seems to be in handling his or her affairs?
	Does the client seem relatively productive?
Identity vs. Identity Confusion	Do you think the client is comfortable bonding with others?
	Does the client have a relatively good sense of self?
Intimacy vs. Isolation	Does the client say things that make you believe that he or she is comfortable loving and sharing with others?
Generativity vs. Stagnation	How willing is the client to care for others and be cared for himself or herself?
Integrity vs. Despair	Do you think the client passes along his or her ideas to the next generation?
	Has the client come to terms with his or her life and with others close to him or her?
	Does he or she have relative comfort with his or her mortality?

Note. Adapted from: Greene, R. R. (2008).

Table 4.4.
Questions for a life history self-evaluation: Erikson

Topic	Questions
Trust/ autonomy	To what extent do you think you were well cared for and well guided through your first years?
	How easily do you interact with others without feeling shy or ashamed?
Initiative	To what extent do you enjoy starting new activities?
	Were you easily kept back by feelings of guilt in your preschool years?
Industry	Were you a hard-working pupil in the early school years?
	Did your teachers indicate that you were good enough?
Identity	Did you belong to a group of friends in your teens?
	Did you feel like you knew yourself?
	Did you know how to behave toward other people?
Intimacy	Do you remember your first love?
	Did you establish a close relationship with anyone?
	How do you remember that person?
Early generativity	In the first half of your working life, did you do things that were meaningful for other individuals? For the next generation?
Late generativity	In the second half of your working period, did you do things for other people? For the next generation?

Note. Rennemark and Hagberg (1997).

Intervene With Individuals, Families, Groups, Organizations, and Communities

As you have seen, assessment in the Eriksonian tradition distinguishes whether the client has been relatively successful in resolving eight psychosocial crises. Interventions are designed to help with those resolutions: Teenagers may be in counseling because they are striving to develop their identity (Identity vs. Identity Confusion), whereas older adults may be coming to terms with the meaning of their lives (Integrity vs. Despair).

> ➤ *Change strategies selected obtain a developmental history and illuminate what is interfering with social functioning.*

A major Eriksonian intervention is engaging the client in self-analysis that results in a developmental history. This in turn sheds light on what may be interfering with social functioning. The developmental history is interpreted and mutually confirmed with the client. In this way, the client can use his or her *ego strengths* to explore how to cope more effectively with the environment and put these ideas into action. In addition, the social worker will delve into which client social supports can be improved (Greene 2008).

A Contemporary Intervention

Life review, or the process of recalling the past, is one widely used contemporary intervention for working with older adults to further resolve Erikson's life crises, particularly Integrity versus Despair. Life review is not to be confused with oral history or guided autobiography. Rather, it is a "naturally occurring mental process characterized by the progressive return to consciousness of past experiences" (Butler 1963, 66). The purpose of the social work interview is to tap into this process to allow for the expression and resurgence of unresolved conflicts so that they can be reintegrated (Butler 1963; see the case study below).

Case Study

➤ Mr. L. (age seventy-nine) was brought to a family service agency by his daughter because he seemed depressed about the death of his companion, Sarah. He had been Sarah's caretaker for two years prior to her death from cancer. He had also cared for his wife until her death from cancer eight years prior.

➤ When he got to the agency, he changed his mind about "talking to a stranger" (the social worker, Ms. Rubin): "This is too personal." The social worker suggested that they could begin by her getting to know Mr. L. She asked whether Mr. L. would mind sharing some of his history with her.

➤ The first session began with Ms. Rubin asking Mr. L. about his past: Where did he and his family come from? What did he do for a living? This began a series of meetings focused on what became a ten-week life review.

➤ Mr. L. began his story as a little boy living in a Russian village. He reflected on how his mother went out to work in the market where she sold aprons the family made at home on their sewing machines. Mr. L. and Ms. Rubin discussed what the aprons looked like and how they fit! Mr. L. recalled waiting for his mother to come home from the market and how he would offer her a hot cup of tea when she returned.

➤ Mr. L. went on to say that he attended the gymnasium in Russia, the equivalent of an advanced high school. When the family immigrated to the United States, he went to college at night to become an engineer. At the next meeting with the social worker, Mr. L. brought in a picture of himself supervising a crew building the U.S. Pentagon. A week later, he showed Ms. Rubin pictures of his wife and then one of Sarah. He concluded that he had "worked hard to keep them comfortable until the end."

Critique of Diversity Issues in Social Work Practice

Erikson's theory attempted to engage diversity and difference in practice. He suggested that membership identities, such as ethnicity, social class, culture, and national affiliation, give people the collective power to create their own environments. Because each society at a particular time and place has its own ideological frameworks, roles, tasks, rituals, and initiations, the society and its various institutions bestow "strength and a sense of identification on the developing individual" (Erikson 1964, 91). The idea that "life histories are inextricably interwoven with history," or what Erikson termed a *psychohistorical account* (Erikson 1975, 20), is important, reminding us of the person–environment perspective in social work practice.

Not only was Erikson known for his interest in the differences among life histories and the viability of societal institutions, he also took views on public matters. For example, at the end of World War II, he argued against the use of nuclear weapons, saying that the human race had "overreached itself" and that nuclear bombs were a "historical maladaptation" in species evolution (Erikson 1975). In a lecture in 1972, he said that the Vietnam War had turned the "American dream" into a "nightmare."

Section III.
Piaget's Cognitive Theory

Professional Purpose and Well-Being

Earlier in the *Handbook,* you learned how a person's personality evolves over time through interaction with the environment. Freud limited his theory to development within the family and did not explore growth beyond adulthood. Erikson had a more expansive view of significant relationships throughout the life span. Both were concerned with *ego mastery,* or a person's ability to cope with the environment. When using these theories or their contemporary adaptations, such as ego psychology and life review, attending to emotions plays a critical role in practice.

In the case of the next theorists, Piaget and Kohlberg, consideration is given to abstract symbolic reasoning or stages of *cognitive development,* which is not directly applicable to social work practice. However, these theories provide the social worker with different ways of thinking about the processes of engagement, assessment, and intervention.

Applying Terms and Assumptions in Social Work Practice

According to Vourlekis (2008), cognitive theories emphasize "the acquisition and function of human thought and knowledge: how and what one comes to think and know, and the role this plays in what one does and feels" (p. 133; see Chapter 5).

Piaget, a biological psychologist, studied cognitive development from birth to late adolescence. He suggested that children filter their experiences within the environment through existing cognitive structures. They draw on two complementary mental processes: (a) *assimilation,* which uses cognitive processes to integrate new perceptual information; and (b) *accommodation,* which takes into account new information to create new cognitive *schemas.* For example, a child may be able to apply his or her knowledge of what a horse looks like to how a zebra is different. This two-part complementary process contributes to the ongoing *adaptation* of children in their environment (Vourlekis 2008). One may thus think of adaptation as a cognitive coping process that makes for well-being.

Another developmental concept suggested by Piaget is *object permanence,* or knowing that an object is still there even when one is not present. For example, Baby

Sarah likes to play peek-a-boo because she really thinks her mother is not there when she hides. She later develops permanence when she is able to leave her favorite blanket at home when she goes to school. Object permanence becomes more sophisticated as the child matures. For example, children must be able to separate from a parent who may be temporarily far away, such as someone deployed in the military.

Engage With Individuals, Families, Groups, Organizations, and Communities

Each of Piaget's cognitive stages involves a new psychological/cognitive reorganization that stems from the maturation of biological functions and abilities. Piaget (1948) outlined how a child grows from being an infant who uses reflexes to act on the environment to an adolescent who is able to use abstract reasoning and formal logic. This growing ability allows the child to engage with helping professionals from an increasingly more sophisticated point of view.

Stages of Cognitive Development

Piaget contended that children go through four distinct universal stages in which they exhibit a greater ability to process more complex conditions and better understand their natural everyday environment.

1. *The sensorimotor stage.* The sensorimotor stage occurs from birth to two years of age. In this stage, infants must learn to distinguish themselves from their environments. Infants are born using reflexive motor activity, including sucking and grasping. They grow cognitively by repeating motor skills and manipulating objects. By the end of this stage, children have an internal representation or schema of essential objects around them, such as a cat or dog. However, they have limited ability to use language or symbols.

   This knowledge about development can be helpful when you are working with parents of young children. Educational information can reassure parents that children are on the right developmental path. Children with developmental delays can be provided with toys that enhance motor skills. This in turn is useful in fostering further cognitive growth.

2. *The preoperational stage.* During the preoperational stage from two to seven years of age, children begin to master language and the use of symbols. They view their world only from their own perspective. This thought pattern, known as *egocentrism,* is a preoccupation with one's personal worldview. At this age, a child has limited ability to exchange ideas with others.

   Social workers practicing with this age group often involve children in play activity to deduce areas of difficulty in social functioning. At this time, children usually display parallel play, playing alone, and not being able to follow the rules of a game. They may also need to be taught empathy or that they have hurt the feelings of another person. Making a professional judgment about a child's ability to get along with others may be needed.

3. *The concrete operational stage.* During the concrete operational stage, children mature and become more logical. Children come to understand the principle of *conservation,* or the fact that the amount of matter remains the same regardless of changes in its shape.

Piaget's example of this stage was helping a child realize that an eight-inch tumbler and an eight-inch highball glass hold the same amount of milk. A child who can realize this concept may be better at deciding what is a fair amount (see the section on Kohlberg below).

4. *The formal operational stage.* The formal operational stage begins at about age twelve. It is characterized by more logical, abstract thought. Children can also use more symbols and abstract concepts in this stage. The adolescent has moved from egocentric thought to socialized thinking, at which time he or she exchanges his or her thoughts with others. By adulthood, people use deductive, hypothetical reasoning.

According to Piaget, a competent adult should be capable of "hearing" others, "'thinks socially' or has his mind's eye on his collaborators or opponents" (Gruber and Voneche 1995, 83).

Assess Individuals, Families, Groups, Organizations, and Communities

Assessing a client's relative ability to reason is important to practitioners working with clients in crisis situations. In addition, according to Piaget's model, intellectual development represents what people believe is the true nature of learning. Consequently, helping professionals can assist clients to interact more positively with their environment, developing their ability to think creatively. Piaget's theory argues that "to know something is to act upon it and/or interact with it" (Renner et al. 1976, 7). Therefore, a professional's role is to ascertain clients' levels of language and intellectual development and to provide experiences that correspond with their stage of intellectual development.

Intervene With Individuals, Families, Groups, Organizations, and Communities

Social workers should try and select interventions related to a client's level of intellectual development. For example, an adolescent is expected to have moved from egocentric thought to socialized thinking. He or she is then able to exchange abstract thoughts with others. When this ability is impaired, perhaps because of developmental delays, children have less empathy for others.

> ➤ *Mr. and Mrs. Roberts are playing a game of Chutes and Ladders with their children, Steven (age ten) and Stanley (age three). Steven expects to win all the time, whereas Stanley cries. Have the parents chosen a game suitable for their children's respective ages?*

Critique of Diversity Issues in Social Work Practice

Piaget's theory has had a great influence, particularly in the field of education. Piaget and his colleagues tested his work in many different cultures, and concluded that his stages of development are universal (Dasen 1994). However, other studies suggest that not all children and adults reach the final operational stage of development (Kuhn et al. 1977). Therefore, the social worker should apply these stages with caution.

Section IV.
Kohlberg's Theory of Moral Development

The Story
Heinz Steals the Drug in Europe

> ➤ *A woman was near death from a special kind of cancer. There was one drug that the doctor thought might save her. It was a form of radium that a druggist in the same town had recently discovered. The drug was expensive to make, but the druggist was charging ten times what the drug cost him to produce. He paid $200 for the radium and charged $2,000 for a small dose of the drug. The sick woman's husband, Heinz, went to everyone he knew to borrow money, but he could only get together about $1,000, which is half of what it cost. He told the druggist that his wife was dying and asked him to sell it cheaper or let him pay later. But the druggist said, "No, I discovered the drug and I am going to make money from it." So Heinz got desperate and broke into the man's store to steal the drug for his wife. Should Heinz have broken into the laboratory to steal the drug for his wife? Why or why not? (Kohlberg, 1981)*

Professional Purpose and Well-Being

Kohlberg's theory of moral development can be used to understand how moral reasoning relates to individual and community well-being. His various stages illustrate how as an individual develops, he or she becomes more morally responsible and possibly more responsive to the social order.

Applying Terms and Assumptions in Social Work Practice

Kohlberg (1981) used the imaginary story of Heinz's situation to determine how individuals would justify their actions if faced with such a moral dilemma. As an example, seventy-two boys were asked to give their answers and justifications about what they would do if they were Heinz. Kohlberg classified each boy into three developmental stages or levels of moral reasoning, each made up of two substages:

1. The *preconventional stage* of moral reasoning usually is found among children. People think about the direct consequences of their actions. The preconventional stage consists of two substages in which children
   • assume an obedience and punishment orientation: "Can I avoid punishment?"
   • take a self-interest orientation: "Can I avoid getting arrested?"

2. The *conventional stage* of moral reasoning generally takes place during adolescence. Youth compare themselves to societal norms and expectations. Two substages are involved in which youth
   - maintain interpersonal accord and conformity: "I do not want to incur the disapproval of others."
   - comply with authority and social order: "I want to live by the law."
3. In the *postconventional stage* of moral reasoning, people take on their own perspectives, developing abstract principles about right and wrong. They do not obey the law unquestioningly. The two substages propose that people who have reached this stage
   - view the world through social contracts composed of multiple opinions, rights, and democratic values: "I don't agree but can accept what you are saying."
   - universalize ethical principles, resulting in a commitment to social justice: "If we do this, we all will benefit."

Kohlberg (1973) contended that most people remain at Stage 2 of development, in which moral reasoning is controlled by outside forces.

Engage With Individuals, Families, Groups, Organizations, and Communities

Social workers work with clients of all ages. As we saw in the case of Piaget's stages of intellectual development, professionals need to adapt their interventions to the client's developmental stage. In a similar vein, there will be times when helping professionals will want to be ready to engage and assess a client's level of moral reasoning. For example, social workers who are developing reports about who will be a custodial parent following a divorce need to determine a parent's level of responsibility toward a child.

Assess Individuals, Families, Groups, Organizations, and Communities

Because Kohlberg's theory of moral development is an explanatory theory, social workers will have to make a professional judgment about a client's level of moral reasoning. This judgment is made by inferring the essence of client meaning: Do you hear the client saying, "I want to live by the law?" "I don't want to receive disapproval?" or "I can accept the views of others?"

Intervene With Individuals, Families, Groups, Organizations, and Communities

As stated previously, interventions using Kohlberg's theory may be useful in legal settings. Intervention strategies are also used by teachers and school personnel (see below).

Critique of Diversity Issues in Social Work Practice

Kohlberg's study was first conducted with a limited sample of young boys (Gilligan 1982). It has been criticized for suggesting that boys who agreed with stealing the medicine had a higher personal moral code. Psychologist Carol Gilligan wrote *In a*

Different Voice (1982) to speak out against the use of an all-male sample in Kohlberg's study. She proposed that because of Kohlberg's sample bias, the idea that women and girls usually place a high value on caring relationships was not explored.

On a different note, Kohlberg's theory has been used to address problems of bullying. In response to the suicide of eight Massachusetts youth of ten to fourteen years of age, Erhardt Graeff (2012), a student at the Harvard Graduate School of Education, decided to conduct research on cyberbullying and moral reasoning. He wanted to know why few youth stand up for victims (upstanders) and most do not (bystanders). His research found that upstanders were more likely to use high-order moral reasoning than bystanders. Graeff concluded,

> Ideally, students should be able to play out these hypothetical dilemmas through mock social networks and text messages designed to simulate being online. Using actual digital media to navigate a variety of examples, with ample opportunities for educators to draw parallels and prompt reflection, may help orient students struggling to make moral judgments in the absence of "proper distance." (p. 17)

Finally, it should be noted that the step by step progression of "normal" developmental theory may ignore the social dynamics that contribute to resilience in human development (Saleebey 2006). In addition, factors related to race, ethnicity, social class, and sexual orientation may be ignored if further research is not conducted to understand how difference life experiences influences practice (CSWE 2015).

Glossary

Freud

Anal stage. Freud's psychosexual stage during which the focus of tension and gratification shifts to the anal area and toilet-training activities are central.

Anxiety. A state of tension that is always present at some level that motivates one to act.

Conscious. Mental processes of which one is aware.

Defense mechanisms. Unconscious mental processes that distort reality to ward off anxiety and safeguard the ego from id impulses and pressures of the superego.

Ego. The executive arm of the personality; its chief function is to interact with the environment.

Genital stage. Freud's final psychosexual stage during which psychological identity is integrated.

Id. The innate subsystem of the personality made up of unconscious representations of sexual and aggressive drives.

Identification. A person tries to replicate the personality features of another person; matching mental representation with physical reality.

Insight. Conscious recognition of previously repressed memories or fantasies.

Interpretation. The process of the helping person listening, observing, and clarifying a client's meaning of events.

Life cycle development. The biopsychosocial-spiritual behaviors that affect a client's everyday function.

Medical model. A perspective with an emphasis on diagnosis, treatment, and cure.

Object. An internal representation of a person, place, or symbol.

Object relations theory. A body of concepts of individual personality development emphasizing attachment and separation in the final individuation of the self.

Oral stage. Freud's psychosexual stage covering the period from birth to 18 months when activity and gratification are centered around the mouth, lips, and tongue.

Phallic stage. Freud's psychosexual stage occurring at about age 3 years when tensions and gratification shift to the genitals. Gender identification and superego formation occur as a result of the resolution of the Oedipal conflict.

Projection. A defense mechanism in which the source of anxiety is attributed to something or somebody in the external world rather than to one's own impulses; attempts to get rid of one's own unacceptable characteristics by assigning them to someone else.

Psychoanalysis. A method of psychotherapeutic treatment for emotional disturbance; a method of studying and developing a theoretical explanation for behavior.

Psychosexual stage. A period of predetermined time in which there is a shift in the focus of sexual and aggressive energy during the course of maturation. As each stage unfolds, emotional patterns are formed that determine the adult personality.

Rationalization. A defense mechanism in which there is an offering of reasonable-sounding explanations for unreasonable, unacceptable feelings or behavior.

Reaction formation. A defense mechanism in which there is a replacement in consciousness of an anxiety-producing impulse or feeling by its opposite.

Reductionism. A thought process that reduces an explanation of complex events to elementary phenomena or events.

Regression. A defense mechanism in which there is a return to behavior patterns characteristic of earlier levels of functioning, often precipitated by stress.

Repression. A basic defense mechanism in which ideas are pushed out of awareness.

Structural model. Freud's concepts about the three major subsystems of the personality: the id, ego, and superego.

Transference. The irrational feelings a client has for the helping person brought about by the irrational intrusion of early childhood relationships.

Unconscious. Mental processes outside of awareness and not subject to direct observation.

Erikson

Autonomy. A sense of self-control without loss of self-esteem.

Care. A concern with adhering to irreversible obligation that overcomes self-concern.

Competence. The ability and skill to complete tasks successfully.

Crisis. A critical period that demands that an individual become reoriented, make a radical change in perspective, and face new opportunities.

Despair. A feeling of lack of integration and meaninglessness.

Development. A maturational process involving social and environmental factors that produces changes in thought and behavior.

Developmental stage. A period in life with an underlying organizational emphasis involving the need to adopt a new life orientation.

Ego. The executive arm of the personality that relates to the outer world.

Ego psychology. A school of psychology that places an emphasis on the striving ego and the individual's efforts to attain mastery of his or her environment across the life cycle.

Ego strength. The capacity to unify experience and take actions that anticipate and overcome self-concerns.

Fidelity. An ability to sustain loyalties despite contradictions in value systems.

Generativity. Concern with establishing and guiding the next generation.

Guilt. A feeling of fear that punishment will occur.

Hope. Belief in the attainability of primal or basic wishes.

Identity. Accrued confidence gathered over the years.

Industry. A sense of the technology of one's culture.

Inferiority. A feeling of being unworthy or unprepared to deal with technology.

Initiative. The ability to move independently and vigorously.

Integrity. The ability to transcend the limits of self-awareness and the relativity of all knowledge.

Intimacy. An ability to commit to affiliations and partnerships even though they may call for significant sacrifice and compromise.

Isolation. The avoidance of contacts that commit to intimacy.

Life cycle. A developmental perspective that explores the tendency of an individual's life to form a coherent, lifetime experience and be joined or linked to previous and future generations.

Life review. A natural process of reminiscing in old age involving a restructuring of past events; a helping process based on the progressive return to consciousness of past experiences in an attempt to resolve and integrate them.

Love. A mutuality of devotion that is greater than the antagonisms and dependency needs inherent in a relationship.

Psychosocial development. Development is understood as the relationship between inner agency and social life.

Psychosocial crisis. A crucial period or turning point in life when there is increased vulnerability and heightened potential; a time when particular efforts must be made to meet a new set of demands presented by society.

Psychosocial theory. A theoretical approach that explores issues of growth and development across the life cycle as a product of the personality interacting with the social environment.

Purpose. An ability to pursue valued and tangible goals guided by conscience.

Radius of significant relationships. The developing individual's expanding number of social relationships through life.

Shame. A feeling of being exposed and of being looked at disapprovingly.

Trust. A feeling of certainty about one's social ecology.

Wisdom. Active concern with life in the face of death; mature judgment.

Piaget

Accommodation. The taking into account of new information and creation of new cognitive schemes.

Adaptation. The use of cognitive processes such as assimilation and accommodation to increase or enhance person–environment fit.

Assimilation. The cognitive process by which a person integrates new perceptual information into existing ways of thinking.

Cognitive processes. The mental processes with which a person perceives, organizes, remembers, and evaluates available information.

Cognitive structures. That which provides the information to interpret reality and engage in problem-solving behavior.

Concepts. The organization of information from multiple experiences into a class or category.

Concrete operational stage. The third of Piaget's stages, occurring between seven and eleven years of age, when a child's reasoning becomes logical in concrete situations.

Conservation. One of the concrete operations; the conceptualization that the amount or quantity of matter stays the same regardless of changes in shape or position.

Egocentric. A person who is egocentric is preoccupied with one's personal worldview rather than the exchange of ideas.

Formal operational stage. The fourth of Piaget's cognitive developmental stages, occurring from eleven to fifteen years of age, when the ability to solve all classes of problems develops, including hypothetical and scientific problems.

Object permanence. A child's awareness that objects continue to exist even when they cannot be seen.

Preoperational stage. The second of Piaget's cognitive stages, occurring between two and seven years of age, during which a conceptual symbolic approach emerges in the child.

Sensorimotor stage. The first of Piaget's stages of cognitive development, occurring from birth to two years of age, when reflexive behaviors are noted.

Social justice. Fairness in terms of the distribution of wealth, opportunities, and privileges within a society.

Stage. A new psychological reorganization that can result from maturational forces, deep insights, and changed demands and opportunities of the environment accompanying life shifts.

Kohlberg

Conventional stage. When teenagers identify with societal norms for moral reasoning.

Post conventional stage. People who use abstract reasoning to obtain moral reason.

Preconventional stage. A time when children obey authority as a means to moral reasoning.

References

American Psychological Association. 2009. *Report of the APA Task Force on Appropriate Therapeutic Responses to Sexual Orientation.* Washington, DC: American Psychological Association.

Bowlby, J. B. 1969. *Attachment and Loss: Vol. 1. Attachment.* New York: Basic Books.

Bowlby, J. B. 1973. *Attachment and Loss: Vol. 2. Separation: Anxiety and Anger.* London: Hogarth Press.

Boyle, S. W., Hull, G. H., Mather, J. H., Smith, L. L., and Farley, O. W. 2008. *Direct Practice in Social Work.* Boston, MA: Allyn & Bacon.

Butler, R. N. 1963. "The Life Review: An Interpretation of Reminiscence in the Aged." *Psychiatry* 26:65–76.

Corey, G. 2005. *Theory and Practice of Counseling and Psychotherapy.* Monterey, CA: Thomson Brooks/Cole.

Council on Social Work Education. 2015. *Educational Policy and Accreditation Standards.* Alexandria, VA: Council on Social Work Education.

Dasen, P. 1994. "Culture and Cognitive Development from a Piagetian Perspective." In *Psychology and Culture,* edited by W. J. Lonner and R. S. Malpass, 37–63. Boston, MA: Allyn & Bacon.

Drescher, J. 2012. "The Removal of Homosexuality from the *DSM*: Its Impact on Today's Marriage Equality Debate." *Journal of Gay & Lesbian Mental Health* 16:124–35.

Erikson, E. 1962. *Young Man Luther.* Glouster, MA: Peter Smith Publishing.

Erikson, E. H. 1963. *Childhood and Society.* 2nd ed. New York: Norton.

Erikson, E. H. 1964. *Insight and Responsibility.* New York: Norton.

Erikson, E. H. 1968. *Identity,Youth, and Crisis.* New York: Norton.

Erikson, E. H. 1969. *Gandhi's Truth.* New York: Norton.

Erikson, E. H. 1975. *Life History and the Historical Moment.* New York: Norton.

Erikson, E. H. 1977. *Toys and Reason.* New York: Norton.

Erikson, E. H. 1978. *Adulthood.* New York: Norton.

Erikson, E. 1980. *Identity and the Life Cycle.* New York: Norton. (Original work published 1959)

Erikson, E. H. 1982. *The Life Cycle Completed.* New York: Norton.

Erikson, E. H., Erikson, J. M., and Kivnick, H. Q. 1986. *Vital Involvement in Old Age.* New York: Norton.

Freud, S. 1933. "New Introductory Lectures on Psychoanalysis." In *The Standard Edition of the Complete Psychological Works of Freud,* edited by J. Strachey, Vol. 22, pp. 1–267. London: Hogarth.

Freud, S. 1951. "A Letter from Freud." *American Journal of Psychiatry* 107:786–87. (Original work published 1935)

Freud, S. 1956. "Four Unpublished Letters of Freud." *The Psychoanalytic. Quarterly* 25:147–54.

Freud, S. [SE 18:223] 1923. "Certain Neurotic Mechanisms; Jealousy, Paranoia and Homosexuality." *International Journal of Psychoanalysis* 4:1–10.

Freud, S. 1963. "Introductory Lectures on Psychoanalysis." In *The Standard Edition of the Complete Psychological Works of Sigmund Freud,* edited by J. Strachey, Vols. 15–16, pp. 9–463. London: Hogarth. (Original work published 1916–1917)

Gay, P. 1988. *Freud: A Life for Our Time.* New York: Norton.

Gilligan, C. 1982. *In a Different Voice.* Cambridge, MA: Harvard University Press.

Goldstein, E. G. 1984. *Ego Psychology and Social Work Practice.* 1st ed. New York: Free Press.

Goldstein, E. G. 1995. *Ego Psychology and Social Work Practice.* 2nd ed. New York: Free Press.

Goldstein, E. G. 1996. "Ego Psychology Theory." In *Social Work Treatment: Interlocking Theoretical Approaches,* edited by F. Turner, 191–217. New York: Free Press.

Graeff, E. February 2012. *Tweens, Cyberbullying, and Moral Reasoning: Separating the Upstanders from the Bystanders.* Retrieved from http://thegoodproject.org/pdf/76-Tweens-Cyberbullying-And-Moral-Reasoning.pdf.

Greene, R. R. 2008. "Eriksonian Theory." In *Human Behavior Theory and Social Work Practice,* edited by R. R. Greene, 3rd ed., pp. 85–112. New Brunswick, NJ: Aldine Transaction Press.

Greene, R. R. 2012. "Psychosocial Theory." In *Human Behavior in the Social Environment,* edited by B. Thyer, C. Dulmus, and K. Sowers, 193–224. Hoboken, NJ: Wiley.

Gruber, H. E., and Voneche, J. J. 1995. *The Essential Piaget.* Northdale, NJ: Jason Aronson.

Hepworth, D. H., Rooney, R. H., Larsen, J., Rooney, G. D., and Strom-Gottfried, K. 2010. *Direct Social Work Practice: Theory and Skills.* 9th ed. Belmont, CA: Wadsworth.

Hoare, C. H. 2002. *Erikson on Development in Adulthood: New Insights from the Unpublished Papers.* New York: Oxford University Press.

Hodge, D. R. 2001. "Spirituality Assessment: A Review of Major Qualitative Methods and a New Framework for Assessing Spirituality." *Social Work* 46:203–14.

Horney, K. 1939. *New Ways in Psychoanalysis.* New York: Norton.

Jones, A. 1955. *Sigmund Freud: Love and Work the Years of Maturity 1901–1919.* London: Hogarth Press.

Kohlberg, L. 1973. "The Claim to Moral Adequacy of a Highest Stage of Moral Judgment." *Journal of Philosophy* 70:630–46.

Kohlberg, L. 1981. *Essays on Moral Development: Vol. 1. The Philosophy of Moral Development.* San Francisco, CA: Harper & Row.

Kuhn, D., Langer, J., Kohlberg, L., and Haan, N. S. 1977. "The Development of Formal Operations in Logical and Moral Judgment." *Genetic Psychology Monographs* 95:97–188.

Mahler, M. S. 1968. *On Human Symbiosis and the Vicissitudes of Individuation.* New York: International Universities Press.

Mahler, M. S., Pine, F., and Bergman, A. 1975. *The Psychological Birth of the Human Infant: Symbiosis and Individuation.* New York: Basic Books.

Newman, B. M., and Newman, P. R. 2005. *Development Through Life: A Psychosocial Approach.* 9th ed. Belmont, CA: Wadsworth/Thomson.

Ogbu, J. U. 1999. "Cultural Context of Children's Development." In *Children of Color: Research, Health, and Policy Issues,* edited by H. E. Fitzgerald, B. M. Lester, and B. S. Zuckerman, 73–92. New York: Garland.

Piaget, J. 1948. *Moral Judgment of the Child.* Glencoe, IL: Free Press.

Rennemark, M., and Hagberg, B. 1997. "Social Network Patterns Among the Elderly in Relation to Their Perceived Life History in an Eriksonian Perspective." *Aging & Mental Health* 1:321–31.

Renner, J., Stafford, D. G., Lawson, A. E., McKinnon, J. W., Friot, F. E., and Kellogg, D. H. 1976. *Research, Teaching, and Learning with the Piaget Model.* Norman: University of Oklahoma Press.

Richmond, M. 1917. *Social Diagnosis.* New York: Russell Sage Foundation.

Rogers, C. R. 1982. *Life-span Human Development.* Monterey, CA: Brooks/Cole.

Saleebey, D. 1993. "Notes on Interpreting the Human Condition: A Constructed HBSE Curriculum." In *Revisioning Social Work Education: A Social Constructionist Approach*, edited by J. Laird, 197–217. New York: Haworth Press.

Saleebey, D. 2006. *The Strengths Perspective in Social Work Practice.* Boston, MA: Pearson: Allyn & Bacon.

Schriver, J. M. 2015. *Human Behavior and the Social Environment: Shifting Paradigms in Essential Knowledge for Social Work Practice.* 6th ed. New York: Pearson.

Sheafor, B. W., and Horejsi, C. J. 2011. *Techniques and Guidelines for Social Work Practice.* 9th ed. Boston, MA: Allyn & Bacon.

Vourlekis, B. 2008. "Cognitive Theory for Social Work Practice." In *Human Behavior Theory and Social Work Practice*, edited by R. R. Greene, 3rd ed., pp. 133–64. New Brunswick, NJ: Aldine Transaction Press.

Weick, A. 1993. "Reconstructing Social Work Education." In *Revisioning Social Work Education: ⁰A Social Constructionist Approach*, edited by J. Laird, 11–30. New York: Haworth Press.

Zijlstra, I. 2014. "The Turbulent Evolution of Homosexuality: From Mental Illness to Sexual Preference." *Social Cosmos* 5:29–35.

5

Human Behavior and the Social Environment Theory: Social Work Practice with Individuals

> ➤ This chapter presents human behavior and the social environment theory for engaging, assessing, and intervening with individuals in social work practice. It first outlines the historical evolution of the cognitive movement, applying the terms and assumptions of behavioral, social learning, and cognitive behavior theory—part of the positivist scientific paradigm. Research influences on theory-building are discussed. These ideas are then contrasted with social constructionism, a school of thought linked to the shift in paradigm to postmodern thinking. Each theory provides a different way of viewing the social work helping process.

In the previous chapter, human behavior and the social environment was organized around stages of *normative development,* focusing on an individual's expected passage from one phase of growth to another. In this chapter, selected theories are discussed that center on cognitive function. In general, cognitive aspects of human behavior and the social environment address the role of cognition in thought processes—what we think and know, and how we see reality. This in turn influences feelings and behaviors. Selected cognitive principles were chosen for this chapter to illustrate their utility in clinical social work practice, providing different ways for social workers to apply theoretical principles in their practice.

To clarify how various theoretical positions are used in social work, the chapter is divided into two sections, each focusing on a different paradigm: One focuses on behavioral, social learning, and cognitive behavior theory, stemming from the positivist tradition and emphasizing how people learn; the other centers on social constructionism, originating from the postmodern way of thinking and focusing on what people know and how they create their own reality (Anderson and Goolshian 1988; Blumer 1937).

Paradigm Shift

The theories presented in this chapter stem from two different scientific/practice paradigms. Each *paradigm,* or configuration of beliefs, values, and techniques that are shared by members of a professional community, is a reconstruction of prior thinking that moves the professional community to a different worldview about the nature of knowledge (Schriver 2014). The following chart summarizes these differences:

Positive Tradition	Postmodern Thinking
Emphasizes universal laws	Focuses on local reality
Uses knowledge based on science, logic, and reason	Finds knowledge through conjecture
Strives for objectivity	Attempts to find personal and collective meaning

Postmodern theorists contend that although social worker objectivity would be ideal, many realities are created at the local level through human interaction (Dean 1993; Foucault 1980; McNamee and Gergen 1992). Not only can no one be objective, but truth is often decided by those in power—even as the social worker has power over a client. In these instances, the social worker's goal is to individualize client meanings. You will learn how interviews may differ depending on the epistemology or philosophical assumptions of the theory a social worker applies (Kuhn 1962; see below).

Section I.A.
Behavior Theory

Historical Background of Behaviorism

An understanding of cognitive theory requires a review of its major historical roots, beginning with some of the basic tenets and terms of behaviorism. Behaviorism stems from a positivist tradition that values the scientific method. It follows then that a central behaviorist premise is that people's mental events cannot be observed. This premise sets the stage for gathering objective evidence about how people learn by studying behavior(s) under controlled conditions.

Pavlov

Behaviorism began with the physiologist Ivan Pavlov (1927), well known for the concept of the conditioned reflex and his experiments with dogs. Pavlov observed that the dogs he used to conduct experiments salivated when his assistants entered the research laboratory (without the presence of food for them to smell). Pavlov concluded that this was not an inborn reflex response but a learned reaction. When the dogs saw laboratory assistants dressed in white—who often did bring food with them into the laboratory—this brought about a *conditioned reflex* (p. 142; Table 5.1).

This observation prompted Pavlov to train his dogs to salivate when hearing the ticking of a metronome or the ringing of a bell (neutral stimulus). The dogs learned by repeatedly associating these sounds with a nonneutral stimulus (meat powder). The Pavlovian conditioning experiments demonstrated that an environmental stimulus (a bell) was not sufficient to produce a response (salivation) without being paired with an *unconditioned stimulus* (meat powder). That is, a conditioned stimulus is "a previously neutral stimulus [that] comes to evoke a specific response by being

Table 5.1.
Selected theoretical foundations of cognitive thought

Time adopted	Major theorist(s)	Theme	Concepts for practice
1927	Ivan Pavlov: Pavlovian conditioning	Experiments are needed to determine how learning occurs.	Learning through repetition of conditioning
1913	John Watson: Classical Conditioning	Prediction and control of behavior is necessary for objectivity.	Using conditioning in child care settings
1957	B. F. Skinner: Neobehaviorism	People have evolved to respond to stimuli from the environment.	Using behavior modification in treatment
1934	Lev Vygotsky: Cultural biosocial development	People are biological beings whose activity should be studied in their cultural environment.	Applying language as a cultural tool
1968	Noam Chomsky: Linguistics, analytic philosophy	Rules of grammar are found in deep structures of the brain.	Connecting aphasias, neurolinguistics, with interventions
1934	G. H. Mead: Symbolic interaction	The self is formed in interaction with others.	Using language as a vehicle of change
1937	Herbert Blumer: Symbolic interaction	The mind is a process rather than a structure.	Interacting people form societies and meaning
1971	Albert Bandura: Social learning theory	Learning is an outcome of person–environment exchanges.	Attaining self-efficacy and self-regulation
1980	Sharon Berlin: Social work	Social functioning depends on meaning making.	Meaning making as problem solving of everyday life difficulties

repeatedly paired with another stimulus that evokes that response" (Random House College Dictionary 2010; www.freedictionary.com).

Skinner

B. F. Skinner was another historical figure in the development of the field of behaviorism. Although Skinner believed that the mind had cognitive structures, he thought that human actions needed to be studied through observable behaviors. According to Skinner (1957),

> If we are to use the methods of science in the field of human affairs, we must assume that behavior is lawful and determined. We must expect to discover that what a man does is the result of specifiable conditions and that once these conditions have been discovered, we can anticipate and to some extent determine his actions. (p. 6)

Skinner believed so much in his view that behavior is predictable (and universal) that he wrote a novel, *Walden Two* (Skinner 1948/2005), in which he claimed that parents could raise ideal children using his approach. This view of behavioral change has been criticized as social engineering and is now not part of mainstream psychology (Robbins, Chatterjee, and Canda 2011).

Skinner based his theoretical concepts on Edward Thorndike (1898), who studied the causes and consequences of an action in experiments with cats. In his experiments, Thorndike put a cat into a puzzle box with a loose latch and a labyrinth of paths to escape. The cat, which was bribed to try and escape with a fish outside the door, quickly learned the right path to a positive consequence. Thorndike called this relationship between cause and consequence the *law of effect.*

Continuing work in his Skinner box, Skinner (1938) coined the term *operant conditioning*, or changing behavior through reinforcement (a reward that is given after the desired response is made). *Reinforcement,* an act that strengthens or encourages behavior, as used in Skinner's work evolved into what is termed *behavior modification: Positive reinforcement* strengthens a response, *negative reinforcement* weakens a response, and *punishment* eliminates negative actions.

> ➤ *Change strategies selected modify behavior with reinforcement.*

Only a brief description of the behavior modification approach to engagement, assessment, and intervention is warranted here. The strategies begin with the trainer assessing and targeting a specific behavior to change. Usually the practitioner gives reinforcements to either strengthen or extinguish the targeted behavior, bringing about an increase or decrease in its frequency. For example, social workers who practice with children in child care settings may teach a child a desired behavior by using the procedure of *time out,* a negative reinforcement. Other related procedures include *biofeedback,* which is used to control body functions, and *imagery,* which is applied to deal with vivid emotions. Through these intervention strategies, clients learn to monitor, identify, and control stressful behavioral cues.

Critique of Diversity Issues in Social Work Practice

Although many of Skinner's ideas about conditioning are not part of mainstream psychology today (Robbins, Chatterjee, and Canda 2011), the technique of *operant conditioning,* in which rewards and punishments are applied, continues to be used to change the behaviors of clients in residential treatment and correctional facilities (Sheafor and Horejsi 2012).

The Bridge to Social Learning Theory

Behaviorists generally derived their theory from animal studies or experiments with one person. They were sometimes criticized for their mechanistic focus on stimulus–response (Thomas 1999). In the early to mid-1900s, other cognitive theorists began taking an approach centered more on the person and his or her environment. For example, Lev Vygotsky (1934/1986), a Russian psychologist, promoted the idea that children's behaviors could be understood by examining them under everyday rather than laboratory conditions. He proposed that language and symbols were mediating factors between cause and effect and originated a cultural, biosocial view of development. At the same time, G. H. Mead's (1934) theory of *symbolic interactionism* called further attention to the idea that humans are social actors responding to the environment through interaction and language. More recently, Noam Chomsky (1968), a linguist, associated learning with children's innate ability—hence the overlap in concepts and disciplines alluded to earlier.

Section I.
B. Social Learning Theory

> ➤ *Well-being is considered a lessening of cognitive distortions.*

Professional Purpose and Well-Being

Although the theories presented here fall under the broad umbrella of cognitive theory and share similarities, the schools of thought vary in their view of person and environment as well as in how their tenets are applied in practice (Council on Social Work Education [CSWE] 2015, 1). Broadly speaking, behavioral, social learning, cognitive behavioral, or cognitive learning approaches emphasize an individual's response to environmental stimuli. Interventions, such as exposure therapy or stress inoculation training, are usually systematic procedures. Practitioners use evidence-based methods whenever possible to teach clients how to monitor themselves and their thoughts, feelings, and behaviors. This can bring about a shift in beliefs and a lessening of cognitive distortions. For example, these techniques can be used to minimize mood disorders, eating disorders, and substance abuse, thereby contributing to client well-being (CSWE 2015; Lambert, Bergen, and Garfield 2004).

We will see below that CBT has evolved into a point of view increasingly more focused on person and environment, exploring the relationships of clients' thoughts, feelings, and behaviors (National Alliance on Mental Illness 2015) to their environments. The purpose of the exploration process in CBT is to guide the client in reaching an understanding of his or her destructive actions and beliefs, determine how this influences social functioning, and make the necessary changes. When negative perceptions are modified, coping and social functioning improve, and the client is better able to meet his or her own goals, thereby becoming a more effective person in his or her environment (CSWE 2015).

Applying Terms and Assumptions in Social Work Practice

There is no one theory of cognitive function; rather, what can be thought of as the cognitive movement—or even the cognitive revolution—resulted in a knowledge base "replete with overlap in assumptions and concepts," with some theories that sharply "diverge" from others (Vourlekis 2008, 193). Movement in the cognitive sciences resulted in a complex interaction among multiple disciplines, including philosophy, psychology, anthropology, computer science, and neuroscience (Figure 5.1). All contributed to the multifaceted foundation of the cognitive sciences, branching out into numerous schools of thought, some of which have been applied in a variety of practice settings (Miller 2003).

Applications of these many streams of thought can vary. For example, Jean Piaget (1948), a developmental psychologist and one of the first developmental cognitive theorists, studied how children process information in order to foster learning and the maturation in their thinking processes (see Chapter 4). Albert Ellis (1962), a psychologist, considered a forefather of cognitive behavior therapy (CBT), was interested in how irrational thoughts and beliefs contribute to anxiety disorders and depression. He developed rational emotive therapy, in which he directly confronted patients' unreasonable ideas in order to improve their social functioning. Aaron Beck (1976), a psychiatrist, linked errors in thinking to depression, working to correct the poor judgments in a patient's core belief system in order to alleviate mental illness. One outcome was the creation of the Beck Depression Inventory, a twenty-one-question survey still frequently used today (Beck et al. 1961).

Albert Bandura (1971, 1986, 1997), a central figure in the development of social learning theory, also proposed that learning is not just behavioral but a cognitive process. He suggested that a person's cognitive function could be understood in the social context of language, culture, values, and customs, espousing a person-and-environment view of human behavior and the social environment known as *reciprocal determinism*. This means that there is a change in both person and environment as one influences the other.

Figure 5.1.

Cognitive science in 1978. Each line joining two disciplines represents interdisciplinary inquiry that already existed in 1978. (From Miller 2003, 143.)

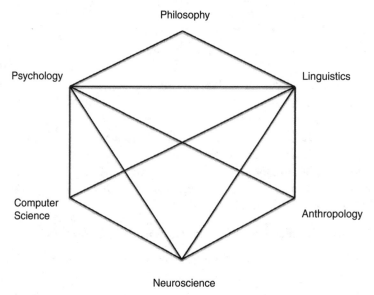

> ➤ *The client–social worker relationship is collaborative, working on modifying negative perceptions of life events and thereby improving social functioning.*

Engage With Individuals, Families, Groups, Organizations, and Communities

Forming a Relationship

According to the National Association of Cognitive-Behavioral Therapists (2014), CBT practitioners collaborate with their clients to bring problem thoughts and behaviors to light. However, unlike in Freudian therapy, the therapeutic relationship *alone* is not sufficient to be the basis of change. Rather, the client must learn to think and act differently.

Self-Counseling

The social worker's task during the initial part of the helping process is to teach the client how their time together is to be spent. The worker asks about the client's reasons for distress; the client tells the social worker why he or she believes these difficulties are occurring. Clients are encouraged to write down thoughts that pop into their minds (*automatic thought*) and bring them to the next session with the practitioner. When clients monitor their thoughts in this way, it puts them in a *self-counseling* mode. This may be likened to the notion that when social workers monitor their social work practice, they are using a form of self-regulation (CSWE 2015).

Modeling

Bandura (1982) contended that people learn by observing, imitating, and modeling one another. That is, learning can be achieved through watching a live model; through listening to verbal instruction; or through symbolic means, such as reading literature. For a person to learn, he or she must undertake four steps: (a) pay attention, (b) retain the information, (c) reproduce the content, and (d) develop motivation. The same process between teacher and learner may be undertaken in the social worker–client relationship and, in the cases of specific learning situations, might be thought of as *role play*. Embedded in these four steps of learning is how a person develops *perceived self-efficacy*, or a sense of his or her own confidence or ability to control life events.

> ➤ *The client–social worker relationship is defined as a teaching-learning process.*

Assess Individuals, Families, Groups, Organizations, and Communities

In CBT, the collaboration between client and social worker during assessment generally follows five steps:

1. Assessing distorted thinking patterns
2. Questioning the safety of self-destructive thoughts and behaviors
3. Establishing the meaning of circumstances and events
4. Determining person–environment fit
5. Arriving at intervention goals

Assessing Distorted Thinking Patterns

The purpose of monitoring or examining a client's thought processes is to change his or her distortions of reality:

> That reality may be distorted as judged by facts as others know them; it may include generalized self-deprecating notions of ability that overlook specific performance success; it may include a set of rules about how to do things that is not shared by a colleague; it may lead to feelings of hopelessness when demands of a task outstrip knowledge and skills; and it also may be a realistic appraisal of an unfair or not welcoming organization or agency. (Vourlekis 2008, 195)

Questioning the Safety of Self-Destructive Thoughts and Behaviors

Inquiring about client thoughts is a major means of conducting an assessment. Because CBT is based on the idea that thought processes are linked to actions, an assessment involves the social worker questioning clients about negative feelings and self-destructive behaviors. Once this screening has taken place, work begins on learning how the client interprets his or her environment.

> ➤ *Assessment content addresses distortions in reality and self-destructive behaviors.*

Establishing the Meaning of Circumstances and Events

In CBT, the social worker and client want to learn the meaning that a client ascribes to the events, circumstances, and behaviors of people that make up his or her outer world. In essence, the social worker wants to know how the client is mentally processing personal meaning from environmental information and to use this knowledge to help the client become self-aware. This cognitive ability eventually becomes the mechanism of change (Berlin 1980; Vourlekis 2008).

Determining Person–Environment Fit

Determining person–environment fit is a matter of asking what negative meanings a client has ascribed to the surrounding events, circumstances, and behaviors of others. When the client sees certain matters as a problem, more positive solutions may be generated.

Arriving at Intervention Goals

In CBT, the focus of intervention is to reduce the effects of the client's negative thoughts and behaviors mutually learned during the assessment. Therefore, the ability of social workers to collect, organize, and critically analyze and interpret this information from client system(s) (CSWE 2015) is critical to reaching intervention goals.

> ➤ *Change strategies selected increase a client's self-efficacy and self-perception.*

Intervene With Individuals, Families, Groups, Organizations, and Communities

Anxiety, panic disorders, compulsions, and phobias are treated using CBT. Treatment may be given in conjunction with medication. Research shows that, depending on the individual, a combination of talk therapy and medication can be more effective than medication alone.

The cognitive behavioral approach to helping may be thought of as psycho educational (Williams and Garland 2002). CBT tends to be brief, time limited, and structured. The social worker often gives homework, such as the client recording the amount of pleasure he or she receives from his or her actions. The belief is that the brain is actually improving as a result of these educational procedures as well as the adoption of new behaviors (National Alliance on Mental Illness 2015). However, the idea that neurobiological changes accompany CBT is still under study (Porto et al. 2009).

> ➤ *Change strategies selected foster the adoption of more positive behaviors and establish new meanings.*

Adopting New Behaviors

The social worker's inquiry can be likened to the Socratic method of teaching, in which the worker engages the client in critical thinking to solve his or her problems. Directing the client to practice new behaviors while the practitioner is giving reinforcement and encouragement is also important. These techniques can lead to a client being more realistic about reality and functioning better in his or her environment.

To reach this goal the client hopes to

- learn new self-management skills,
- give up second guessing,
- become less self-critical,

- have a more positive view of the future, and
- gain more self-efficacy (Williams and Garland 2002).

A Personal Problem-Solving Model

Social worker Sharon Berlin (2002) is known for her work in adapting CBT to clinical social work practice. Her nine-step personal problem-solving model suggests that people who seek help usually are managing a variety of life concerns that are largely derived from their environments. Therefore, clients must first establish the meaning of events associated with their difficulties and then use this information to operate more effectively in their daily lives. This aim is realized if the client can

1. develop *self-awareness* of early warning signs of difficulty (cues),
2. *expect* that he or she can solve his or her problem,
3. *define the problem* or what is wrong,
4. *think of solutions* that are under his or her control,
5. *analyze options* and make *decisions* required for various tasks,
6. take *action* and *persevere*,
7. *attribute success* to [himself or herself] and figure out what remains to be done,
8. *analyze progress* and *modify* plans, and
9. *maintain* changes made. (Berlin 1980, 1099)

Finally, CBT interventions are also used in social work practice with families and groups.

Critique of Diversity Issues in Social Work Practice

Bandura's concept of self-efficacy is important in social work practice because both the client and practitioner have to be confident and self-regulated: The social worker needs to "use reflection and self-regulation to manage personal values and maintain professionalism in practice situations" (CSWE 2015, 4), whereas the client hopes to become aware of and overcome "self-debilitating behaviors" (Bandura and Locke 2003, 89). This view of human behavior in the social environment maintains that *all* people can anticipate events and be purposeful, proactive, and self-evaluating (Bandura 2001, 2002).

For example, Bandura (1999) applied his concept of self-efficacy to a psychosocial program to prevent the spread of HIV/AIDS. The health education program, sponsored through a grant from the National Institute of Mental Health, consisted of four parts:

1. Providing information, knowledge, and self-awareness about HIV
2. Fostering self-regulation, skills, and preventive action around the spread of the disease
3. Enhancing resilient self-belief through self-direction, guided practice, and corrective feedback
4. Enlisting social supports

The case of Maria described below illustrates how the program can be used to further what Bandura called resilient self-efficacy, a combination of the ability to overcome adversity and the power to produce effects (see Chapter 10). This illustrates another example of reciprocal determinism, in which individual, group, community, and environment all influence and possibly change one another.

> ➤ Maria is an eighteen-year-old woman who lives in Washington, DC (the District). Her boyfriend contracted HIV six months ago but has not engaged in safe sex practices or talked about this with Maria. Maria has little self-esteem or self-efficacy. She is afraid that she will lose her boyfriend to another girl in their housing development. She has taken no steps to reduce her risk of contracting HIV.
>
> ➤ Unfortunately, Maria is one of many young adults, women, and people of color living in the District who are caught up in the HIV epidemic. The District has the largest percentage of untreated HIV cases in the United States. Clinics have long been seeking preventive approaches to the problem. A social worker at one of these clinics researches what has already been done to alleviate this difficulty. Her review uncovers a paper given by Albert Bandura at the National Institute of Mental Health and Drug Abuse Research Conference Women and AIDS: Promoting Health Behaviors in Bethesda, Maryland, in September 1987. She discusses the paper's implications for the District's underserved population at the clinic's next staff meeting.

Section II.
Social Constructionism

Social constructionism is an outgrowth of the postmodern shift in paradigm that dramatically affected the arts and sciences as well as political, economic, cultural, and ideological points of view. The shift involves questioning existing knowledge and calls for multiple ways of knowing (Schriver 2014). In 1966, Peter Berger and Thomas Luckman introduced the term *social construction* to describe this theoretical position.

During the late 1980s and early 1990s, the social work profession became increasingly engaged with this philosophical shift, which challenged the notion of fixed identities and rigid political and social categories (Freud 1994; Laird 1989; Weick 1987). Also debated was how to conceptualize curriculum (Blundo, Greene, and Gallant 1994,) and "the basic concept of what constitutes treatment and outcome" (Edinburg and Cotter 1995, 1641).

Theory Redefined

In the previous section it was shown that cognitive theorists stress the use of testable hypotheses to study behaviors under question. Theoretical (scientific) categories are then derived from direct, controlled observations. Social constructionists offer an alternative view of psychological inquiry. Social constructionists contend that there are no fixed truths, only alternative realities (Shotter 1993).

Saleebey (1993) has suggested that theories

- are associated with power and the dominant culture, and are thereby socio-cultural, political, and relational in nature;
- offer multiple, not singular, views, considering the uniqueness of individuals and cultures;
- best address individuals as social phenomena, interdependent beings, living as persons-in-environments;
- reflect language and intersubjectivity, using language as the basis for the exchange and creation of meanings.

Theories also imply or reflect values (pp. 205–212).

In short, knowledge is something that people create together at the local level, and reality is socially constructed. A summary of the contrasting views of cognitive and social construction theories appears in Table 5.2.

Professional Purpose and Well-Being

As stated earlier in the *Handbook,* according to the CSWE *Educational Policy and Accreditation Standards,* "The purpose of social work is actualized through its quest for social and economic justice" (p. 1). Several of the tenets of social

Table 5.2.
Contrasting cognitive and social construction theories

Cognitive theory

- An individual's emotions are based on how he or she thinks.
- Most people have irrational thoughts about themselves and their social situation.
- Individuals can overcome irrational beliefs and self-defeating patterns of behavior.
- Social workers facilitate a cognitive process that identifies and challenges misconceptions.
- Helping strategies are primarily educational in nature.
- The purpose of intervention strategies is to help clients develop cognitive skills to foster their sense of mastery and control.

Social construction theory

- There are no universal truths and no singular reality. Rather, knowledge is created through people interacting at the local level.
- Social constructionists provide a safe environment so that clients can explore their own meaning of events.
- Reflective questions help clients construct and reconstruct their sense of self.
- Clients are prompted to externalize their problem or view themselves as free of a difficulty. They develop alternative understandings and solutions.
- Clients may choose not to accept negative attributions, such as racism.
- Language and culture are the mechanisms for the exchange of ideas and meaning.
- By creating new meaning, individuals and communities can overcome life challenges.

Note. Adapted from Greene (2007).

constructionism relate to this professional purpose. For example, social constructionists recognize that individual and family meanings are "socially constituted within the context of the present sociopolitical juncture" (Lowe 1991, 47). Therefore, social constructionist therapies have the potential "to relate to themes of justice, poverty, gender, politics, and power" (p. 47, as cited in Blundo and Greene 2008).

Another social constructionist assumption related to the purpose of social work is to give attention to the formation of personal and communal identity (CSWE 2015). Given the opportunity in the helping process, clients can directly address their identity—"the interweaving of a particular gender, race, religion, age, socio-economic position, sexual orientation, and life experience and so forth" (Blundo and Greene 2008, 238)—and the role societal power plays in their social functioning and well-being (Foucault 1965, 1980; McNamee and Gergen 1992; see the case study of George below).

Social work practice from a social constructionist perspective centers around listening to a client's story or narrative to question and clarify the meaning of life events. Well-being is enhanced as the client reframes meaning through dialogue with the social worker. This approach is congruent with the "social worker as learner" stance suggested by CSWE (2015, 4).

> ➤ *Well-being is considered a positive identity within a cultural/political context.*

Applying Terms and Assumptions in Social Work Practice

Contrasting Social Constructivism and Social Constructionism

To avoid confusion, before discussing social constructionism it is necessary to define some similar terms. *Social constructivism* is a school of thought that flows from a social learning perspective and espouses the importance of cultural experiences in acquiring knowledge. People are said to generate their own rules and meanings based on social experiences (Granvold 2004). For example, the term is used in education to understand how people learn together or collaborate by having a dialogue about the subject matter (e.g., a museum docent may ask, "What is this picture about?").

In contrast, the term *social constructionism* as used here stems from a postmodern tradition that rejects universal laws. Constructionists hope to explicate "the process by which people come to describe, explain, and otherwise account for their reality" (Gergen 1985, 266) while dealing with local complexities.

A Multitheoretical Foundation

The basic tenets of social construction can be traced to a number of different theorists (Table 5.3). For example, G. H. Mead, a sociologist and one of the founders of social constructionism, is credited with calling attention to people as social beings (see Section I. A). Kenneth Gergen (1982, 1985), a social psychologist, proposed a postmodern means of viewing personal identity as self-in-relationship. Michael White (with David Epston; White and Epston 1990), founder of narrative therapy, claimed that therapy is a conversation between practitioner and client. Finally, Steven de Shazer and Kim Insoo Berg contributed *solution-focused therapy*, a step-by-step problem-solving process used in social work practice with individuals, families, groups, and organizations.

Biological Base

Social constructionists assume that people come into the world with temperaments and sensitivities—that they are wired and their minds naturally put things into categories (Table 5.4). A person's subsequent development is a process of person–environment interactions as well as interactions among people in a particular time and place.

Table 5.3.
Selected theoretical foundations of social constructionism

Time adopted	Major theorist(s)	Theme	Concepts for practice
1934	G. H. Mead: Symbolic interaction	People create reality through interaction.	Learning about a client's personal meanings
1946	Michael Polanyi: Philosophy of science	The scientific method is its own social construct.	Critically analyzing theory
1959	Erving Goffman (sociologist): Dramaturgical analysis	People create their life script through interactions with others.	Realizing that stigmatized roles are only social constructs
1966	Jerome Berger and Thomas Luckman: Sociology of knowledge	People–environment interactions form roles that are institutionalized; communal meanings and socialization result.	Helping people change their personal meanings and knowledge of the environment
1965, 1980	Michael Foucault (philosopher): Social critique	Power relations are part of people's interactions and discourse.	Infusing power relations as part of clinical and community practice
1985	Kenneth Gergen: Social construction/social psychology	The self is formed in relationship to others.	Living life in authentic relationships
1990	White and Epston: Narrative therapy/ social work	The client's narrative is the mechanism of change.	Recognizing the client as expert
1995	de Shazer and Insoo Berg: Solution-focused therapy/social work	The client's solution is embedded in his or her story.	Listening and prompting for solutions
1988, 1992	Anderson and Goolishian: Linguistics and role creation	Clinical practice may be thought of as a linguistic system.	Using the conversation as a problem dissolving process

Table 5.4.
Social construction theory: basic assumptions

- People are biological organisms that differentiate and categorize the stimuli they receive.

- People are proactive and construct or create meaning over time through interactions with other people and with their environment.

- People use language to contemplate and evaluate events and construct personal meanings. People are able to consider alternative meanings because those new versions of reality are less disruptive to their sense of self.

- Personal meanings are created in the context of the individual's life and historical moment.

- Core personal meanings are experienced by the individual as a sense of self.

- A person's sense of self can be reconstructed as meanings in his or her life narrative are rewritten or restoried.

- Culture is a system of meaning created through the use of language and communal action.

Note. Adapted from Blundo and Greene (2008, 237–64).

Language and Meaning Making

Another assumption of social construction theory is the importance of the linkage between language and meaning making. This idea was reflected in the writings of Polanyi (1946/1974), a philosopher who argued that people participate in their own knowledge making. He described language as central to people's existence and how they come to know themselves and their worlds. He went on to state, "We are born in language, and we are also born into a set of beliefs about the nature of things" (p. 75).

Consequently, self-awareness grows as people interact with their physical, cultural, and interpersonal environments. In turn, meaning is constructed through a process of dialogue in a specific cultural tradition and within the context of a particular locality (Blundo and Greene 2008; Gergen and Gergen 1983a, 1983b).

You may understand this better if you think of yourself as active in creating your own narrative and worldview (a belief system) through the use of language. This process involves recognizing and identifying what is important and designating it by giving it a name. A familiar example concerns the Inuit—indigenous peoples of the Arctic—who have fifty words for *snow,* depending on whether it is crusty or powdery, drifting or blowing, and so forth. Through the creation and use of language, the Intuit are able to evaluate their surroundings and effectively act on their environment (Mendosa 2015).

Self-Identity

According to social construction theory, clients may come to social work agencies because their version of reality and sense of personal integrity have been disrupted. Social workers can help them reconstruct a more positive sense of self by recognizing that self-identity is related to a person's beliefs, frames of reference(s), and culture/language. As seen in the case of George below, social workers can help clients reject negative attributions associated with racism and homophobia as they act as an expert on their own life events (O'Hanlon 1993).

> ➤ *Universality is realized as part of the helping process.*

Meaning

Because social construction provides an understanding of how people gain a higher sense of consciousness about their inner selves, it is sometimes associated with *transpersonal theory.* "From this perspective, people not only form their personalities in unity with others; they connect with meaning beyond their own immediate personal concerns" (Greene and Kropf 2011, 95). Transpersonal theory is described further in Chapter 7.

Engage With Individuals, Families, Groups, Organizations, and Communities

Unconditional Regard

As social workers get ready to practice with clients from a social construction point of view, they may have to step out of their comfort zone, eliminating stereotypes about different types of clients or preconceived views and explanations of events (Freire 1993). They also must try to be careful not to impose their own views.

> ➤ *The client–social worker relationship is egalitarian, and participants engage in a conversation.*

An Egalitarian Relationship

The client–social worker relationship in a social constructionist approach is a collaborative process. Because clients are believed to contemplate and self-evaluate, they are able to consider who they are while they engage in the interview or conversation. The practitioner deliberately goes about the interview thinking whether his or her questions are therapeutic, nontherapeutic, or countertherapeutic (Tomm 1994).

> ➤ *Interview goals intend that clients be reflective.*

The Interview

Interview questions from a social constructionist perspective tend to be reflective. Tomm (1994) distinguished four major groups of questions that social workers may ask depending on the particular aim(s) of the interview:

1. Lineal orienting questions are those that presuppose that normative data can be collected about each client, such as, "What problems brought you to see me today?"
2. Circular questions are primarily exploratory, such as, "How is it we find ourselves together today?"
3. Strategic questions are based on an assumption the practitioner holds about the client, such as, "When are you going to take charge of your life and start looking for a job?"
4. Reflexive questions are intended to place the client in a reflexive position or to trigger the consideration of new options, such as, "If your depression suddenly disappeared, how would your life be different?"

The Practice Context

In a social constructionist approach to the helping process, the social worker acknowledges the therapeutic context of an agency or practice setting—the structure and procedures. As in the case of George below, environmental influences affecting the client are explored explicitly so that the client does not attribute the problem to himself or herself (e.g., "I am a loser").

Assess Individuals, Families, Groups, Organizations, and Communities

Assessment as Four Levels of Narrative

Listening to the client tell his or her narrative is key to the assessment process. A person's life story contains self-knowledge about how he or she has met life's critical events. According to Kenyon and Randall (2001), narratives can be understood on four different levels: personal, interpersonal, sociocultural, and societal.

1. The *personal* level of the narrative examines biological, psychological, sociological, and spiritual factors across a person's life course.
2. The *interpersonal* aspects of the narrative explore nurturing and mentoring between people across generations.
3. The *sociocultural* level examines the positive influences of society—its mores, attitudes, and values.
4. The *societal* characteristics of the narrative address historical, social, and economic concerns, such as poverty, potable water, child and maternal health, and laws.

Assessment Assumptions

The following are assumptions to remember when conducting an assessment:

1. As people create meaning in interaction with others, they develop a life story.
2. People are proactive and self-organizing.
3. People's behavior is shaped by the meaning they give to events. (Greene 2007)

Assessment begins with the social worker taking a "not-knowing" position (Anderson and Goolishian 1992, 29). This means that predetermined social categories are not used. Rather, the practitioner aims to arrive at an understanding of the client's particular story within the context of his or her culture (Bruner 1987a, 1987b; Gergen and Gergen 1983a, 1983b).

> ➤ *George (age thirteen) is a sophomore in high school. He comes from a traditional midwestern family composed of his father Joseph; his mother Susan; and siblings Margaret (age seventeen), Stephanie (age fifteen), and Steven (age eight). George is accustomed to his dad being in charge of the family. They attend their house of worship every week. The children are expected to do their chores and attend either the Girl Scouts or Boy Scouts.*
>
> ➤ *George is struggling with his emerging teenage identity. He is comparing himself with his peers and feels like an outsider. He confides in his sister Margaret, who is a senior at the same school and serves as a peer counselor. Margaret refers her brother to Mrs. Gilbert, a school social worker, who has been hired after a series of suicides among youth in the community.*
>
> ➤ *Learning that some of these suicides might have been prompted by bullying and questions of sexual orientation, Mrs. Gilbert has held Parent–Teacher Association and town council meetings to try and devise intervention strategies. She has gathered information from the American Psychological Association, the Family Acceptance Project, and Lambda Legal.*
>
> ➤ *George decides to talk with Mrs. Gilbert, who uses a postmodern approach to helping. Mrs. Gilbert begins by listening to George's story: She asks about the events and the sequence of events across time that have led to the appointment. She learns that after being called a "geek," a "nerd," and a "queer" for the past two years, George has come to think of himself as a "loser." He says, "It makes me tired and sad."*

> ➤ *The goal that Mrs. Gilbert sets, given George's description, is to reconstruct George's story line (restorying). Restorying will involve mapping a history of the problem, searching for already-made positive initiatives, and defining hopes for the future. From this conversation, George will externalize the problem, or realize that the problem is not part of his personal identity. George has decided to be active in the founding of a support group for youth who are questioning their sexual orientation.*

Assessment as Self-Definition

Assessment reveals whether a client's story gives his or her life coherence and continuity (Greene 2007). What is his or her self-definition? George begins the helping process with a negative sense of self, but the social worker focuses on interventions that help him reauthor his story.

Intervene With Individuals, Families, Groups, Organizations, and Communities

Social constructionist social workers do not believe that there are right interventions. The coconstructed client story will point the way to mutually agreed-on interventions.

Restorying and Externalizing

If a client's story is problem saturated, he or she can be helped to reconstruct it and discover alternative realities (White 1993; White and Epston 1990). This process is achieved through the "conversation" between client and practitioner (White and Epston 1990, 41). Techniques are applied to *externalize the problem,* or to make the problem separate from the client's identity, and to *restory* life events, or to write a new favorable personal script. That is, social workers use social constructionist interventions to transform a client's core meaning about his or her self and life context.

George's story is rewritten through deconstructing what he believes is normal or the right way of life, allowing him to come to his own ideas. Cary and Russell (2004) of the Dulwich Centre in Australia (www.dulwichcentre.com.au/) have called this "responding to yourself." The social worker knows that George has accomplished his goals for the future when he no longer considers himself "a loser" and takes on an alternative solution, such as creating a school support group.

Solution-Focused Treatment

In order to find future solutions, social workers can use solution-focused treatment methods, an outgrowth of the social constructionist approach. In this school of thought, practitioners take the conversation step by step to find positive solutions.

Client–social worker conversations are intended to help the client gain control by recalling past successes and imagining a positive future (Franklin, Garner, and Berg 2007). Solution-focused treatment offers two major interview techniques for arriving at alternative solutions:

1. The Miracle Question: "If in the middle of the night, there was a miracle and the problem you described is resolved, when you awake what would be your first small sign that would make you wonder—Did a miracle occur?" (de Shazer 1988)
2. The Scaling Question: "Can you tell me, on a number between 1 and 10, when 10 stands for the best and 1 the worst, how much confidence you have that you can solve the issue that brought you to seek help?" (de Shazer and Insoo Berg 1995, 249)

> ➤ *Change strategies selected focus on solutions within the conversation.*

Critique of Diversity Issues in Social Work Practice

Social constructionists do not believe that people have fixed personal characteristics; rather, attention is given to how clients' social, cultural, and historical environments affect them and how they in turn affect their environment. In addition, a person's characteristics are seen as a result of these person–environment exchanges in a given time and place.

Social constructionists believe that personal identity is fluid and multidimensional. That is, people create and negotiate their intersecting identities within a particular sociohistorical context (Frable 1997; Gubrium, Holstein, and Buckholdt 1994). In addition, according to the social constructionist perspective, there are no fixed life stages (see Chapter 4). Rather, the idea that an individual has grown from being a child to an adolescent is itself considered a social construct.

> ➤ *Universality is realized through attention to difference and human rights.*

Social constructionists contend that communal meanings are established over time as the roles people create through reciprocal person–environment interactions and with one another are institutionalized (Berger and Luckman 1966). These roles may have power differentials associated with them as well as the amount of and access to resources associated with that power position (see Chapter 3). Hence, there is a need for social workers to "advocate for human rights at the individual and system levels" (CSWE 2015, 5).

The process of construction and reconstruction does not affect only the individual. The process can result in new meanings for family and societal roles, modifications of institutions and culture(s), as well as changes to sociopolitical environments. Consequently, engagement in policy practice necessitates a dialogue within larger social systems. A recent example is a U.S. military policy that banned discrimination of gays who did not reveal their sexual orientation. This fight against discrimination ended in the repeal of Don't Ask, Don't Tell.

Glossary

Attributions. Beliefs about the causes of behavior.

Biological propensities. A person's inborn sensitivities and temperament; the core of the self.

Cognition. Knowledge, thinking, and problem solving; higher mental processes.

Cognitive processes. The mental processes with which a person perceives, organizes, remembers, and evaluates available information.

Culture. The expression of historically shared meanings of a community of people. People create culture through the use of language within a locality.

Deconstruction. A social work technique that disrupts a client's typical frames of reference, listens for multiple meanings, and reconstructs negative meaning.

Externalization. Separating the person from the problem.

Information exchange. Reciprocal exchanges between personal and environmental realities.

Intentionality. The initiation of goal-directed behavior.

Intervention. A client's organizing of old meanings into newly constructed consciousness or new meanings. Change necessitates transformations of meaning about the self and the world.

Language. A means of conceptualizing, representing, and communicating experiences. Language is a communal act.

Meaning. People know their world through their perception, interpretation, and characterization of stimuli. Meaning represents a person's ability to separate out and characterize the world.

Not-knowing position. A social worker's learning stance in which he or she listens for the client's views and explanations.

Reality. A socially constructed view. There is no final, true explanation of the world.

Reciprocal determinism. One system's influence on another.

Self. The person one experiences in oneself from day to day over a lifetime.

Self-efficacy. The belief system about oneself with respect to capability for performance.

Story. A person's way of coherently organizing experiences into personally meaningful conceptualizations of his or her life.

References

Anderson, H., and H. Goolishian. 1988. "Human Systems as Linguistic Systems: Preliminary and Evolving Ideas about the Implications for Clinical Practice." *Family Process* 27 (4): 371–93.

Anderson, H., and H. Goolishian. 1992. "The Client Is the Expert: A Not-knowing Approach to Therapy." In *Therapy as Social Construction*, edited by S. McNamee and K. J. Gergen, 25–39. Newbury Park, CA: Sage.

Bandura, A. 1971. *Social Learning Theory*. New York: General Learning Press.

Bandura, A. 1982. "Self Efficacy a Mechanism in Human Agency." *American Psychologist* 37 (2): 122–47.

Bandura, A. 1986. *Social Foundations of Thought and Action*. Upper Saddle River, NJ: Prentice Hall.

Bandura, A. 1997. *Self-efficacy: The Exercise of Control*. New York: Freeman.

Bandura, A. 1999. "Perceived Self-efficacy in the Exercise of Control over AIDS Infection." *Evaluation and Program Planning* 13:9–17.

Bandura, A. 2001. "Social Cognitive Theory: An Agentic Perspective." *Annual Review of Psychology* 52:1–26.

Bandura, A. 2002. "Growing Primacy of Human Agency in Adaptation and Change in the Electronic Era." *European Psychologist* 7:2–16.

Bandura, A., and E. A. Locke. 2003. "Negative Self-efficacy and Goal Effects Revisited." *Journal of Applied Psychology* 88 (1): 87–99.

Beck, A. T. 1976. *Cognitive Therapy and the Emotional Disorders*. New York: International Universities Press.

Beck, A. T., C. H. Ward, M. Mendelson, J. E. Mock, and J. Erbaugh. 1961. "An Inventory for Measuring Depression." *Archives of General Psychiatry* 4:561–71.

Berger, P., and T. Luckman. 1966. *The Social Construction of Reality*. New York: Anchor.

Berlin, S. B. 1980. "Cognitive-behavioral Approaches." In *Handbook of Clinical Social Work*, edited by A. Rosenblatt and D. Waldfogel, 1095–119. San Francisco, CA: Jossey-Bass.

Berlin, S. B. 2002. *Clinical Social Work Practice: A Cognitive-integrative Perspective*. Oxford: Oxford University Press.

Blumer, H. 1937. *Social Psychology: Man and Society*. New York: Prentice Hall.

Blundo, R., and R. R. Greene. 2008. "Social Construction." In *Human Behavior Theory and Social Work Practice*, 3rd ed., edited by R. R. Greene, 237–64. New Brunswick, NJ: Aldine Transaction Press.

Blundo, R., R. R. Greene, and P. Gallant. 1994. "A Constructionist Approach with Diverse Populations." In *Human Behavior Theory: A Diversity Framework*, edited by R. R. Greene, 115–32. Hawthorne: Aldine de Gruyter.

Bruner, J. 1987a. "Life as Narrative." *Social Research* 54 (1): 11–22.

Bruner, J. 1987b. "The Narrative Construction of Reality." *Critical Inquiry* 18 (1): 1–21.

Cary, M., and S. Russell. 2004. *Narrative Therapy: Responding to Yourself*. Adelaide, Australia: Dulwich Centre.

Council on Social Work Education. 2015. *Educational Policy and Accreditation Standards*. Alexandria, VA: Author.

Chomsky, N. 1968. *Language and the Mind*. Sydney, Australia: Harcourt Bruce Jovanovich.

de Shazer, S. 1988. *Clues Investigating Solutions in Brief Therapy*. New York: Norton.

de Shazer, S., and K. Insoo Berg. 1995. "The Brief Therapy Tradition." In *Propagations: Thirty Years of Influence from the Mental Research Institute*, edited by J. H. Weakland and W. A. Ray, 249–52. Binghamton: Haworth Press.

Dean, R. 1993. "Teaching a Constructivist Approach to Clinical Practice." In *Revisioning Social Work Education: A Social Constructionist Approach*, edited by J. Laird, 55–75. New York: Haworth Press.

Edinburg, G. M. and F. Cotter. 1995. "Managed Care." In *Encyclopedia of Social Work*, vol. 2, edited by R. Edwards (Ed.-in-Chief), 1635–42. Washington, DC: NASW Press.

Ellis, A. 1962. *Reason and Emotion in Therapy*. New York: Lyle Stuart.

Foucault, M. 1965. *Madness and Civilization*. New York: Vintage.

Foucault, M. 1980. *Proper/Knowledge: Selected Interviews and Writings*. New York: Pantheon.

Frable, D. 1997. "Gender, Racial, Ethnic, Sexual, and Class Identities." *Annual Review of Psychiatry* 48 (24): 1–18.

Franklin, C., J. Garner, and I. Berg. 2007. "At Risk Youth: Preventing and Retrieving High School Drop Out." In *Social Work Practice: A Risk and Resilience Perspective*, edited by R. R. Greene, 115–39. Monterey, CA: Brooks/Cole.

Freire, P. 1993. *Pedagogy of the Oppressed*. New York: Continuum.

Freud, S. 1994. "The Social Construction of Gender." *Journal of Adult Development* 1 (1): 37–45.

Gergen, K. J. 1982. *Toward Transformation in Social Knowledge.* New York: Springer.

Gergen, K. J. 1985. "The Social Constructionist Movement in Modern Psychology." *American Psychologist* 40 (3): 266–75.

Gergen, K. J., and M. J. Gergen. 1983a. "Narratives of the Self." In *Studies in Social Identity*, edited by T. R. Savin and K. E. Scheibe, 254–73. New York: Praeger.

Gergen, K. J., and M. J. Gergen. 1983b. "The Social Construction of Helping Relationships." In *New Directions in Helping*, vol. 1, edited by J. D. Fisher and B. DePaulo, 143–63. New York: Academic Press.

Granvold, D. 2004. *Cognitive Behavioral Treatment.* Pacific Grove, CA: Brooks/Cole.

Greene, R. R., ed. 2007. *Social Work Practice: A Risk and Resilience Perspective.* Monterey, CA: Brooks/Cole.

Greene, R. R., and N. P. Kropf. 2011. *Competence: Select Theoretical Concepts.* New Brunswick, NJ: Aldine Transaction Press.

Gubrium, J. F., I. A. Holstein, and D. R. Buckholdt. 1994. *Constructing the Life Course.* New York: General Hall.

Kenyon, G. M., and W. Randall. 2001. "Narrative Gerontology: An Overview." In *Narrative Gerontology*, edited by G. Kenyon, P. Clark, and B. de Vries, 3–18. New York: Springer.

Kuhn, T. S. 1962. *The Structure of Scientific Revolutions.* Chicago, IL: University of Chicago Press.

Laird, J. 1989. Women and Stories: Restoring Women's Self-constructions." In *Women in Families: A Framework for Family Therapy*, edited by M. McGoldrick, C. M. Anderson, and F. Walsh, 427–50. New York: Norton.

Lambert, M. J., A. E. Bergen, and S. L. Garfield. 2004. *Handbook of Psychotherapy and Behavior Change*, 5th ed. New York: Wiley.

Lowe, R. 1991. "Postmodern Themes and Therapeutic Practices: Notes towards the Definition." *Dulwich Centre Newsletter* 3:41–53.

McNamee, S., and K. J. Gergen, eds. 1992. *Therapy as Social Construction.* Newbury Park, CA: Sage.

Mead, G. H. 1934. *Mind, Self, and Society.* Chicago, IL: University of Chicago Press.

Mendosa, D. 2015. *Inuit Words for Snow.* Accessed October 15, 2015. http://www.mendosa.com/snow.html

Miller, G. A. 2003. "The Cognitive Revolution: A Historical Perspective." *Trends in Cognitive Sciences* 7 (3): 141–4.

National Alliance on Mental Illness. 2015. *NAMI National Alliance on Mental Illness.* Accessed October 15, 2015. http://www.nami.org/

National Association of Cognitive-Behavioral Therapists. 2014. *Cognitive-Behavioral Therapy.* Accessed October 15, 2015. http://www.nacbt.org/whatiscbt.htm

O'Hanlon, W. H. 1993. "Possibility Therapy: From Iatrogenic Injury to Estrogenic Healing." In *Therapeutic Conversations*, edited by S. Gilligan and R. Price, 3–17. New York: Norton.

Pavlov, I. P. 1927. *Conditioned Reflexes: An Investigation of the Physiological Activity of the Cerebral Cortex.* Translated and Edited by G. V. Anrep. London: Oxford University Press.

Piaget, J. 1948. *Moral Judgment of the Child.* Glencoe, IL: Free Press.

Polanyi, M. 1974. *Science, Faith, and Society.* New York: Oxford University Press. (Original work published 1946).

Porto, P. R., L. Oliveira, J. Mari, E. Volchan, I. Figueira, and P. Ventura. 2009. "Does Cognitive Behavioral Therapy Change the Brain? A Systematic Review of Neuroimaging in Anxiety Disorders." *Journal of Neuropsychiatry and Clinical Neuroscience* 21 (2): 114–25.*Random House College Dictionary.* 2010. New York: Random House.

Robbins, S. P., P. Chatterjee, and E. R. Canda. 2011. *Contemporary Behavior Theory: A Critical Perspective for Social Work.* Boston, MA: Allyn & Bacon.

Saleebey, D. 1993. "Notes on Interpreting the Human Condition: A Constructed HBSE Curriculum." In *Revisioning Social Work Education: A Social Constructionist Approach*, edited by J. Laird, 197–217. New York: Haworth Press.

Schriver, J. M. 2015. *Human Behavior and the Social Environment: Shifting Paradigms in Essential Knowledge for Social Work Practice*, 6th ed. New York: Pearson.

Sheafor, B. W., and C. J. Horejsi. 2012. *Techniques and Guidelines for Social Work Practice*, 9th ed. Boston, MA: Allyn & Bacon.

Shotter, J. 1993. *Conversational Realities: Constructing Life through Language.* London: Sage.

Skinner, B. F. 1938. *The Behavior of Organisms.* Oxford: Appleton-Century Press.

Skinner, B. F. 1957. *Verbal Behavior.* New York: Appleton-Century-Crofts.

Skinner, B. F. 2005. *Walden Two.* Indianapolis, IN: Hackett. (Original work published 1948).

Thomas, R. M. 1999. *Comparing Theories of Child Development,* 5th ed. Belmont, CA: Wadsworth.

Thorndike, E. L. 1898. "Animal Intelligence: An Experimental Study of the Associative Processes in Animals." *Psychological Monographs: General and Applied* 2 (4): 1–109.

Tomm, K. 1994. "Interventive Interviewing: Part III. Intending to Ask Lineal, Circular, Strategic, or Reflexive Questions?" In *Constructivism and Family Therapy,* edited by K. Brownlee, P. Gallant, and D. Carpenter, 117–56. Thunder Bay, ON: Lakehead University.

Vourlekis, B. 2008. "Cognitive Theory for Social Work Practice." In *Human Behavior Theory and Social Work Practice,* 3rd ed., edited by R. R. Greene, 173–200. New Brunswick, NJ: Aldine Transaction Press

Vygotsky, L. 1986. *Thought and Language.* Cambridge, MA: MIT Press. (Original work published 1934).

Watson, J. 1913. "Psychology as the Behaviorist Views It." *Psychological Review* 20:158–77.

Weick, A. 1987. "Reconceptualizing the Philosophical Perspective of Social Work." *Social Service Review* 61:218–30.

White, M. 1993. "Deconstruction and Therapy." In *Therapeutic Conversation,* edited by S. Gilligan and R. Price, 22–61. New York: Norton.

White, M., and D. Epston. 1990. *Narrative Means to Therapeutic Ends.* New York: Norton.

Williams, C., and A. Garland. 2002. "A Cognitive Behavioral Therapy Assessment Model in Everyday Life." *Advances in Psychiatric Treatment* 8:172–9.

6

Human Behavior and the Social Environment Theory: Social Work Practice with Families

> ➤ *This chapter presents the use of structuralist human behavior and the social environment theory to engage, assess, and intervene with families. The primary assumptions discussed are derived from general systems theory and are augmented with selected theoretical frameworks and practice strategies taken from the family therapy literature. The knowledge, attitudes, and skills necessary for competency-based practice are applied to illustrate family-centered social work practice.*

This chapter discusses the basic tenets and terms associated with general systems theory (GST). Developed by biologist Ludwig Von Bertalanffy (1968), GST is a model that was originally developed to explain the working of cells. Its rules underpin much of the structure of family-focused treatment (Nichols and Schwartz 2001). The model is augmented by other structuralist ideas, such as role theory and ideas related to schools of family therapy.

Models are high-level abstractions that are universal in their application. They may be thought of as simple representations of complex realities. Analytical models guide theorists or practitioners in recognizing which factors to consider in their analysis and in identifying the relationships between these factors (Greene 2008).

You will see here how the GST model acts as a blueprint for action in social work practice with families. The limitations of the model are also discussed.

Professional Purpose and Well-Being

Family-centered social work practice is central to the field's historical professional purpose to improve individual and community well-being. In 1917, Mary Richmond espoused the idea that it was necessary to understand an individual or family within a person–environment context of community, work, education, health, and social policy. Friendly visitor pioneers often helped families within their homes with issues of resettlement and poverty, and Charity Organization Societies were an earlier version of today's United Way. In 1918, the American Association for Organizing Charity declared that aiding "disorganized" families was its primary area of work. Family caseworkers obtained client physical and mental evaluations and gathered social histories to develop a plan for intervention, which often involved financial aid. In addition, schools of social work were created with curriculum content that included such topics as economics, sociology, social psychology, criminology, casework, community problems, and the family (Lubove 1965).

> ➤ *The well-being of families is historically related to stability and financial security.*

Tribal Nations and Ethnic Minority Services

The *Educational Policy and Accreditation Standards* of the Council on Social Work Education (CSWE 2015) have added the requirement that tribal nation status be considered among the differences that social workers address in practice. Prior to the arrival of the Europeans in North America, each *tribal nation* had its own governmental structure to provide for its decision making and the welfare of its members. Following the disruption of colonization and the formation of the United States, tribal nations were recognized and had their own sovereignty. Yet the actual right of tribal nations to govern their own affairs has often come under question (Associated Press 2014). At the same time, social services have become a mix of local, state, and national activity. Today few special agencies exist specifically to assist or inform indigenous populations, but one such agency is the National Indian Child Welfare Association, founded to support children and families.

As early as the 1600s, social welfare services to assist families were developed in *ethnic minority communities.* For example, mutual aid was given in African American communities under slavery and during and after the Civil War. Many of these services are still available today, including faith-based services, with African American pastors playing a pivotal role in mental health care (Taylor and Chatters 1988, 1991). The provision of social services in the Jewish American community began in 1654, and the United Jewish Charity was organized in 1869. Services historically included financial assistance and counseling for needy children and families. More recent examples of family-focused social work services include Fanm Ayisyen nan Miyami (or Haitian Women of Miami; http://fanm.org) and Korean Community Services of Los Angeles (www.koreancommunity.org/e_about.aspx).

The Family Therapy Movement

Social workers influenced and were influenced by the family therapy movement. This movement grew out of the child guidance approach to treatment as practitioners realized that mental health outcomes were more positive when children and parents were treated as a unit. Although a description of the many ideas and interventions that were developed as a result of the movement is beyond the scope of this chapter, the schools of thought may be viewed as forming an artificial continuum from A to Z (Table 6.1). At the A end of the continuum, treatment involves psychodynamic approaches characterized by attention to the emotional life of the family (Ackerman 1958). The process of the family developing insight is considered an important intervention. At the Z end of the continuum, interventions are designed to change the structure and function of the family (Haley 1971). Modifying the family's communication and organization patterns in order to alleviate dysfunction is the goal (Greene 2008). As can be seen, each school of family treatment offers various methods of intervention from which to choose when augmenting the GST model. For example, how active a role the practitioner will take to effect change within a family is a matter of theoretical orientation and a key professional decision.

Table 6.2 provides more details about various family theorists' points of view on assessment and practice interventions that may be combined with social work techniques in family-focused treatment. For example, Murray Bowen (1978) suggested that therapists enhance the differentiation of the self in the family of origin, Salvador Minuchin (1974) contended that practitioners should try to change dysfunctional organizational patterns, and Virginia Satir (1972) proposed

Table 6.1.
Polarities of family treatment forms

Type A	Type Z
Adopts concepts from the psychoanalytic approach and the medical model	Uses ideas from small-group and systems theories
Explores emotional/affective relationships within the family	Focuses on structural or behavioral relationships
Proposes that family relationships are influenced by emotional tension/anxiety	Suggests that relationships are influenced by structural and communication patterns of the family group
Retains the idea that transference and interpretations are therapeutic	Rejects the idea of transference
	Promotes the idea that the therapist remains detached from the family system except for interventive input
Promotes the development of insight in family members through the interpretation of unconscious processes	Emphasizes understanding of interactive behavioral patterns
Strives to alleviate "interlocking emotional disorders" of the family group	Works to alleviate dysfunctional family patterns
Fosters health and growth by contributing to insight and relieving pathogenic conflict and anxiety	Enhances functional behaviors by educating members and altering structural arrangements of the family

Note. Adapted from Greene (2008, 187).

Table 6.2.
Selected theoretical foundations of family theories

Time adopted	Major theorist(s)	Theme	Concepts for practice
1958	Nathan Ackerman: Psychoanalytic family therapy	The goal is to deal with the family as an emotional system, resolving emotional conflict.	Uses psychodynamic theory, including object relations, to diagnosis and treat.
1962	Albert Ellis: Rational emotive behavior therapy	The goal is to replace destructive emotions and thoughts with positive ones.	Suggests that attitude change precedes behavioral change.
1971	Jay Haley: Strategic family therapy	The goal is to directly deal with symptoms and problems.	Works on symptom relief to solve family problems.
1972	Virginia Satir: Experiential family therapy/social work	The goal is to create a warm, accepting environment so that the self-esteem of all is enhanced.	Emphasizes the natural ability of people to thrive. Sculpts family positions.
1974	Salvador Minuchin: Structural family therapy	The goal is to identify and when necessary modify patterns of family structure.	Clarifies boundaries, subsystems, and hierarchies.
1978	Murray Bowen: Nuclear family emotional process	The goal is to balance togetherness and individuality.	Works to achieve each family member's differentiation of self.
1985	Lynn Hoffman: Social construction/social work	The goal is to facilitate meaning making in families.	Gives attention to family belief systems.
1990	Michael White and David Epston: Narrative therapy/social work	The goal is to reframe and restory negative family narratives.	Emphasizes the social construction of the self. Addresses the effects of sexism, homophobia, poverty, and so forth.
1994	Harry Aponte: Ecostructuralist approach/social work	The goal is to make connections across ethnic, racial, socioeconomic, and cultural boundaries.	Focuses on the person of the therapist.

that social workers create a warm therapeutic environment to foster self-esteem. Often such techniques are not mutually exclusive and can be used in conjunction with one another.

> ➤ *Family interviews are often an integration of family theories and social work practice methods.*

Applying Terms and Assumptions in Social Work Practice

Theoretical Base

Systems theory is composed of a rich multidisciplinary theoretical base that has developed over time. Its theorists include social worker Mary Richmond (1917), known for family casework and a systemic view of problem resolution; anthropologist Claude Lévi-Strauss (1948), associated with describing the influences of the organizational structure of society; sociologist Talcott Parsons (1968), recognized for his explanation of family roles; biologist/ecologist Ernst Haeckel (1904), acknowledged for his attention to a unified environment; and cyberneticist/anthropologist Gregory Bateson (1971, 1979), credited with exploring how information flows through a family system. Finally, Ludwig Von Bertalanffy's (1968) work is central to many family therapy approaches, offering social workers a unifying systems theory approach that provides rules for the functionality of systems.

Systems Thinking

This chapter uses systems thinking as a lens for understanding and intervening in families. *Systems thinking* is a means of examining living systems as interacting, complex wholes. A key principle is that "the whole is more than the sum of its parts" (Buckley 1968, 490). You have already learned that ecological systems are composed of subsystems that reciprocally influence one another. Similarly, systems thinking is not *linear*—where *a* causes *b*. It is *recursive* or circular in its approach, in which mutual transactions and shared effects among members of a system are taken into account (Tomm 1994; see Chapter 5).

Systems thinking was a primary means of taking social work practice from the medical model, with its linear view of causation, to a more multicausal context (Buckley 1967; Petr 1988). Therefore, family-centered social workers view the family as more than a collection of individuals. They focus on family processes and how members relate to one another. In addition, the assumption is made that the problem or behavior in question rests in the overall functioning of the family group.

According to this way of thinking, change in a family can best occur when members are viewed as a dynamic, evolving social system. Furthermore, the practitioner recognizes that family difficulties may rest anywhere in the larger ecological space (see Chapter 2). In short, from this point of view, a family "is [composed] of interrelated members who constitute a unit or whole," functioning together to meet life goals (Greene 2008, 48).

> ➤ *Change strategies selected start at the beginning of the helping process when the family realizes all members are a target for change.*

Family Forms

The original idea that systems thinking is *universal* or applied neutrally to any family form is increasingly under discussion (Franklin and Jordan 1999; Laird 1996). Nonetheless, the multicultural nature of the family suggests that social workers need to be prepared to work with diverse family forms. The question can be asked: What constitutes a family? This is important to the social worker, who has to consider whom to invite to work on family difficulties.

Families may include those constituted by *birth*, or consanguinity; *marriage*, or affinity; *lineage*, or generation; or *household*, or residency. A family may also be defined by its organizational pattern, including *single parent*, or a parent and his or her child(ren); *grandparent led*, or grandparents raising their grandchild(ren); *nuclear*, which usually includes parents and their child(ren); or *extended*, which includes related individuals not in the nuclear group. Families may also be augmented by adoption and/or provide foster care. In addition, families may be *childless*, when couples decide or prefer not to have children, or *blended*, when two people who already have children marry. On July 25, 2015, gay or same-sex marriage was approved by the Supreme Court under Obergellfell v Hodges.

> ➤ Dona calls the agency to make an appointment because her twelve-year-old son recently started having trouble at school. His grades have fallen. She is living with her new boyfriend, but her ex-husband will pay for the service. Who should be invited to the first family-focused meeting? What theoretical assumption(s) can help you make a professional judgment? Decide now and again after reading the chapter.

Engage With Individuals, Families, Groups, Organizations, and Communities

> ➤ Engagement is accomplished when the social worker creates an environment in which the family does the work.

Forming a Relationship

The client–social worker relationship takes on different characteristics when one is working with families. The practitioner role may be seen as active in the ways in which the social worker puts the family to work on its own issues. Listening to, observing, and deciding when to intervene in family interactions is at the core of the process. Depending on the school of thought, the social worker may be a distant coach, an energetic teacher/advocate, or a transpersonal helper. For example, Harry Aponte (1994), a structural family therapist, created the person-of-the-therapist model, in which a practitioner uses personal feelings and stories to understand the client family. He contended that this use of professional self-understanding of oneself and one's own woundedness allows social workers to connect with their clients, especially those who are ethnically, socioeconomically, or culturally different from themselves (Aponte 1992). This idea is congruent with the CSWE (2015), which expects "social workers [to] understand how their personal experiences and affective reactions may impact their ability to effectively engage with diverse clients and constituencies" (p. 6).

> *Assessment content is gathered through setting boundaries and mapping the family history and relationship with other social systems.*

Setting Boundaries

Setting the boundaries for your family sessions is another practice issue to keep in mind. Boundaries may be pictured as a dotted or broken line drawn around the members of a social system or family. By drawing a genogram of all of the people in the system, the family identifies its *membership,* or those who belong. Ann Hartman's (1978) well-known visual representations of the genealogy and ecology of the family (Figures 6.1 and 6.2) can be used directly with the family as engagement, assessment, and intervention tools. The genogram is placed in a circle in the center of the Ecomap. Together, they are a dynamic way of understanding the ecological system. The boundaries encompass a *family in its life space* or the major systems that are part of the family's relationship with its environment.

Figure 6.1.
A sample genogram. Adapted from Hartman and Laird (1983, 473.)

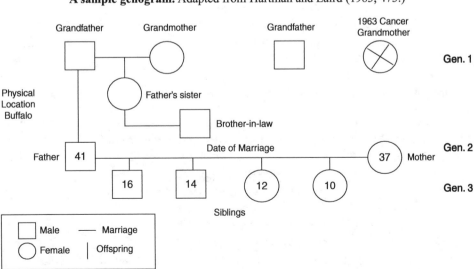

Figure 6.2.
A blank Ecomap. (From Hartman 1978, 465.)

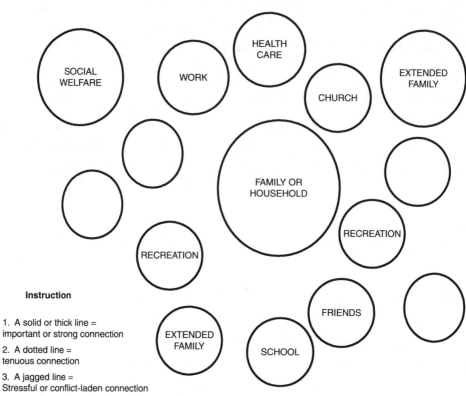

Instruction

1. A solid or thick line =
important or strong connection

2. A dotted line =
tenuous connection

3. A jagged line =
Stressful or conflict-laden connection

4. Arrows indicate the direction of energy flow

That is, an Ecomap gives an overview of the family in its life space; it pictures the important nurturant or conflict-laden connections between the family and its immediate world. It also demonstrates the flow of resources back and forth between the family and other social systems (or the lack thereof). Furthermore, this mapping procedure highlights the points of conflicts to be mediated. Consequently, its use continues after engagement, providing assessment information and suggesting interventions.

The instructions for drawing an Ecomap are as follows:

- Engage the family by completing a *genogram*—a drawing of the immediate family members attending family sessions and their generational composition. Symbols on a genogram traditionally represent family members, their ages, and their relationships to one another (e.g., dates of marriage or geographical location). You may want to go to the website of the Multicultural Family Institute (Highland Park, New Jersey) to see a more comprehensive listing of symbols developed for diverse family forms (http://www.multiculturalfamily. org). For example, some tribal nations have a *mother clan system* in which children are connected through their mothers' lineage. Such a generational configuration might be depicted on a family's genogram.

- Continue with the Ecomap by asking the family members about their relations with other social systems. Work together with the family members to add lines that connect them to different social systems in their environment. The nature of the connection between the family and the other social systems is expressed by the type of line drawn between them:
  - A solid line indicates a strong/important connection.
  - A dotted line means there is a tenuous connection.
  - A jagged line stands for a stressful, conflict-laden connection (Figure 6.3).

Remember that although the Ecomap is used as a thinking tool for the worker, it is also a way for the family system and the social worker to collaborate, hopefully leading to active participation in the helping process.

Figure 6.3.
A sample completed Ecomap. (From Hartman 1978, 473.)

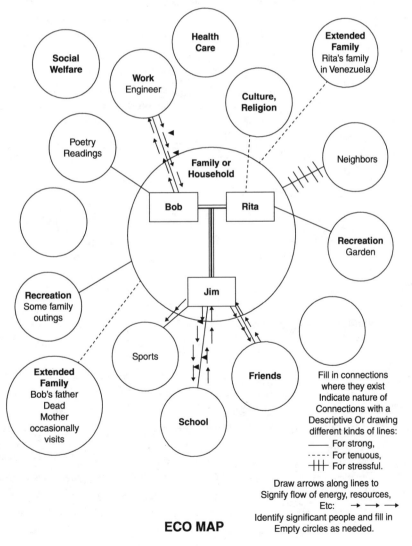

Assess Individuals, Families, Groups, Organizations, and Communities

The social worker assesses a family using a blend of communication and observational techniques inferred from the chosen school of thought. Various GST concepts discussed here are applicable.

> ➤ *Assessment content addresses family–environment fit.*

Family–Environment Fit

According to the assumptions of GST, social systems must carry out several functions to maintain themselves as a unit. Family functions needed to keep the system viable generally include the provision of economic resources, protection or safety, and care. Family functions have also historically included the legitimization of sexual activity, reproduction, the socialization of children, and the provision of status. In addition, families may provide access to health, education, welfare, and recreation.

Family–environment fit addresses how well family functions are being met, exploring contributions from and to other social systems within the environment. The social worker and family have created an Ecomap and now can explore whether there is a correspondence between the family's environmental quality and its internal functions and needs. Namely, are the resources needed by the family supported by a nurturing environment? For example, how does the workplace environment fit with family needs? Is there maternity leave?

> ➤ *Major assessment content addressed includes the family's ability to stay together in a balanced state.*

Family Adaptiveness

When working with diverse family forms, the social worker needs to keep in mind the concept of *equifinality*. This suggests that a system has a variety of ways of reaching a single goal. It is also assumed that systems are naturally goal oriented (Buckley 1968; Von Bertalanffy 1962). Therefore, the social worker should take a strengths perspective and presuppose that the family has come for help because its members want to stay together.

There are different ways for the social worker to increase a family's adaptiveness. An *adaptive family system* maps and discriminates which factors members may use in their environment. By helping families develop a pool of alternative ideas and behavior, social workers assist them to become better at problem solving (Minuchin 1974). This allows families to maintain a *steady state* or dynamic balance. Increased positive interaction within a system is called *synergy;* when families have less positive interaction within the system, they exhibit *entropy,* or become disordered or run down. As seen in the case study below, the Rogers family appears to be running down and in need of better communication and problem-solving strategies. The practitioner tests out these presumptions while working with the family.

Relatively Open or Closed Families

Whether a family's boundaries are relatively opened or closed affects its access to and use of resources. *Closed systems* have less active exchange with their environment. Therefore, family members are less flexible and may be less open to one another's and the social worker's ideas as well as to change. Members of a relatively closed family are less individuated or autonomous. Such families are sometimes considered *dysfunctional* (Bowen 1978; Goldenberg and Goldenberg 2003).

Open systems have a more efficient flow of *energy* or information and resources in and out of the system, such as using the public library or food pantry. They are more goal oriented. This enables the system to better carry out its functions and to adapt to changing circumstances. To begin getting an impression of the openness of the family, the social worker interprets its Ecomap with the family, confirming issues about the flow of energy into and out of the system (see Chapter 2). He or she also observes the family members' interactions in the here in now during their time together, asking about how well they talk together about family problems.

Case Study

> The Rogers family is composed of four members: uncle John, mother Sally, daughter Rosemary, and son Everest. Everest has been having temper tantrums while doing homework. John has just lost his job. Rosemary is hanging out late with her friends. Sally has threatened to take the family's only income, move out, and go live with her mother. Everest's tantrums have increased, and he recently pushed his fist through the wall. Growing tired of the family's noisy conflict, their neighbor called the police. This precipitated the Rogers family "trying out" the help available at the local community mental health center. What does the social worker want to learn when they attend the first family counseling session?

> As the family sessions progress, the social worker learns that the Rogers family lives in a crime-ridden neighborhood. Sally "supervises" all homework to "be sure her son earns his way out of the housing development." John is tired of being "dissed."

Internal Family Patterns

In addition to family–environment fit and the need for resources, the social worker next explores internal family patterns to identify possible solutions for family difficulties. A GST assumption is that a family has unique communication and structural/organizational patterns that support or negate the family's ability to deal with problems or crises. The social worker's role is to discern and clarify these patterns with the family.

Communication is the flow of information between and among systems and between family members. Through communication, family members learn the expectations they have of one another, also known as *rules* (Jackson 1965). If rules are not explicit, *triangulation,* or siding with one family member against another, may occur.

Through these various positive and negative interactions, a *family culture*—a belief system and values—is formed. In addition, the *socialization* of children, or the preparation of children to participate in society, occurs. Families that have a communication pattern conducive to using information effectively, known as a *positive feedback loop,* are more effective in carrying out their functions. Families that do not are less effective and bring about negative behaviors in family members (Bowen 1978). Dysfunctional families often know but do not obey their rules or may have a family secret (Satir 1972).

> ➤ Assessment content addressed includes whether a family is rela-
> tively functional. Functional families are relatively open, have clear
> communication, and have an organizational structure (roles) that
> carries out their functions.

Social workers use their interpersonal helping skills to help model more functional communication skills (CSWE 2015). They listen for communication patterns and simultaneously observe family structure or organization. *Structure* refers to "the pattern of stable relationships among family systems members based on the functions that each person carries out" (Greene 2008, 56). There may also be *subsystems,* or smaller systems in their own right. For example, most theorists agree that in a functional family the child subsystem is subordinate to the parent subsystem. Social workers also observe hierarchy as a feature of family organization. *Hierarchy* is the ranking of family members by power and control. Who are the family decision makers? In what situations? When a family's organization is dysfunctional, the social worker will work with it to become more adaptable and goal oriented.

In addition, the organization of families refers to how members carry out their *reciprocal roles* (see Parsons 1968; Thompson and Greene 2008). As can be seen in Figure 6.4, people play roles derived from personal characteristics, how they behave in a group, and what level of social system is involved. The social worker's assessment examines the extent to which roles are *complementary* or fit well together. As seen in the case study of the Klein family, the social worker explores the fit of family roles.

Figure 6.4.
Types of roles: Levels and categories. Adapted from Thompson
and Greene (2008, 101–22, 106.)

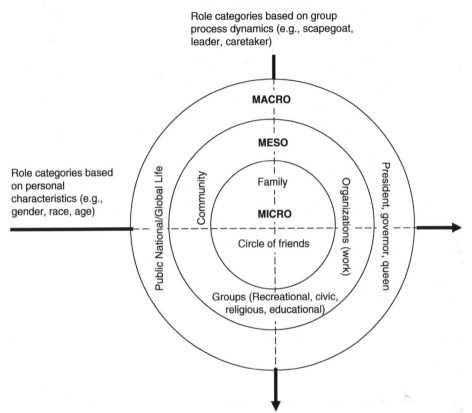

> ➤ The Klein family has four members: dad Arnold (age fifty), mother
> Ruth (age forty-seven), daughter Magnolia (age fourteen), and
> daughter Kimberly (age twelve). They have been remanded by the
> court for family counseling because Magnolia has stolen a car.
> The social worker learns during the first family meeting that Arnold
> is a wealthy businessman. He says, "Why would she steal a car
> when she knows I can buy her one?"
>
> ➤ The children whisper to each other as the parents speak. As the
> meeting progresses, the social worker learns that Arnold has
> already taught Magnolia to drive without Ruth's knowledge. "I'm
> too young to get a learning permit. So I just went out with the guys
> and got me a car!" Ruth is appalled and says, "Arnold has always
> allowed Magnolia to get away with everything."

(Continued)

> ➤ As the family sessions continue, Ruth reveals that she is experiencing conflict about her role as a stay-at-home wife and mother. Arnold wants her to continue being his "homemaker." Now that her daughters are older, Ruth says that she wants to go back to college.

> ➤ What family systems communication assumptions do you see at play? What role conflicts do you observe in the Klein family? Do the parents collaborate on their parental role?

When *role conflict* occurs, a family may or may not restructure itself naturally as it faces crises and times of transition across its life cycle. Turning points or *family developmental tasks* have traditionally been births, marriages, and deaths—times when members reconfigure themselves to take on new roles and obligations. Examples may include someone obtaining a second job, an adult child moving back home, or a new father becoming a stay-at-home dad.

> ➤ Assessment content addressed considers role complementarity and family patterns.

Diversity in Family Patterns

Social workers need to be aware that families may have different family patterns based on their configuration, including *grandparent-headed families.* In the United States today, 2.7 million grandparents have sole responsibility for the care of their grandchildren (U.S. Census Bureau 2011), and this number is growing fast. Grandparents who raise their grandchildren maintain family cohesiveness and provide love and security, which are foundation for the children's lives (Hayslip and Kaminski 2005). Their caregiving may contribute to grandchildren overcoming experiences of early abuse and domestic violence. Yet despite their significant role as caregivers, custodial grandparents tend to have more negative emotional and physical health (Luo et al. 2012), experience depression more (Baker and Silverstein 2008), and have limited support from and involvement with family and friends (Musil et al. 2009).

More important, custodial grandparents face inadequate access to legal, financial, community, and educational resources (Yancura 2013) and a lack of understanding from their grandchildren's schools about their unique family dynamics (Shakya et al. 2012). Custodial grandparents want more of a connection and better communication with their children's schools. Grandparents raising grandchildren note that the hierarchy of the intergenerational family and their role as a major caregiver and authority with their grandchildren are sometimes not recognized by teachers and school staff in parent–teacher conferences.

> Assessment content addressed and change strategies selected may vary by family form.

> Mr. and Mrs. Baker have been raising their eight-year-old grand-daughter since she was born. Lucy's parents were divorced right after Lucy's birth, and the father has been incarcerated for the past three years. Lucy's mother, Kristin, lives in the same town but has very limited contact with Lucy. However, Kristin has insisted on retaining shared custody of Lucy with Mr. and Mrs. Baker.

> On a parent–teacher conference day, Mr. and Mrs. Baker request a meeting with the school social worker and principal. The grand-parents share that the teacher only wants to talk to Lucy's biolog-ical mother, even though the grandparents are the ones raising Lucy. The grandparents also say that they are frustrated with some school activities that are not sensitive to a variety of family com-positions, such as a father–daughter dance and a class project to create Mother's Day cards.

Assess Individuals, Families, Groups, Organizations, and Communities

As the assessment process unfolds, social workers develop mutually agreed-on intervention goals and objectives based on the critical assessment of strengths, needs, and challenges within clients and constituencies (CSWE 2015). Areas of assessment with families include the following:

1. Viewing the family as a unit
2. Determining boundaries or membership within the family
3. Evaluating family–environment fit
4. Developing a picture of the family structure (subsystems, hierarchy, roles)
5. Exploring the family's communication processes (feedback loops, rules)
6. Asking what is bringing about dysfunction
7. Exploring strengths
8. Understanding the family culture
9. Mutually evaluating how responsive the family is to stress

Intervene With Individuals, Families, Groups, Organizations, and Communities

Family Stress

Family interventions are called for when the family is unable to use its natural ability to overcome stress and continue to function effectively. Ironically, systems theory sug-gests that stresses and strains on the organizational and functional capabilities of the family are natural characteristics even of adaptive systems. That is, tensions are part of everyday life. Responding to stress and attempting to reach goals is also a natural tendency. The tendency for families to overcome stress can be seen in many military families, who must restructure with each deployment, putting pressure on relationships or the attachment network (Riggs and Riggs 2011). However, when a family appears in a state of instability, the social worker can enhance communication flow and foster reorganization so that *homeostasis,* or the ability to maintain balance, is restored.

The Family Adjustment and Adaptation Response Model

A visual representation of Patterson's (1988) family adjustment and adaptation response model can be seen in Figure 6.5. This is a means of understanding a family's attempts to use its resources to meet the burden of stress. There are two phases to this process:

1. In the *adjustment phase,* the family experiences relative stability. The *demands* placed on the system—stressors, strains, and hassles—are met with existing *capabilities,* coping skills, and resources. If a *crisis* occurs, demands may be too great and exceed capabilities. This can bring about a state of disequilibrium. The *meaning,* or interpretation of these demands derived from the family's belief system, is a major influence in the family's ability to remain or regain balance.
2. In the *adaptation phase,* the family tries to restore its balance by obtaining new resources and developing new coping strategies. The family may also reduce demands by changing its perception of its situation.

Family Assets and Adaptation

Rothwell and Han (2009) combined Patterson's (1988) family adjustment and adaptation response model and Sherraden's (1991, 2008) asset-based theory of social welfare to examine the relationship between family assets and stress. They found that the availability of family assets correlated with less financial strain and stress.

Sherraden (1991) proposed that at least nine positive effects associated with family assets need to be taken into account in policy formation: (a) household stability, (b) an orientation toward the future, (c) development of other assets, (d) focus and specialization, (e) risk taking, (f) personal efficacy, (g) social influence, (h) political participation, and (i) the welfare of future generations. They concluded that assets were important to family stress management and that social welfare policymakers should design programs to promote the acquisition of assets among low-income families.

> ➤ *Change strategies selected primarily focus on reducing family stress and obtaining resources.*

Family Intervention Techniques

Family intervention techniques borrowed from the family therapy literature discussed here have been divided into five treatment goals: (a) obtaining goods and services, (b) attempting structural modifications, (c) improving communication

Figure 6.5.
The family adjustment and adaptation response model.
Adapted from Patterson (1988, 236.)

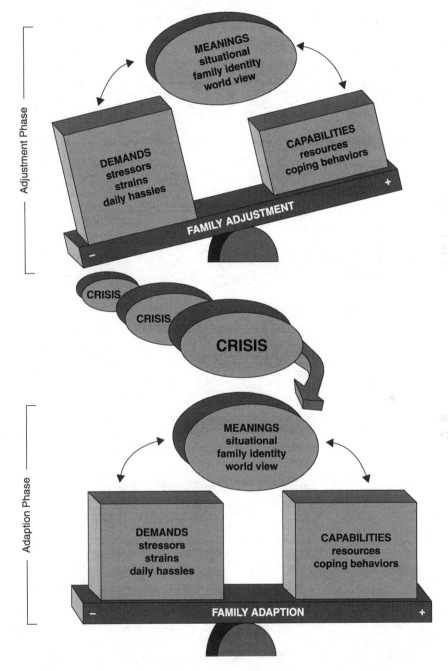

skills, (d) dealing with emotional and role conflict, and (e) reframing meaning. You can apply them to the cases studies presented previously to see the overlap or crossover between these possible techniques and outcomes.

Obtaining goods and services. As seen in the discussion of family–environment fit, family treatment can be a time for the social worker to address oppressive structural barriers to ensure that social goods and responsibilities are distributed equitably and that civil, political, economic, social, and cultural human rights are considered (CSWE 2015). When a family reveals that it has limited resources, it is identifying possible areas of intervention. How can members learn about available environmental resources? The answers to these questions may lead "the social worker to negotiate, mediate, and advocate on behalf of client and constituencies" (CSWE 2015, 8).

Attempting structural modifications. Treating structural problems in a family generally involves a modification of the family's hierarchy and subsystems. The social worker sets the stage by asking adults in the family to describe the family's difficulties. Then all family members are coached to speak among themselves so that interactions in the here and now can be observed (Minuchin 1974). What does the social worker see played out in the interaction? Is one member of a couple aligned with the other? Do children ignore what adults say? In the case of the Klein family, you might ask the parents to address their children's whispering while they, the adults, talk. You will also have to decide whether to remain neutral about Mrs. Klein's educational aspirations (McGoldrick, Gerson, and Petry 2008).

Improving communication skills. Improved communication skills go hand in hand with structural modification. Depending on the problems raised by the family, the social worker should have a plan for how he or she wants to enhance family communication. Are family rules known by all? Is there a family secret that needs to be shared? Teaching family members to speak to one another using "I" statements can be helpful: Perhaps, depending on the family culture, Mrs. Klein can be coached to say to her husband, "I feel you are taking me for granted."

Dealing with emotional and role conflict. Emotional and role conflict in a family is an indication that the social worker may need to look for triangulation and less differentiation of self among members. However, the social worker needs to first establish a calm and safe environment. Observations will tell who has aligned with whom. Are family members caught up in a cycle of violence, reacting to one another with anger and conflict? When this information becomes apparent in the here-and-now interacting family group, the social worker takes a stance that minimizes emotionality (Bowen 1978). For example, family therapist Virginia Satir might have said to Sally Rogers, "It looks like you are wearing many hats in this family—wife, mother, wage earner, and school principal. Can you tell your family how you feel about that?"

Reframing meaning. Determining the reason for violence among family members may require reframing the family problem. John and Everest Rogers are in increasing conflict with each other because they do not recognize that John feels disrespected and Everest believes he has been abandoned to his mother's tyranny. By changing these interpretations of events surrounding Everest's homework, they may interrupt their cycle of violence. A postmodern technique that can be used in reframing meaning is the frequently quoted miracle question. The social worker asks, "Suppose one night when you were asleep, a miracle took place and your problem would be solved. What would be different?" (De Shazer 1991).

Critique of Diversity Issues in Social Work Practice

> ➤ *Assessment content and change strategies in family-focused social work may vary by cultural context.*

Nichols and Schwartz (2001) considered the period from 1970 to 1985 the golden age of family therapy, when most renowned theorists made their theoretical contributions. These concepts combined with the GST model as described here were viewed positively by many practitioners. The continued development of family practice into the 21st century provides the social worker with numerous choices to make when using GST as a foundation in family-centered practice (Franklin and Jordan 1999). Can the model truly be effective with the range of families social workers serve? Is the model applicable across cultures? More evidence-based information is needed.

Feminist social workers such as Lynn Hoffman (1985) have argued that applying GST in family treatment maintains the status quo of unequal treatment of women within families. She contended that *first-order change,* or the modification of behavior, was insufficient for women to gain equal treatment. Rather, *second-order change,* in which the family is restructured, was necessary. Does this argument suggest that the practitioner may need to take sides?

In a similar vein, social constructionists lodged another critique against GST. They proposed that GST could not be neutral, nor should it be. Rather, the social worker should introduce societal inequities reflected in the family into family meetings, such as Mrs. Klein's wish to further her education.

However, the role of women may differ according to cultural traditions. For example, family caregivers play a significant role as a resource for older adults. This role is more important in many immigrant communities because of their limited utilization of social services. The experiences of immigrant families and their needs can be expected to differ depending on norms, practices, and expectations concerning their role.

For example, in Asian culture, Confucianism, filial piety, and familism are major determinants in establishing family caregiving dynamics and the caregivers' perception of caregiving. The traditional philosophy emphasizes the importance of family cohesion, the parent–child relationship, and continuity in sustaining both the community and the state. These cultural traditions rooted in filial piety dictate that children are supposed to respect and take care of their aging parents within the family network. In addition, the lack of trust toward social services (Lee and Smith 2012) contributes to limited interaction with the majority social service community.

Elaine Congress (1994) has created the culturagram, which can be used with immigrant families such as the Lius to increase ethnic-sensitive practice (Figure 6.6). Through mutual exploration with the family, the social worker can ascertain reasons for immigration, length of time in the community, legal status, age at the time of immigration, and language spoken at home and in the community. By obtaining answers to these questions, the social worker is more likely to appreciate the client's and constituency's culture.

Figure 6.6.
The culturagram. (From Congress 1994, 53).

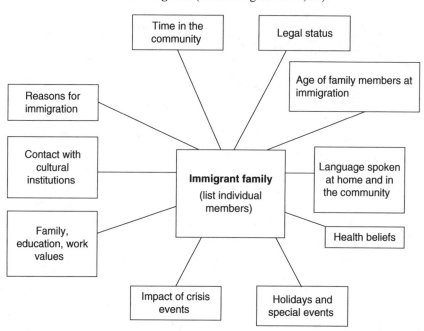

> ➤ Mr. Liu's father was diagnosed with dementia five years ago. His father did not present problem behaviors until recently, but now he has started wandering during the night. His primary physician recommended that the Liu family put the father in a nearby nursing home. However, the father refuses to go to a nursing home because the home does not have a Chinese-speaking doctor. Mr. Liu thinks it would be disrespectful and shameful to send his father to a nursing home. Because the family needs someone who can speak Chinese and take care of the father at home, the Liu family thinks Mr. Liu's wife needs to quit her job and take care of her father-in-law.

Glossary

Adaptive systems. Systems that discriminate well and act effectively on their environments. Adaptive systems are more complex because they have a greater capacity to grow and to elaborate their structures.

Boundary. A permeable limit to the system that defines what is considered inside or outside the system. Boundaries regulate the flow of energy into (inputs) and out of (outputs) the system.

Closed systems. Systems characterized by a less active exchange with the environment. They are less goal oriented and have less ability to modify behavior.

Communication. The flow of information between and among system members and between and among systems.

Complementarity of roles. The fit of role relationships.

Culture. A way of life that binds a group together.

Differentiation. The developmental sequencing or elaboration of a system. It is the way in which members take on organizational roles. Differentiation or change in behavior is based on expectations of the members, the needs of the individual, and the system.

Dysfunctional systems. Systems that have relatively closed boundaries and primarily operate within their own boundaries. These systems are apt to be inflexible, undifferentiated, and less effective.

Energy. The flow of information and resources in and out of the system that makes it able to perform its functions.

Entropy. Disorganization within the system, or the running down of performance.

Environment. Everything external to or outside a system's boundaries.

Equifinality. A property of a system that allows it to arrive at its goals from a number of different vantage points, or the ability of a system to reach the same final state from different initial conditions and in different ways.

Equilibrium. The ability of a system to maintain balance without input from the environment. This may bring about temporary instability; this instability, however, may lead to growth and development.

Family. A social system of interdependent persons with its own unique structure, pattern of differentiated roles, and communication that may exist in different forms in different cultures.

Family developmental task. A major turning point for the family that brings about a new set of circumstances to which the system must adapt.

Feedback. The ability to monitor a system's operation; make a judgment if adaptive action is needed; and, if so, make corrections.

Feedback loop. A response to information gathered by the system.

Functional systems. Systems that are more open to outside energy sources and are more flexible, adaptable, and goal achieving.

Hierarchy. The ordering or ranking of people within a system that is based on power or control.

Homeostasis. The inclination of a system to maintain a balance and to attempt to restore it when threatened.

Individuation. The ability of a system to provide for individual development.

Interaction. The exchange of information or resources between and among systems and system members. Interaction is a continuous and reciprocal series of contacts between two or more persons who take each other into account.

Model. An abstraction or visual representation of the reality of how things work under ideal conditions. Models present a frame of reference for analyzing a phenomenon.

Open systems. Systems that are characterized by the active exchange of energy (information and materials) with their environment, are more goal oriented, and have a greater ability to adapt. All living systems are by definition relatively open.

Organization. The way in which systems members work together, or their established patterns for achieving systems goals.

Rules. Guidelines for the way in which a family maintains defined behaviors among its members.

Social system. A structure of interacting and interdependent people.

Socialization. A process of bringing about reciprocity between individual and social needs so the individual may participate effectively in societal systems.

Steady state. A system's dynamic balance. Systems that maintain a steady state are better able to adapt and grow through the effective use of inputs and outputs.

Structure. A pattern of stable relationships among family systems members based on the functions that each person carries out.

Subsystem. A component of any system that is a system in its own right.

Synergy. Increased positive interaction in a system or among systems.

System. A complex whole made up of component parts in mutual interaction.

Tension. Normal stresses or strains on the structural organization of systems.

References

Ackerman, N. 1958. *The Psychodynamics of Family Life.* New York: Basic Books.

Aponte, H. 1992. "Training the Person of the Therapist in Structural Family Therapy." *Journal of Marital and Family Therapy* 18 (3): 29–81.

Aponte, H. 1994. *Bread and Spirit: Therapy with the New Poor: Diversity of Race, Culture, and Values.* New York: Norton.

Associated Press. June 14, 2014. *President Obama Visits Indian Country.* Accessed October 15, 2015. http://www.heraldnet.com/article/20140614/NEWS02/140619571

Baker, L., and M. Silverstein. 2008. "Depressive Symptoms among Grandparents Raising Grandchildren: The Impact of Participation in Multiple Roles." *Journal of Intergenerational Relationships* 6 (3): 285–304.

Bateson, G. 1971. *Steps toward the Ecology of the Mind.* New York: Ballantine.

Bateson, G. 1979. *Mind and Nature.* New York: Dutton.

Bowen, M. 1978. *Family Therapy in Clinical Practice.* New York: Jason Aronson.

Buckley, W. 1967. "Systems and Entities." In *Sociology and Modern Systems Theory*, edited by W. Buckley, 42–66. Englewood Cliffs, NJ: Prentice Hall.

Buckley, W. 1968. "Society as a Complex Adaptive System." In *Modern Systems Research for the Behavioral Scientist*, edited by W. Buckley, 490–511. Chicago, IL: Aldine.

Congress, E. P. 1994. "The Use of Culturagrams to Assess and Empower Culturally Diverse Families." *Families in Society* 75:531–40.

Council on Social Work Education. 2015. *Educational Policy and Accreditation Standards.* Alexandria, VA: Council on Social Work Education.

De Shazer, P. 1991. *Putting Difference to Work.* New York: Norton.

Ellis, A. 1962. *Reason and Emotion in Therapy.* New York: Lyle Stuart.

Franklin, C., and C. Jordan. 1999. *Family Process.* Monterey, CA: Brooks/Cole.

Goldenberg, I., and H. Goldenberg. 2003. *Family Therapy: An Overview.* Monterey, CA: Brooks/Cole.

Greene, R. R. 2008. *Social Work with the Aged and Their Families.* New Brunswick, NJ: Aldine Transaction Press.

Haeckel, E. 1904. *The Wonders of Life: A Popular Study of Biological Philosophy.* London: Watts.

Haley, J. 1971. "Family Therapy: A Radical Change." In *Changing Families: A Family Therapy Reader,* edited by J. Haley, 20–26. New York: Grune & Stratton.

Hartman, A. 1978. "Diagrammatic Assessment of Family Relationships." *Social Casework* 59:466–76.

Hartman, A., and J. Laird. 1983. *Family-centered Social Work Practice.* New York: Free Press.

Hayslip, B., and P. L. Kaminski. 2005. "Grandparents Raising Their Grandchildren: A Review of the Literature and Suggestions for Practice." *The Gerontologist* 45:262–9.

Hoffman, L. 1985. "Beyond Power and Control: 'Second order' Family Therapy." *Family Systems Medicine* 3 (4): 381–96.

Jackson, D. D. 1965. "Family Rules: Marital Quid pro Quo." *Archives of General Psychiatry* 12:589–94.

Laird, J. 1996. "Family-centered Practice with Lesbian and Gay Families." *Families in Society* 77:559–72.

Lee, Y., and L. Smith. 2012. "Qualitative Research on Korean American Dementia Caregivers' Perception of Caregiving: Heterogeneity between Spouse Caregivers and Child Caregivers." *Journal Human Behavior in the Social Environment* 22:115–29.

Lévi-Strauss, C. 1948. *The Elemental Structure of Kinship.* Paris, France: Societe des Americanistes.

Lubove, R. 1965. *The Professional Altruist: The Emergence of Social Work as a Career, 1890–1930.* Cambridge, MA: Harvard University Press.

Luo, Y. Y., T. A. LaPierre, M. E. Hughes, and L. J. Waite. 2012. "Grandparents Providing Care to Grandchildren: A Population-based Study of Continuity and Change." *Journal of Family Issues* 33:1143–67.

McGoldrick, M., R. Gerson, and S. Petry. 2008. *Genograms: Assessment and Intervention,* 3rd ed. New York: Norton.

Minuchin, S. 1974. *Families and Family Therapy.* Cambridge, MA: Harvard University Press.

Musil, C., C. Warner, J. Zauszniewski, M. Wykle, and T. Standing. 2009. "Grandmother Caregiving, Family Stress and Strain, and Depressive Symptoms." *Western Journal of Nursing Research* 31:389–408.

Nichols, M. P., and R. C. Schwartz. 2001. *Family Therapy: Concepts and Methods.* Needham Heights, MA: Pearson.

Parsons, T. 1968. *Knowledge and Society: American Sociology.* New York: Basic Books.

Patterson, J. M. 1988. "Families Experiencing Stress: The Family Adjustment and Adaptation Response Model." *Family Systems Medicine* 6:202–37.

Petr, C. G. 1988. "The Worker-client Relationship: A General Systems Perspective." *Social Casework* 69:620–6.

Richmond, M. E. 1917. *What Is Social Casework?* New York: Russell Sage Foundation.

Riggs, S. A., and D. S. Riggs. 2011. "Risk and Resilience in Military Families Experiencing Deployment: The Role of the Family Attachment Network." *Journal of Family Psychology* 25:675–87.

Rothwell, D., and C. -K. Han. 2009. *Assets as a Resource Variable in the Stress Management of Low Income Families* (CSD Working Paper No. 09-50). St. Louis, MO: Washington University, Center for Social Development.

Satir, V. 1972. *People Making.* Palo Alto, CA: Science and Behavior.

Shakya, H. B., P. M. Usita, C. Eisenberg, J. Weston, and S. Liles. 2012. "Family Well-being Concerns of Grandparents in Skipped Generation Families." *Journal of Gerontological Social Work* 55:39–54.

Sherraden, M. 1991. *Assets and the Poor: A New American Welfare Policy.* Armonk: M. E. Sharpe.

Sherraden, M. 2008. *IDAs and Asset-building Policy: Lessons and Directions* (CSD Working Paper No. 08-12). St. Louis, MO: Washington University, Center for Social Development.

Taylor, R., and L. Chatters. 1988. "Church Members as a Source of Informal Social Support." *Review of Religious Research* 30:193–203.

Taylor, R., and L. Chatters. 1991. "Religious Life." In *Life in Black America,* edited by J. Jackson, 105–23. Thousand Oaks, CA: Sage.

Thompson, K., and R. R. Greene. 2008. "Role Theory." In *Human Behavior: A Diversity Framework,* 2nd ed., edited by R. R. Greene, 101–22. New Brunswick, NJ: Aldine Transaction Press.

Tomm, K. 1994. "Interventive Interviewing: Part III. Intending to Ask Lineal, Circular, Strategic, or Reflexive Questions?" In *Constructivism and Family Therapy,* edited by K. Brownlee, P. Gallant, and D. Carpenter, 117–56. Thunder Bay, Canada: Lakehead University Printing Services.

U.S. Census Bureau. 2011. *2011 American Community Survey*. Accessed October 15, 2015. http://factfinder2.census.gov/faces/tableservices/jsf/pages/productview.xhtml?pid=ACS_11_1YR_B10056&prodType=table

Von Bertalanffy, L. 1962. "General Systems Theory: A Critical Review." *General Systems Yearbook* 7:1–20.

Von Bertalanffy, L. 1968. *General Systems Theory: Human Relations*. New York: Braziller.

White, M., and D. Epston. 1990. *Narrative Means to Therapeutic Ends*. New York: Norton.

Yancura, L. 2013. "Service Use and Unmeet Service Needs in Grandparents Raising Grandchildren." *Journal of Gerontological Social Work* 56:473–86.

7

Human Behavior and the Social Environment Theory: Social Work Practice with Groups

> ➤ *This chapter presents human behavior and the social environment theories for social work practice with groups. Mutual aid in social work groups and Yalom's existential group therapy processes are contrasted, illustrating the sociohistorical context of theory construction. Transtheoretical content is also explored.*

There are a myriad of theoretical and methodological approaches to social work practice with groups. Groups may vary by problem addressed, membership, length, setting, structure, composition, and goals. Populations served encompass the full spectrum of clients seen by social workers. Social work with groups is conducted in many agencies and can meet human needs that are not always met through individual help, such as the need to belong.

This chapter specifically contrasts two approaches for social workers to use in group practice: (a) social group work and (b) Irvin Yalom's existential group therapy. Social group workers perceive groups as a form of mutual aid and tend to focus on clients' interpersonal relationships and social skills, whereas therapeutic group leaders view the group process as a treatment method and emphasize corrective emotional experiences (Corey 2009). These schools of thought were selected to illustrate the way in which human behavior and the social environment theory reflects the era in which a particular theory was constructed and, in turn, to reformulate the ideas that social workers can call on in practice. This self-reflection calls for critical thinking and the ability to synthesize multiple sources of knowledge (Council on Social Work Education [CSWE] 2015).

Section I.
Social Group Work

This section discusses the historical development of social group work with its emphasis on mutual aid. Like community organization, *social group work* is a social work practice method that attends to people in small groups. *Small groups* are generally defined as two or more persons (up to a membership of about twenty) who interact with one another with mutual influence and interdependence (Garvin and Reed 1994). Generally speaking, participating in a group allows members to share common experiences and to work with others on tasks. Groups can validate their members through group feedback and provide the opportunity to share ideas and explore the universality of human problems (Toseland, Jones, and Gellis 2004). In addition, group experiences provide the opportunity to work toward making individual and common decisions (Anderson, Carter, and Lowe 1999).

Professional Purpose and Well-Being

Historical Background

Just like social work practice with families, social group work has historical significance. Social group work rests on a foundation of mutual aid with roots in many world religions. Early community-based services sprang from the tradition of helping people within their faith communities.

During the nineteenth and twentieth centuries, various forms of government-sponsored and private charity organizations increasingly emerged to assist people in poverty and those who suffered from mental illness. Unfortunately, the recipients of such services were frequently viewed as unworthy or shameful. A philosophy of social Darwinism prevailed, which suggests that people survive through the natural selection of the fittest; that is, animals who are more fit live to reproduce and rise to the top.

> ➤ Social work with groups began with the intent to promote democracy and improve life conditions.

A countervailing thought was spearheaded by the settlement house movement, whose members made a major contribution to social services based on a philosophy of mutual aid and well-being (CSWE 2015). The movement began in the 1860s in London, with activists who were concerned with improving people's daily lives. It was a historical response to industrialization, the displacement of people from rural areas, as well as the increase in the number of urban poor (Table 7.1). For example, social philosopher and activist John Ruskin worked to advance living conditions, whereas economist Arnold Toynbee founded Toynbee Hall, a center of learning amid urban poverty. Thus, in the broadest sense, group participation was seen as a means of helping people learn to relate to others and to better their life conditions.

In a similar fashion, U.S. pioneer social worker Jane Addams established the well-known Hull House in Chicago in 1899. The number of settlement houses in the United States eventually reached more than four hundred, providing courses on a variety of topics intended to promote middle-class values and offering health care and day care services.

Group workers were interested in helping new Americans adapt to life in the United States. Socializing them to the American way of life was the ideal. Group workers viewed their professional purpose as improving clients' social functioning

Table 7.1.
Selected theoretical foundations of social group work: mutual aid

Time adopted	Major theorist(s)	Theme	Concepts for practice
1860	John Ruskin: Social philosopher	The excesses of industrialism brought about poverty and poor living conditions.	Undertaking activism and social reform
1884	Arnold Toynbee: Economist	Education and discussion can lead to opportunity and the eradication of poverty.	Addressing the ills of capitalism and marginalization
1889	Jane Addams: Philanthropist, social worker	People have a natural longing for fellowship.	Eliminating poverty and class distinctions through philanthropy and aid Building citizenship
1902	Peter Kropotkin: Sociobiologist	Mutual aid is part of evolution.	Giving and receiving aid, focusing on altruism
1963	Gisela Konopka: Social work educator	Social work with groups is multidisciplinary.	Combining theories in practice
1948	Grace Coyle: Social work educator	Groups conducted in the mutual aid model foster leadership.	Providing support for women and girls in leadership
1961	William Schwartz: Social work educator	People form alliances that support one another.	Ensuring the group does the work
2005	Alex Gitterman: Social work educator Lawrence Shulman: Social work educator	Investment in others is the purpose of social work with groups.	Reducing isolation and stigma

within their families and respective communities. Practice was often carried out at youth organizations, summer camps, and settlement houses, embodying education, recreation, and social action. Along with charity organizations, these services formed an incipient social welfare system (Scheuer 1985). Although the number of settlement houses has declined over the years, many major cities still retain community centers to support individual and community well-being.

Contemporary Mutual Aid Groups

Over time, contemporary theorists broke new ground in terms of the purpose of mutual aid groups. The idea of social work groups as a form of mutual aid was integrated into the social work curriculum (Konopka 1966; Schwartz 1961, 1986). Their use as a therapeutic method was affirmed (Coyle 1948), and their use in assisting people with many different issues—bereavement, trauma, mental illness—has come to fruition (Gitterman and Shulman 2005).

Applying Terms and Assumptions in Social Work Practice with Groups

> ➤ Mutual aid groups are based on group cohesion, trusting relation-
> ships, and mutual support and demand.

The social worker leading a mutual aid group will apply several terms and assumptions. A major assumption of social work practice with groups is that group participation or *membership* is a natural part of human existence (Falk 1988). Another
is that a group is a microcosm of society and part of the person–environment
configuration (Lewin 1943). Given these precepts, social workers can expect that
group members will eventually come together as a unit, working to solve mutual
problems and addressing one another's needs (Schwartz 1986). Consequently, the
assumption is made that *altruism* is another human instinct carried out in groups.
This means that practitioners can anticipate that a mutual aid group will become a
forum in which clients engage and care for other members of the group (Northen
and Kurland 2001).

> ➤ Engagement is accomplished through group cohesion, with
> human behavior and the social environment principles guiding
> techniques.

Engage With Individuals, Families, Groups, Organizations, and Communities

Adapting Theories for Group Practice

Group work is a method for social workers to use as part of engagement, assessment, and intervention (CSWE 2015). Yet group practice requires more from a
social worker than the ability to carry out a leadership role and work through group
phases. Such tasks as defining the role of the leader in social group work depend on
the human behavior and the social environment theory the social worker adopts (see
below). Consequently, the first rule of client engagement is for the social worker to
adopt a human behavior theory suitable for the purposes of the group. The leader
need not use only one human behavior and the social environment theory to guide
group practice. Rather, he or she may select key principles from several theories that
can be used to bring about change, known as *transtheoretical practice* (Prochaska
and Velicer 1997).

For example, social workers may elect to follow assumptions derived from
theories they know from practice with other systems and modify them for group
practice. That is, the social worker may want to reformulate some of the concepts
used in social work practice with individuals or families for work with groups (see
Chapters 5 and 6). For example, cognitive behavior theory aims to free clients of
problematic thoughts and establish sound cognitive processes. This strategy can
be used with group members, asking them to address faulty thinking and to adopt
problem-solving strategies. Problems that are learned can be unlearned through

such activities as improving social skills and learning to manage stress. The role of the group leader remains engaging and assessing the client group and setting mutual therapeutic goals. Methods used by the leader may include rehearsal, coaching, homework, feedback, and reinforcement.

Another example of modifying theory for work with groups is adapting solution-focused principles to a group format. In solution-focused treatments, clients do not examine problems but pay attention to life's positives and future solutions. When asked to attend to what is working well in their lives, group members can then define what it is they want to accomplish in the group. The group leader facilitates each group member's speaking to how the group can achieve goals for meaningful change.

> *Engagement involves group members learning to care about the functioning of other group members.*

Engagement in Mutual Aid Groups

Engagement, or the *beginning phase* of a mutual aid group, may be thought of as a contract between group members and among group members themselves. Members are wondering what the group leader is like and who other members of the group are. What is the group's purpose? The social worker can introduce himself or herself and ask group members to do the same. The agency's and group's purpose can be explored. How this fits with the reason a particular group member is attending can begin to clarify the work to be done. This clarification can also begin to alleviate concerns about the safety of the group (Gitterman and Salmon 2009).

Leadership in Mutual Aid Groups

As stated previously, leaders of mutual aid groups may adopt a *transtheoretical* approach to the helping process—one in which they infuse a number of theories into their group practice to give guidance to their role (CSWE 2015). For example, social work group theorist Lawrence Shulman (2009a, 2009b) illustrated how principles from a number of schools of thought can provide information on how to lead mutual aid support groups. He looked to Nathan Ackerman (1958), a psychodynamic psychiatrist, who contended that when people join a group, they must become aware of how their private inner self performs as a social outer self. This awareness of role performance is fostered by the group leader as well as by group members. In addition, Shulman used the general systems theory assumption that the whole is more than the sum of its parts to guide his examination of the group-as-a-whole phenomenon (see Chapter 5). This holistic perspective of group dynamics allows the leader to observe and interpret the group as a system in which there are issues related to norms, rules, taboos, and roles.

> *Assessment content explores the readiness of the group members to assist one another.*

Assess Individuals, Families, Groups, Organizations, and Communities

A Working Group

In group work, assessment is also theory based and relates to the purpose of the group. In the *middle phase* of a mutual aid group, the group leader is primarily concerned about helping members assist one another. Are members engaged in a culture of caring? Is mutual aid work going on within the group?

Theorists who discuss whether mutual aid group members are working together sometimes refer to Bion (1961), a British psychoanalyst who developed his ideas while treating soldiers following World War II. Bion argued that the leader's role is to assess and interpret three basic assumptions or postures that make up a *non-working group*:

1. A *dependency* position, when members hope for the leader to take care of all of their anxiety
2. A *pairing* assumption, which expects two members of the group to join together to rescue the other group members by producing a new (more effective) leader
3. A *fight-or-flight* assumption, when the group members find a common enemy or scapegoat inside or outside the group

From Bion's point of view, the sole role of the leader is to interpret these assumptions:

1. The group is acting as if they expect me to rescue them.
2. The group is acting as if they expect Robert and Jane to save them.
3. The group is acting as though if they can only get away from or fight the general of their unit, they will be okay.

You will see later in the chapter that this thinking about the leadership role may be considered too limited.

Tasks of a Working Mutual Aid Group

Alex Gitterman and Lawrence Shulman (2005) proposed that mutual aid groups are appropriate when people experience life transitions, trauma, and environmental pressures and when they go through maladaptive interpersonal processes. They suggested that social workers use in assessment the following principles characteristic of mutual aid groups:

- Engage group members in discussing issues of day-to-day functioning. Are group members learning more effective ways of dealing with their lives?
- Lead members in an exploration of their concerns from various (dialectical or contrasting) points of view. Are group members discovering new ideas? Can they see their own issues from a different perspective?
- Provide a safe environment for members to reveal taboo topics. Are group members able to trust one another and let their guard down in the group?

- Help the group find common ground. Does the group develop an agenda that helps most members?
- Assist group members in learning that most feelings/problems are universal. Can group members realize that others feel like they do?
- Use group dynamics to form a mutually supportive and demanding environment. Do group members expect to have give and take in their group? Does the group have cohesion?

In short, the social worker acts to ensure that the group is a place of healing. The authority of the leader's role also extends to reaching for the underlying meaning of behaviors enacted by members of the group, thus deepening group members' understanding. In addition, social workers also seek ways to strengthen resilience (see Chapter 10). The satisfaction or lack thereof with this group approach should be evaluated as the group progresses (CSWE 2015).

Because client-sensitive concerns are often explored with members of the group, trust, safety, and group cohesion are paramount. This is particularly difficult when vulnerable populations or traumatic events are part of the group experience (Schiller and Zimmer 2005). As seen in the case of Martha, feminist groups are one more transtheoretical example of a form of mutual aid group that can be a source of empowerment.

> ➤ Martha, a college freshman, has recently attended a fraternity party where she heard about a sexual assault. This has triggered a painful childhood memory of an uncle who abused her. She decides to join a mutual aid feminist group. Through the sharing of the group members, she learns that rape is an act of one person wielding power over another. Martha realizes that she is not to blame for what happened in her childhood. With positive group interaction, she has grown from victim to survivor.

Intervene With Individuals, Families, Groups, Organizations, and Communities

> ➤ Change strategies in mutual aid groups depend on the work of group members.

Populations Served

Mutual aid groups may be established for people with many different concerns: chemical dependency, mental illness, HIV/AIDS, and so forth. The case of Marvin illustrates how participating in a group can help individuals traverse social service delivery systems. For example, two of the most important factors in the medical environment that determine the effectiveness of personal treatment for HIV/AIDS are continuity of care and systems integration. *Continuity of care* involves maintaining the quality of care over time, whereas *systems integration* encompasses both formal and informal case management, which allows patients to maintain needed treatment (Greene and Kropf 2014). Therefore, mutual aid group leaders may collaborate with others in the social service delivery system (CSWE 2015).

> ➤ *Marvin was recently diagnosed with HIV at a San Francisco clinic that houses a number of health and human services. He has many questions to consider: How should he tell his partner about the diagnosis? How should he tell his teenage daughter? Should he tell his family of origin? Will his employers accept him? What will be the reaction of his faith community? Can he persevere through months or years of treatment?*
>
> ➤ *Marvin is referred for individual and group counseling for help in answering his concerns. His social worker, Patricia, serves as his case manager so that he does not drop out of the care system. In her monthly followups, Patricia learns that Marvin considers his group sessions very effective in keeping him on track in a complicated medical system. He also has been referred to additional helpful services.*

Purposes of Intervention

Interventions in mutual aid groups are designed to foster healing, promote empowerment, strengthen resilience, and provide mutual support. According to Gitterman and Salmon (2009), these change strategies occur when the forces of the group offer a minilab for solving life problems. They suggested that change strategies include

- universalizing group members' situations
- connecting with and nurturing others
- promoting consciousness raising
- sharing personal identities
- enhancing interpersonal communication
- accepting differences
- challenging issues of power and privilege
- providing a nonstigmatizing atmosphere
- advocating against oppressive policies and institutional structures

Evaluating group effectiveness is important as group *ending*, or termination, takes place. Members can be encouraged to reminisce about their participation in the group; that is, the group's members evaluate whether the group has been beneficial.

Critique of Diversity Issues in Social Work Practice with Mutual Aid Groups

Intergroup dialogue is a form of social group work intended to resolve community or intergroup conflict and is known as *transformational dialogue*. According to Garvin and Reed (1994), either participation in a small group may promote diversity and social and economic justice, or it can recreate inequities (Table 7.2). They made

Table 7.2.
Basic assumptions of small-group theory: relationship to issues of diversity

Basic assumptions	Relationship to diversity issues
The personality develops, grows, and changes through interaction with other persons, often carried out in small groups.	These interactions are strongly affected by group members' cultural identities and by the identities of others in the group.
Perceived roles and statuses outside the group affect status within the group.	The roles and statuses of people are strongly affected by their previous group experiences, typically with people from their own culture. This affects the assignment of status within the group.
The improvement of mental and social health has to do with actions and experiences within the group, not just with analysis and introspection.	The events that occur in the group are affected by the diversity characteristics of the group. Consequently, efforts to improve mental and social health through groups must attend to these compositional factors.
Joining together to accomplish group purposes is one of the major ways in which problems are solved in a democratic society and people can find meaning and purpose in their lives.	The ability of the group to solve problems is strongly determined by the diversity of the group. How the group goes about solving problems is also shaped by these factors.
Sharing mutually meaningful experience in small groups is one of the most effective ways people create bridges of understanding and learn to work together despite their differences.	The ability of diverse people to share these experiences depends on the creation of group conditions in which people are not hindered by power differentials or a lack of trust. Group members need to experience support and empathy.
It is more useful to help people to grow and change from an assessment of their individual and collective strengths than from a focus on their weaknesses.	This recognition of strength must be driven by a recognition of the strengths of each culture represented in the group.
Through its problem-solving process, each group develops its own structure, communication patterns, and culture.	The group culture must actively attend to diversity issues, or this can recreate structures and processes that perpetuate inequities.
Because groups are a microcosm of society, group members often express beliefs and values of the broader culture.	An important aspect of this broader culture is its regard (or lack of regard) for issues of diversity.
The purpose of social work practice with groups is to promote, enhance, or restore social functioning. The rewards of participation are linked to adaptive functioning.	Social functioning consists in part of a person's ability to develop to his or her full potential as a member of a diverse society. Empowerment is a practice goal.

the case for the group leader consciously considering how multiple dimensions of diversity, or intersectionality, are affected by group members' cultural identities and are related to group interactions. In addition, they encouraged social workers to (a) incorporate social justice goals; (b) respond to and negotiate differences/conflicts within the group; (c) embrace difference and harness various standpoints; and (d) deal with group structure, boundaries, and culture, including power (Reed, Ortega, and Garvin 2010).

Section II.
Yalom's Existential Group Therapy

This section addresses the practice of existential group therapy as developed by Irvin Yalom (1980). It begins with a focus on the historical background of the philosophy of existentialism and concludes with practice strategies for social workers to use to engage, assess, and intervene with clients in small groups.

Professional Purpose and Well-Being

> ➤ Social workers who use existential theory consider well-being to be related to clients finding their true selves and the meaning of life's existence.

Historical Background

As stated earlier, social work is a profession committed to helping people function well within their social environments and to changing environments to make that possible (Sheafor and Horejsi 2012). At the same time, the person–environment constellation and its theory base are dynamic and evolve over time, reflecting historical events and shifts in philosophical and scientific thinking.

René Descartes (1644), the father of philosophy, set the foundation for scientific debate with his statement "I think, therefore I am". He also planted the roots of existential doubt when he said, "If you would be a seeker of the truth, it is necessary that at least one time in your life you doubt, as far as possible, all things." This point of view about the subjective nature of the world was later described by Søren Kierkegaard (1843/1985), who contended that doubt accounts for people's sense of unease or apprehension (Table 7.3).

To understand today's use of existential theory, one must fast-forward and consider the dramatic changes in the way people viewed societal and their own individual well-being following World War II. The unspeakable events of the war precipitated a major shift in the way some people thought about reality: Authors such as Albert Camus and Jean-Paul Sartre wrote about the absurdity of life, nothingness, and life's lack of meaning. Musicians and artists expressed a renewed sense of disillusionment, fear, or dread, and some philosophers contended that there were no universal guidelines for behavior.

Table 7.3.
Selected theoretical foundations of existential group therapy

Time adopted	Major theorist(s)	Theme	Concepts for practice
1648	René Descartes: Father of modern philosophy, mathematician	"I think, therefore, I am."	Exploring freedom of will—the conscious
1843	Søren Kierkegaard: Philosopher/ theologian, father of existentialism	Science/knowledge is not absolute. Life's contradictions exist side by side.	Exploring conflicting choices
1959	Victor Frankl: Psychiatrist, logotherapist	Lack of meaning in life is at the core of stress.	Helping clients establish life's meaning
1971	Abraham Maslow: Psychologist	People have a hierarchy of needs.	Achieving self-actualizing and growth
1980	Irvin Yalom: Existential psychiatrist	Clients strive for freedom from isolation and meaninglessness.	Transcending one's past and establishing choice
1999	Robert Lifton: Psychiatrist	Amorphous anxiety is part of the human condition.	Connecting with others and grounding with sociohistorical events
2000	Kenneth Gergen: Psychologist	People are less grounded today than at other times in history.	Finding one's centered self

➤ *People experience well-being when they understand themselves and deal with the uncertainty.*

Existential Thought and Well-Being

Existential theorists equate people's ability to deal with life's ambiguities and find meaning in life with the key to well-being. This self-acceptance is difficult considering that existentialists believe that anxiety is a natural condition of life. Rollo May (1953), who introduced existential treatment to the United States, argued that "anxiety strikes us at the very 'core' of ourselves . . . when our existence as selves is threatened" (p. 40). He believed that existential therapists should help clients live with this ambiguity and use the debilitating effects of anxiety "constructively" (p. 43).

Dealing with this disquiet, known as *existential anxiety*, was also suggested by other human behavior theorists. Psychiatrist and Holocaust survivor Victor Frankl (1959/2006) responded to his own search for meaning by creating logotherapy, which is based on the idea that people strive to find freedom of will and meaning in life. That is, no matter the circumstances, life has meaning. Irvin Yalom (1980) built on this tradition by developing existential group work.

Recent threats to psychological stability, such as domestic and foreign terrorism, have brought about a demand for theories that are concerned with life's daily uncertainties (Greene 2007; Lifton 1999). In turn, these views on the person and environment have been accompanied by an interest in transpersonal theories of human behavior and the social environment, such as existentialism (Greene and Kropf 2009; see more in Chapter 10 on risk and resilience).

Applying Terms and Assumptions in Social Work Practice With Groups

Existentialism: A Transpersonal Theory

Existentialism is a *transpersonal theory*, or one that emphasizes people's highest aspirations and potential, focusing on "love, meaning, creativity, and communion with others and the universe" (Robbins, Chatterjee, and Canda 2011, 386). Such transcendence can occur more effectively when seemingly autonomous selves connect with others (Cowley 1996). For this reason, a group format is conducive to effecting behavioral change.

Self-transcendence, or the discovery that life is not an end in itself, is explored during the group process. By realizing that there is something greater than oneself that involves self-expression and caring for others, clients can become more adaptive and arrive at a reason to live (Kierkegaard 1843/1985; Maslow 1970; Yalom 1980). It is through such connectedness, sometimes gained in treatment, that people can come to the realization that they have freedom of choice and the responsibility to choose from life's alternatives (Yalom 1980).

Engage With Individuals, Families, Groups, Organizations, and Communities

Irvin Yalom's (1995) principles of existential thought are among the most widely used in group therapy (Lese and MacNair-Semands 2000). He suggested that in the *first stage* of group therapy practitioners orient the group members to the purposes of the group. Members are introduced to the way the group will be conducted and look to the leader for support and approval. As described in Chapter 1, the social worker assists clients through showing concern and acceptance and displaying empathy and genuineness (CSWE 2015). This in turn establishes the therapeutic relationship or alliance between group members and practitioner. This begins the first phase of creating a therapeutic system in which the group acts as the mechanism of change.

> ➤ *Assessment content explores group members' readiness to deal with life's uncertainties.*

Assess Individuals, Families, Groups, Organizations, and Communities

In the *second stage* of Yalom's group therapy, the social worker needs to maintain group cohesion by building a positive culture based on norms of safety and self-reflection. The social worker can set norms either by acting as an expert or by modeling helpful behavior. Meanwhile, group members establish a hierarchy, and hostility may be expressed toward the leader. The social worker's goal is to maintain a working group by dealing with conflict in the here and now.

Major principles that social workers can use in the assessment process include asking whether group members are able to deal with life's uncertainties by doing the following:

- Acknowledging that they are not victims of circumstances; rather, they have the freedom to choose what they want to be.
- Helping others in the group validate one another. Such altruism can leave members feeling that they are useful and have empathy for the aspirations of others.
- Recognizing that people's thoughts and behavior are not fixed. People may not be able to change past events, but they can take responsibility (with the help of the group) to change what they think about them.
- Realizing that as they accept themselves and make choices, they grow.

In sum, social workers help group members resolve conflicts about life's givens and establish meaning. Clients start to answer the question, "How can I live with who I am?" As can be seen in the case study of Joe, this subjective, phenomenological approach can help people who have undergone trauma tell their story from a first-person point of view.

> *Joe has posttraumatic stress disorder. He receives treatment from a psychiatrist at the Veterans Administration and has been referred to a group for additional treatment. Joe is better able to express his concerns about his three deployments to Iraq with other veterans who share similar experiences. They talk about having nightmares about their buddies' deaths and being startled by loud noises. Solving complex situations can make them angry.*

> *Most important, they are able to talk about the meaning of the war. Many remember their sense of pride when they enlisted. Looking back, some members feel they sacrificed too much. Others have lost religious faith. Still others take pride in deposing a dictator. Group members come to respect the differences in meaning each gives to his experiences.*

> *The social worker's goal in therapy is to help clients find meaning in a seemingly meaningless world.*

Intervene With Individuals, Families, Groups, Organizations, and Communities

In the *third stage* of existential group therapy, the practitioner acts on existentialism's principal assumption that existence—and in fact the world—"is contingent on the meaning a person creates" (Yalom 1980, 422). The existential group is intended to help members reach honesty about themselves. The practitioner guides them in the process of discerning what gives them meaning in life (Corey 2009), and clients learn to live with their aloneness and conflicting life contingencies. To achieve these purposes, the group must have a sense of cohesiveness that is based on the therapist–client relationship.

In sum, interventions in existential therapies deal with people's larger than life concerns: isolation, meaninglessness, mortality, and freedom of choice. Existential group psychotherapy promotes self-discovery, prompts self-responsibility, opens up possibilities, and fosters creativity.

Yalom's Therapeutic Factors

Yalom and Leszcz (2005) suggested that a group leader should be sure to provide eleven therapeutic experiences in an existential psychotherapy group:

1. Instilling hope and optimism: Do group members have faith that the group can help them heal?
2. Providing a sense of universality: Do clients learn that they are not alone or that other group members may have similar concerns?
3. Imparting information: Do group members receive instruction or needed information?
4. Practicing altruism: Do group members receive help from and give help to one another? Do they feel useful?
5. Reliving the corrective experience of the primary family group: Does the group configuration allow members to revisit their primary group experience and attend to unfinished/distorted business?
6. Developing interpersonal skills through socialization: Does the group provide opportunities for learning new person-to-person skills? Does it receive feedback?
7. Imitating behavior: Does the group present the possibility of imitating/modeling other members' positive communication skills?
8. Allowing for interpersonal learning: Do group members make human contact with others in the group and give feedback?
9. Providing a feeling of group cohesion: Are clients attracted to the group, and do they receive self-esteem from participation? Do they feel they belong?
10. Expressing emotions through catharsis: Are group members able to release emotions and be heard?
11. Exploring existential factors: Do clients deal with basic life issues, death, and meaning?

The ultimate aim of the therapy is growth or transformation. To evaluate the effectiveness of his group therapy sessions, Yalom often met with group members to obtain their thoughts on their helpfulness, administered questionnaires, and conducted more formal research. He found that participation in such a group

- fostered the formation of interpersonal bonds,
- diminished fear and anxiety,
- enhanced acceptance of others,
- provided useful advice,
- offered knowledge,
- provided opportunities to gain by giving to others, and
- bolstered self-acceptance and self-esteem.

Critique of Diversity Issues in Social Work Practice with Existential Groups

Because existential therapy depends on subjective client phenomenological accounts (Kira 2010), its methodology is likely to "recognize and communicate [clients'] understanding of the importance of diversity and difference in shaping life experiences" (CSWE 2015, 4). However, the midlife existential crisis can be said to be a cultural artifact (Greene 2008).

Glossary

Altruism. Unselfish practice of concern for the welfare of others.

Dependency. A tendency group members have of expecting the group leader to take care of all of their anxiety.

Existential group therapy. A group work model based on existentialism.

Existential theory. A postmodern theory emphasizing the unique experience of an individual, free will, freedom of choice, and personal responsibility.

Feminist group. A type of mutual aid group work model practicing conscious raising, validation, and empowerment based on feminist philosophy.

Fight or flight. A person's reaction in a group that depends on finding a common enemy or a scapegoat inside or outside of the group.

Group cohesion. A bond among group members that is a component of successful group work.

Group leader. A person who leads a group, engages and assesses the group, and sets up mutual therapeutic goals among group members.

Group purpose. A collective and mutual purpose a group attempts to achieve through group work.

Hull House. A settlement house cofounded in 1889 by Jane Addams and Ellen Gates Starr for economically disadvantaged immigrant workers in industrial Chicago.

Mutual aid group. A group work model focusing on group cohesion, trusting relationships, and mutual support and demand.

Mutual therapeutic goal. A goal set by group members with therapeutic purposes.

Pairing. Two group members joining together to rescue other group members by producing a new group leader.

Self-transcendence. The state of a person realizing that there is something greater than himself or herself that involves self-expression and caring for others.

Social Darwinism. The theory that people survive through natural selection of the fittest.

Social group work. A group work model focused on cultivating mutual aid among group members and clients' interpersonal relationships and social skills.

Transformational dialogue. A form of intergroup dialogue that is intended to resolve community or intergroup conflict.

Transpersonal theory. A theory emphasizing people's highest aspirations, potential, love, meaning, creativity, and communion with others and the universe.

Transtheoretical practice. Practice utilizing key principles from several theories to bring about change.

Universality. The existence of universal or similar characteristics across different groups and cultures.

References

Ackerman, N. 1958. *Psychodynamics of Family Life*, 3rd ed. New York: Basic Books.

Anderson, R. E., L. Carter, and G. R. Lowe. 1999. *Human Behavior in the Social Environment: A Social Systems Approach*. Hawthorne: Aldine de Gruyter.

Bion, W. R. 1961. *Experience in Groups*. New York: Basic Books.

Corey, G. 2009. *Theory and Practice of Counseling and Psychotherapy*. Pacific Grove, CA: Brooks/Cole.

Council on Social Work Education. 2015. *Educational Policy and Accreditation Standards*. Alexandria, VA: Council on Social Work Education.

Cowley, A. 1996. "Transpersonal Social Work." In *Social Work Treatment*, edited by F. Turner, 663–98. New York: Free Press.

Coyle, G. 1948. *Group Work with American Youth: A Guide to Practice and Leadership*. New York: Harper & Row.

Descartes, R. 1644. *Principles of Philosophy*. Dissertation.

Falk, H. S. 1988. *Social Work: The Membership Perspective*. New York: Springer.

Frankl, V. 2006. *Man's Search for Meaning*. Boston, MA: Beacon. (Original work published 1959).

Garvin, C., and B. Reed. 1994. "Small Group Theory and Social Work Practice: Promoting Diversity and Social Justice or Recreating Inequities?" In *Human Behavior Theory and Practice: A Diversity Framework*, edited by R. R. Greene, 201–30. Hawthorne: Aldine de Gruyter.

Gergen, K. 2000. *The Saturated Self*. New York: Basic Books.

Gitterman, A., and R. Salmon. 2009. *Encyclopedia of Social Work with Groups*. London: Routledge.

Gitterman, A., and L. Shulman. 2005. *Mutual Aid Groups, Vulnerable and Resilient Populations across the Life Cycle*. New York: Columbia University Press.

Greene, R. R. 2007. *Social Work Practice: A Risk and Resilience Perspective*. Monterey, CA: Brooks/Cole.

Greene, R. 2008. "Human Behavior Theory and Social Work Practice." New Brunswick, NJ: Aldine Transaction.

Greene, R. R., and N. P. Kropf. 2009. *Human Behavior: A Diversity Framework*, 2nd ed. New Brunswick, NJ: Aldine Transaction Press.

Greene, R. R., and N. P. Kropf. 2014. *Caregiving and Care Sharing: A Life Course Perspective*. Washington, DC: NASW Press.

Kierkegaard, S. 1985. *Either/or: A Fragment of Life*. London: Penguin. (Original work published 1843).

Kira, I. A. 2010. "Etiology and Treatment of Post-cumulative Traumatic Stress Disorders in Different Cultures." *Traumatology* 16 (4): 128–41.

Konopka, G. 1966. *The Adolescent Girl in Conflict*. Englewood Cliffs, NJ: Prentice Hall.

Kropotkin, P. 1972. *Mutual Aid: A Factor of Evolution*. New York: New York University Press. (Original work published 1902).

Lese, K. P., and MacNair-Semands, R. R. 2000. "The Therapeutic Factors Inventory: Development of a Scale." *Group* 24 (4): 303–17.

Lewin, K. 1943. "Defining the Field at a Given Time." *Psychological Review* 50:292–310.

Lifton, R. J. 1999. *The Protean Self: Human Resilience in an Age of Fragmentation*. Chicago, IL: University of Chicago Press. (Original work published 1993).

Maslow, A. H. 1970. *Motivation and Personality*, 2nd ed. New York: Harper & Row.

May, R. 1953. *Man's Search for Himself*. New York: Delta.

Northen, H., and R. Kurland. 2001. *Social Work with Groups*. New York: Columbia University Press.

Prochaska, J. O., and W. F. Velicer. 1997. "The Transtheoretical Model of Health Behavior Change." *American Journal of Health Promotion* 12 (1): 38–48.

Reed, B., R. M. Ortega, and C. Garvin. 2010. "Small-group Theory and Social Work: Promoting Diversity and Social Justice or Recreating Inequities?" In *Human Behavior Theory and Practice: A Diversity Framework*, edited by R. Greene and N. Kropf, 201–30. Hawthorne: Aldine de Gruyter.

Robbins, S. P., P. Chatterjee, and E. R. Canda. 2011. *Contemporary Behavior Theory: A Critical Perspective for Social Work*. Boston, MA: Allyn & Bacon.

Scheuer, J. 1985. *Origins of the Settlement House Movement*. Accessed October 15, 2015. http://www.socialwelfarehistory.org/organizations/origins-of-the-settlement-house-movement/

Schiller, L., and B. Zimmer. 2005. "Sharing the Secrets: The Power of Women's Groups Who Were Sexually Abused." In *Mutual Aid Groups*, edited by A. Gitterman and L. Schulman, 290–319. New York: Columbia University Press.

Schwartz, W. 1961. "The Social Worker in the Group. New Perspectives on Services to Groups." In *Theory, Organization, and Practice*, edited by B. Saunders, 7–34. New York: NASW Press.

Schwartz, W. 1986. "The Group Work Tradition and Social Work Practice." *Social Work with Groups* 8 (4): 7–28.

Sheafor, B. W., and C. J. Horejsi. 2012. *Techniques and Guidelines for Social Work Practice*, 9th ed. Boston, MA: Allyn & Bacon.

Shulman, L. 2009a. *The Dynamics and Skills of Group Counseling*. Belmont, CA: Cengage.

Shulman, L. March 2009b. "Leading Mutual Aid Support Groups: Difficult Members and Other Challenges." Paper based on a program presented at the American Counseling Association Annual Conference and Exposition, Charlotte, NC.

Toseland, R., L. Jones, and Z. Gellis. 2004. "Group Dynamics." In *Handbook of Social Work with Groups*, edited by C. Garvin, L. Gutierrez, and M. Galinsky, 13–31. New York: Guilford Press.

Yalom, I. D. 1980. *Existential Psychotherapy*. New York: Basic Books.

Yalom, I. D. 1995. *The Theory and Practice of Group Psychotherapy*, 4th ed. New York: Basic Books.

Yalom, I. D., and M. Leszcz. 2005. *Theory and Practice of Group Psychotherapy*, 5th ed. New York: Basic Books.

8

Human Behavior and the Social Environment Theory: Social Work Practice with Organizations

> ➤ This chapter presents human behavior and the social environment (HBSE) theory for social work practice with organizations. It outlines HBSE theory that informs social work practice with workers and their families at the job site (employee assistance programs). The chapter also provides HBSE theory to guide social workers in carrying out organizational change strategies. It then discusses the application of leadership theory for social workers who carry out administrative or managerial roles as part of organizational change. Policy implications are also raised.

You have seen throughout this book that social workers need to understand theories of human behavior and the social environment and critically evaluate and apply this knowledge to facilitate engagement, assessment, intervention, and evaluation with clients and constituencies, including individuals, families, groups, organizations, and communities (Council on Social Work Education [CSWE] 2015). This chapter is the first in the *Handbook* to provide human behavior and the social environment theories that center on social work practice with organizations. The scope of occupational social work is very broad, ranging from top-level management in government to individual crisis counseling in the workplace. Therefore, we have chosen to focus on several areas of interest. First, we discuss how social workers in organizations may help individuals and families with work-related issues through the organization's employee assistance program (EAP). Social workers who work in EAPs deliver social services to workers who may be having difficulties that interfere with effective job performance and/or may be in jeopardy of losing their jobs (Akabas and Bikson 2000; Van Den Bergh 1995). The practitioner's purpose is to reduce stress and maintain wellness in the workplace, including offering direct counseling and developing programmatic initiatives.

Second, the chapter describes the role social workers may play in leading initiatives that maintain and/or transform organizational culture. Their major goal in this case is to organize workers to modify organizational culture to better provide work satisfaction and to meet the challenges of a changing U.S. and world economy. Finally, the chapter presents leadership theories that can be used by the social worker to configure his or her administrative or managerial interventions.

> ➤ *Wellness in the workplace has historically been linked to working conditions, the philosophy of management, and government policy.*

Professional Purpose and Well-Being

Historical Background: Industrial Organizations

Recognition of the existence of workplace stressors and the need for their amelioration dates back to the nineteenth-century industrial revolution. By the late nineteenth and early twentieth century, the industrial revolution was in full force (see more in Chapter 9). This was a time when farm workers and their families increasingly moved to cities to find work in industrial settings. For the most part, working conditions were poor, to say the least.

With the industrial revolution came the creation of ever larger and more complex organizations with varying approaches to the nature of work. Although the overriding motivation of industrialists was monetary growth or profit, there were countervailing forces that remain in effect today: fairness or equity in pay, work quality, and work satisfaction. At the same time, social workers may want to keep abreast of efforts to destroy unions (such as in Wisconsin), and governmental regulatory mechanisms.

Scientific management. At the beginning of the industrial revolution, science gained prominence in solving many of the problems faced by industry. For example, Frederick Taylor (1911), a mechanical engineer by training, created a management approach based on the study of production processes. His theory came to be known as *scientific management,* also referred to as *classical management theory* or *Taylorism* (Table 8.1).

Taylor focused on the scientific selection and training of workers. Prior to this, workers were simply told what their job was with no attention to training or prior expertise. In other words, workers were expected to figure things out on their own. However, Taylor believed that workers should be trained in production processes to improve efficiency.

Taylor's goal was to create a science of work. He believed that there was "One Best Way" to ensure the maximum efficiency and productivity of workers. The One Best Way was to study work and management processes using human engineers to conduct time and motion studies and to do task and workload analyses. The engineers would observe workers to find ways to make process improvements to increase production. These efforts were aimed at making the worker an appendage of the machines used for production. For example, containers of electrical parts might be moved a few inches closer to employees so it would take less time for workers to complete their part in the production process. While the idea that a person "is the extension of a machine" is less common today in the United States, it remains

Table 8.1.
Selected theoretical foundations of organizational practice

Time adopted	Major theorist(s)	Theme	Concepts for practice
1903 1911	Frederick Taylor: Mechanical engineer	Industrialists and workers are motivated by monetary rewards. Workers are seen as an appendage of machines and as motivated solely by economic rewards.	Organizing workers for fair wages" A fair day's pay for a fair day's work"
1827	Robert Owen: Utopian socialist	Industrialists should promote the social good and shares of production.	Creating cooperative workplaces
1905	Max Weber: Sociologist	An organization is a bureaucracy governed by formal rules.	Protecting rights in the workplace
1964	Amitai Etzioni: Sociologist	Societies need a balance between rights and responsibilities and autonomy and order.	Mobilizing for a positive communal life
1985	Edgar Schein: Psychologist	Fundamental notions of how the organization and its members relate to the environment, time, space, reality, and each other are examined.	Examining the culture of the organization
1987	Benjamin Schneider: Psychologist	Work is redefined to include interpersonal relationships on the job. This support and the rewards of job satisfaction are taken into consideration.	Understanding job satisfaction
1903, 2007	Elton Mayo: Industrial Psychologist	Attention is directed toward noneconomic rewards in the workplace. Management must relate not only to individual workers but to members of a group.	Creating noneconomic rewards in the workplace
2005	Margaret Wheatley: Organizational behavior	Because they are living systems, most people are intelligent, creative, adaptive, and self-organizing.	Letting people (organizations) coordinate themselves
1990 1996 2014	R. Roosevelt Thomas, Jr.: Organizational behaviorist and Joe Schriver: Social worker	Organizations have diverse and similar personnel. These attributes contribute to the social capital of the organization.	Celebrating differences and similarities

a global human rights problem. It reminds us that "social workers [need to] understand the global interconnections of oppression and human rights violations, and are knowledgeable about theories of human need and social justice and strategies to promote social and economic justice and human rights" (CSWE 2015, 6).

Taylor's methods also included studying the role of management in the production process. Prior to this, management and labor had almost no contact with each other. Taylor believed that management and workers needed to be brought together so that the implementation of scientific principles of work would be successful. However, he also argued for a clear division of labor within the organization (Etzioni 1964; Schriver 2014; Taylor 1947)

Although Taylor's focus was on a scientific approach, his theory also included assumptions or beliefs about the workers themselves. Workers were said to be solely motivated by economic rewards. As a result, workers' pay was often directly tied their output using such devices as individual production quotas, still in question by labor unions today (Etzioni 1964; Schriver 2014; Taylor 1947). Although social workers participation in labor unions goes back as far as Jane Adams who particularly supported the organization of garment workers, the commonality of goals between those of unions and those of social worker professional remains unclear (see Karger 1988, 2008). According to Scanlon and Harding (2005), the twenty-first century will see increased alliances.

Welfare capitalism. By contrast, some manufacturers were also philanthropists/reformers who began a social movement called *welfare capitalism*—a form of business that embodies welfare services to employees. For example, in 1827, Robert Owen, a Welshman, took his considerable fortune to New Harmony, Indiana, to further develop a utopian working town. The town was highly successful, and its residents lived in pleasant surroundings with parks and open spaces that are still available to tourists today. Another example of the adoption of welfare capitalism in the mid-nineteenth century was the founding of the Lester Shoe Company in Binghamton, New York. It became the Endicott Johnson Corporation in 1854 and provided housing and medical care for workers until well after World War II.

Critique of welfare capitalism. Welfare capitalism also had its downside and critics. Jacoby (1997) noted that in the early twentieth century "workers labored under the 'drive system,'" a policy of pressuring workers to maximize output. Jacoby further noted that, "the system depended on fear of job loss to ensure obedience, and employers did not hesitate to fire workers." On the other hand, many company founders who had accumulated vast wealth created systems of welfare capitalism out of sense of ethical and, sometimes religious, responsibility for sharing their wealth to benefit workers. However, often the motives for welfare capitalism, also called welfare work, "created company bonds that undermined trade unionism and quieted public critics of concentrated wealth." In addition, he contended that "welfare work was frequently condescending and manipulative. The hope was that firms could recast the intemperate, slothful worker or the ignorant immigrant in a middle-class mold (Jacoby 1997: n. p.).

Government policy. Over time, fair-minded managers created a "square deal" for workers, a policy first announced by President Theodore Roosevelt to ensure

the preservation of natural resources, shared control of corporations, and protection of consumers. By this time, the number of people in the U.S. workforce had
increased dramatically. Employers were overwhelmed by the differing needs of
new groups of employees and the problems that were erupting within the work
environment (Kotschessa 1994). Nonetheless, the welfare capital innovations created a foundational interest in workers' well-being—their health, housing, financial status, and the education of their children—that is still maintained in some
workplaces today.

Historical Background: Human Services Organizations

   Social workers not only work in business and industry, but are employed in
human services organizations. In the broadest sense, social workers employed
by these organizations try to assure people's health, well-being, and quality of life
through the services they deliver. For example, according to the National Association of Social Workers (NASW) Center for Workforce Studies and Social Work
Practice (2011), the Social Security Administration alone employs 26,000 social
workers who engage in program analysis, act as eligibility workers, and serve as
community outreach workers and program administrators. The basis of these formal, often public, organizations dates back to religious charities; civic organizations;
and the 1601 Elizabethan Poor Laws, which provided help to poor families with
children (see Dolgoff and Feldstein 2013). Today, social workers may be employed
at any one of the United States formal, monolithic social welfare institutions that
includes organizations such as the U.S. Department of Health and Human Services,
a cabinet level agency that attends to medical well-being, public health, veterans'
affairs, social services, education, and preparedness and response services. Some
social workers are employed in such settings may take on an administrative and
leadership role (see below).

   Persistence of poverty. However, this system of programs and support has been
unable to appreciably reduce the overall poverty rate or the increase in health,
income, education, and social disparities and inequality in American society. In the
late twentieth and early twenty-first centuries, state and federal legislative and executive branches of government severely cut support for many of these governmental
programs and returned to the much earlier notion of the "unworthy poor." As Hansan
(2011) pointed out, "in effect, the poor laws separated the poor into two classes:
the worthy (e.g., orphans, widows, handicapped, frail elderly) and the unworthy
(e.g., drunkards, shiftless, lazy)." The result has been continuous devolution of the
so-called social welfare system in the United States. Compared to other developed
countries and regions (e.g., Europe, Scandinavia, Australia) the US system may be
considered both more punitive and inadequate.

   Service delivery systems. Even frontline social workers need to "understand the
history and current structures of social policies and services, the role of policy in
service delivery, and the role of practice in policy development" (CSWE 2015, 6).
Social service delivery systems are responsible for coordinating benefits and services
intended to enhance and maintain people's social functioning (Dolgoff and Feldstein

2013). The practice of most social workers is either directly or indirectly influenced by their laws and regulations, requiring them to know the following:

- What are the basic components of the social welfare program in their practice arena?
- Who is eligible for those programs and benefits?
- What policies and funding sources are pertinent?
- Are policies and funding levels consistent with social justice and other social work principles?
- What advocacy and leadership skills are needed to address injustice in the system, its programs, and policies?
- Are innovative methods of providing care emerging and available to clients and constituencies?
- Can I, as a social worker, contribute to those innovations? (Greene and Kropf 2014, 1)

Social workers also must ask what ethical dilemmas and values may need to be resolved in their practice setting and what current research is germane to guide their area of practice (CSWE 2015).

Workplace Well-Being for the Twenty-First Century

Occupational social work policies and services in EAPs have historically been delivered through the auspices of employers or trade unions (Akabas 1995). Practice continues to be characterized by a focus on workers and their dependents at the work site. The social worker's goal is to prevent or remediate a range of problems in order to maintain a high-quality workforce, for example, providing marriage counseling or facilitating support groups for workers involved in elder care.

In addition to its competitive array of health care, income protection, retirement, and time-off benefits, IBM offers a range of other programs to support employee needs (www.ibm.com). These include an EAP, a work-life family resource program, a special care for children assistance plan, an adoption assistance plan, and a transitional medical program based on the Consolidated Omnibus Budget Reduction Act of 1985.

Within the social work profession currently, there has been controversy about the goodness of fit between for-profit social work and the profession's foundational principles of service and poverty reduction. For example, can employee assistance workers effectively advocate for change within a company to reduce worker stress levels? Are workplace expectations for production among the factors contributing to employees' substance abuse, domestic violence, or depression? Can social workers be effective managers, motivating line workers for transformational change?

Applying Terms and Assumptions in Social Work Practice

Definitions and Characteristics of Organizations

Social workers' roles in organizations vary according to the organization's auspices, type, and respective goals (Tables 8.2 and 8.3). *Organizations* are social units (or human groupings) specifically constructed and reconstructed to achieve

Table 8.2.
Types of organizations

Type	Basic premise	Examples
Not for Profit	Goal is service, not profit making	American Red Cross, United Way, Jewish Family Services, Catholic Charities, Lutheran Social Services, Islamic Social Services Association
Public Sector	Goal is government service provision	Division of Family and Children's Services, State Adult Protective Services, U.S. Department of Health and Human Services, county human service offices
For Profit	Goal is to make a profit, even in providing human or social work services	Private practice social work, corporate employee assistance programs, many in- and outpatient mental health companies/hospitals
Nongovernmental Organization	Goal is similar to that of a not-for-profit organization, but the focus is international service provision	Oxfam, Red Crescent, Greenpeace, Amnesty International, Doctors Without Borders

Table 8.3.
Goals of human service organizations

Goal	Central theme	Examples
Well-being	Improve well-being and quality of life	Ideally all social work or human service organizations
Social care	Change the environment	Poverty reduction programs, housing authorities, community gardens, programs implementing the Affordable Care Act
Social control	Contain deviant behavior	Juvenile justice programs, criminal justice programs, jails/prisons
Rehabilitation	Change the individual	Literacy organizations, organizations serving persons with disabilities, organizations serving returning veterans with combat-related mental and physical disabilities

Note. Adapted from Neugeboren, B. (1985). *Organization, policy, and practice in the human services.* New York: Longman.

specific goals (Etzioni 1964). Although brief, this definition is rich with meaning. For example, central to formal organizations is their goal directedness. These social units are created by humans and are built and can be rebuilt, always in pursuit of more efficient and effective goal achievement. For this reason, social workers can play a meaningful role in organizational transformational activities (see below).

Amitai Etzioni (1964) further detailed the characteristics of organizations that prompt questions for occupational social workers. Each characteristic is accompanied here by a question or statement that may help social workers explore what issues clients may be facing in the workplace. Etzioni suggested that organizations have

1. divisions of labor, power, and communication responsibilities, divisions that are not random or traditionally patterned but deliberately planned to enhance the realization of specific goals:
   Does the employee have a clear picture of his or her job description? Does he or she properly carry this out?
2. one or more power centers that control the concerted efforts of the organization and direct them toward its goals; these power centers also must review continuously the organization's performance and re-pattern its structure, when necessary, to increase its efficiency:
   Is the employee caught in a power struggle with other workers or with management? Is labor empowered to contribute to the organization's success?
3. substitution of personnel (i.e., unsatisfactory persons can be removed and others assigned their tasks); the organization can also recombine its personnel through transfer and promotion (p. 3):

   Are workplace rules posted and explicit? Has the employee been removed from his or her position without due process?

Theories and Organizations

Several theorists have contributed to organizational theory for social work practice. This has led to various assessment and intervention strategies.

> ➤ *Organizational theory based on an ideal type.*

Max Weber. Perhaps the oldest and most widely known theory of organizations is Max Weber's idea about bureaucracy. Max Weber presented bureaucracy as an *ideal type,* helping social workers to visualize it as the most efficient and effective way of organizing work in formal organizations. Like ideal types in general, bureaucracy in its pure form is not likely to be found in reality. However, elements of bureaucracy are a part of virtually all organizations, whether simple or complex. In addition, almost every other theory of organizations includes some aspects of bureaucracy theory that can be explored by the occupational social worker. Those key elements include:

- Bureaucratic organizations are supposed to recruit workers based on merit. The organization is expected to have a clear career ladder with specified salaries. The social worker should be aware that these rights are protected by the 1941 Fair Employment Act and the 1964 Civil Rights Act, and help their clients understand their implications (see the case below, in which Norma Wright believes her organization's informal dress codes interferes with her getting a merit raise).
- Perhaps the most fundamental principle of bureaucracy is the notion that the organization must function based on a clear and stable set of rules that are rational. That is, organizations should not operate based on personal beliefs

or tradition. Therefore, clients may see an occupational social worker to deal with their sense of dissonance between organizational rules and personal beliefs. For example, should a clerk in a state office refuse to issue a wedding license to a same sex couple based on his or her religious beliefs?

- People must work in specialized roles within bureaucratic organizations. An employee may be referred to the EAP worker when roles become blurred. In addition, an employee may experience role strain or overload, particularly in organizations that are not family friendly. This calls for the social worker to take systemic change strategies (see below for IBM's programs to help families with adoption issues).

- Employment in the organization requires specialized training and skills suited to the technical rules and norms of the job that workers are assigned to perform. This is true for both managers and workers. When employees are undertrained, EAP workers can advocate for employee training that may lead to better job performance knowledge and skills. For example, workers in the car industry increasingly must use computing knowledge and skills to accomplish their jobs.

- Bureaucratic organizations have a clear hierarchy of authority or chain of command. Each person in the organization has a supervisor to whom he or she is responsible. That supervisor in turn reports to a person who supervises him or her. The notion is that the clarity of the reporting structure facilitates communication throughout the system in an orderly way, so employees know who to go to with questions or information. Furthermore, managers must have the authority to allocate and reallocate resources, including personnel, for maximum efficiency and effectiveness. Social workers in managerial positions will have to use their communication and budgetary skills.

- In order to ensure rationality in operations, Weber argued that owners must be completely separate from the means of production and those who administer the system of production. Nepotism, for example, or hiring one's family member, is not considered viable when seeking rationality. Similarly, impersonality is a central principle. In other words, organization members must separate their personal lives from their work lives to ensure efficiency and focus on the job they are to perform. As a result, EAP social worker may be called upon to assist workers in resolving conflicts resulting from the lack of recognition by the employer that personal or family issues can, in fact, interfere with work performance. The social worker in this context may also struggle with balancing conflict between their personal and work lives.

- All administrative transactions, rules, or policies are to be recorded in writing to prevent redundancy and optimize efficiency and rationality. Some social workers perceive this insistence on written documentation as red tape that takes away from their time to actually perform their jobs; others may see such record keeping as a means of accountability (Etzioni 1964; Schriver 2014).

- Finally, Max Weber considered bureaucratic organizations to be politically neutral—an ideal that is under debate given the U.S. Supreme Court ruling called Citizens United that declared corporations to be individuals. This ruling allows corporations and unions to give unlimited funds to political campaigns (Liptak 2010).

> ➤ *Organizational theory based on research.*

Elton Mayo. Elton Mayo (1933, 2007) was a psychologist and organizational theorist who had a significant impact on *human relations theory* through his research. Mayo and his team conducted their studies at the Hawthorne Works of Western Electric Company in Chicago from 1927 to 1932 and focused on efficiency and effectiveness in the workplace. A well-known study examined workers' performance based on the level of lighting in the factory. The researchers found that performance increased regardless of the differences in light intensity. Mayo and his team were surprised to discover what is now known as the *Hawthorne effect,* in which the workers sensed that the efforts and presence of the researchers indicated that management had concern for them and their working conditions. In contrast to scientific management, Mayo contended that management concern was a significant factor in labor productivity and opened the door to understanding noneconomic rewards in the workplace. For example, giving and receiving praise in the workplace, such as the employee of the month award, can have positive effects on job satisfaction (Sirota, Mischkind, and Meltzer 2005).

Another study in the Hawthorne series was the bank wiring room experiment. In this study, researchers studied a group of fourteen men who wired telephone switchboards. The researchers were examining the relationship between wages and productivity. Pay increases were provided to employees based on their individual high productivity. However, this individual reward system did not seem to significantly improve the productivity of the workers. Mayo concluded that the men had formed an informal group whose members responded to management's plans: They informally determined for themselves what was called a "proper day's work." Social workers can credit Mayo and his team for providing an understanding of the small group theory and the idea that workers are motivated by those who work around them.

> ➤ *Organizational theory is based on complexity and change.*

Chaos theory. Systems theory may be contrasted with chaos theory. *Chaos theory* is "the study of processes that seem so complex that at first they do not appear to be governed by any known laws or principles, but actually have an underlying order" (Krippner 1994, 49). Wheatley (2005) and Wheatley and Kellner-Rogers (1996) used this idea in research in organizations, suggesting that chaotic organizations are distinguished in part by their complexity. Complexity is viewed as a positive aspect that can assist organizations in being more open, creative, and innovative by focusing on information, participation, and self-organization.

According to chaos theory, in order to realize an organization's potential, social workers must let some traditional elements of formal organizational theories go by the wayside. Wheatley (2005) argued that organizations must dispense with "control mechanisms that paralyze employees and leaders alike" (pp. n.p.), thus freeing workers to maximize their potential and contributing to organizational success. This may lead the social worker to wonder how to engage an organization in practice. But it suggests that practitioners must discover and tap into naturally, emergent adaptive processes. This is in keeping with resilience theory is discussed in Chapter 10.

Engage With Individuals, Families, Groups, Organizations, and Communities

To engage with organizations, occupational social workers must first understand their own perception of workers and the organization's culture and climate. This personal reflection (CSWE 2015) contributes to the assessment and intervention processes.

Characteristics of Workers

To know how they perceive employees, social workers can turn to the work of Douglas MacGregor (1960). He sought to understand internal assumptions held by managers about their workers, as well as the impact of those assumptions on productivity and the quality of life in the workplace. Table 8.4 shows two very different sets of assumptions about workers put forth by MacGregor. Theory X is grounded in the belief that people are inherently lazy and will avoid work if they can. Managers who make this assumption often use power and control to exact production from seemingly lazy and recalcitrant workers. Coercion and surveillance are seen as means of increasing productivity, and managers who ascribe to this theory use significant resources in surveillance to monitor workers to force production from them (see leadership interventions below).

Table 8.4.
Defining workers: Douglas MacGregor's theory X and theory Y

Theory	Themes/characteristics
Theory X	1. The average human has an inherent dislike for work and will avoid it if he or she can.
	2. Because of Assumption 1, people must be coerced, controlled, directed, or threatened with punishment to get them to use energy toward the organization's objectives.
	3. The average human prefers to be directed, wishes to avoid responsibility, has relatively little ambition, and wants security above all.
Theory Y	1. The expenditure of physical and mental effort in work is as natural as play or rest.
	2. Humans will exercise self-direction and self-control in the service of objectives to which they are committed.
	3. The most significant reward that can be offered in order to obtain this commitment is the satisfaction of the individual's self-actualization needs.
	4. The average human learns, under proper conditions, not only to accept but to seek responsibility.
	5. Many more people are able to contribute to organizational objectives than actually do so.
	6. At present the potentialities of the average person are not being fully used.

Note. From Pugh, Hickson, and Hinings (1985).

Theory Y, in contrast, makes the fundamental assumption that work is a natural part of human life. Theory Y assumes that the average person will exhibit self-control and self-direction when working for a manager and organization whose values are shared. Not only will people accept responsibility, but they will seek it out. In essence, Theory Y assumes that people are active and curious and seek out challenges in their environments, especially where this is allowed or accepted. Theory Y is quite consistent with social work principles, especially the foundational belief that all people possess potential for growth and have inherent dignity.

Organizational Culture

After using self-reflection to explore your perception of workers, it is important to examine and understand the organizational culture of your workplace. Edgar Schein (1985) is credited with applying the anthropological concept of culture to organizations. He used the term *organizational culture* to refer to a way of thinking, behaving, or working that exists in a workplace or organization, such as a business ("Culture," n.d.). Schein believed that organizations have the attributes of culture by virtue of organizational members' shared values and beliefs. Furthermore, he believed that the physical attributes or artifacts of an organization reflect the culture's beliefs and values. Moreover, he believed that the norms, attitudes, and expectations of members of the culture are so deeply ingrained in day-to-day operations that although these attributes are clear to insiders to the point of being taken for granted, outsiders are likely to be unaware of or confused by them.

Cultural Artifacts

Duden (2011, 220) further elaborated the levels of culture posited by Schein to address cultural artifacts in the workplace. In this conceptualization, artifacts are the most visible representations of an organization's culture. The first level of artifacts includes clothing (dress codes), the physical architecture, and interior design representing the identity projected by the organization. The second level includes organizational values defining behaviors expected of organizational members. Often these expectations are formally spelled out in organizational documents such as staff handbooks and should be understood and carried out by the social worker (CSWE 2015). At other times, these expectations are informal and can interfere with workers' rights as in the situation of informal dress codes.

> ➤ *Norma Wright is an African American woman who has been employed by a major women's department store for four years. She has a high sales record, positive job performance reports, and excellent customer service surveys. However, she feels she has been overlooked for promotion and a salary increase. She decides to discuss the situation with the EAP worker, Mrs. Huntington, a sixty-year old who has cerebral palsy and who has worked for the firm for fifteen years.*

> ➤ Mrs. Huntington is aware that the firm has made the accommodations required to comply with her needs as spelled out in the American with Disabilities Act. She also is aware that the company has a good track record of respecting ethnic differences in the workplace. When Ms. Wright visited the EAP she was wearing large hoop earrings and a multicolored floral print dress. Mrs. Huntington was wearing a black pinstriped suit. Most of the store's personnel tend to dress in black or shades of gray.

> ➤ Given the organizational culture and personal values, how should Mrs. Huntington deal with her client's complaint?

The third level includes very basic and deeply held attitudes and beliefs about the organization and how it operates resulting from socialization to and length of time in the organization. These are the most difficult for outsiders to understand, and longtime members of the organization often have difficulty explaining how the organization works to outsiders because the beliefs and patterns are so ingrained. As seen in the following case description, for the organization and its members, however, they provide a source of stability and predictability.

> ➤ Loretta McDouglas is a senior administrator at a local Department of Human Services office evaluating her own effectiveness. She is aware that artifacts can convey to clients and constituencies either a sense of respect and openness or the fact that clients are undeserving of either value or trust. She asks herself the following: Are there toys or books for clients' children in reception and waiting areas? Is there sufficient and comfortable seating for both adults and children? Are clients separated from workers by high counters or glass or mesh screens (such as those in some all-night convenience stores and gas stations to prevent robberies) through which clients must speak or pass documents? Are physical spaces light or dark?

> ➤ In terms of attitudes and behaviors, has she trained employees to interact with clients respectfully or behave as if the client's motives are suspect? Are eligibility determination policies, documents, and processes customer friendly and tailored to the education level or culture (e.g., language) of the client? Are workers provided with time to effectively assist clients in completing forms or obtaining the necessary documentation? Are workers sensitive to the discomfort and humiliation many clients feel because they need assistance to meet their family's basic needs?

Organizational Climate

Organizational culture and climate theories are related, and both are important in social work engagement. Perhaps the primary difference is that the organizational climate is the feel of the organization held by those working there and is reflected in the experience of people engaging with the organization (i.e., clients, customers, visitors). Schneider, Brief, and Guzzo (1996) suggested that organizational climate consists of four dimensions. These dimensions and illustrative examples are given here for you to use with your clients and constituencies:

1. The nature of interpersonal relationships
   - Is there mutual sharing and trust or conflict and mistrust?
   - Are relationships between functional units (e.g., between production and sales) cooperative or competitive?
   - Does the organization support the socialization of newcomers or exhibit a sink-or-swim approach?
   - Do people feel that their personal welfare is important to those around them and to top management?
2. The nature of the hierarchy
   - Are decisions affecting work and the workplace made only by top management or with participation from those affected by the decision?
   - Is the organization characterized by a team approach to work or strictly an individualistic competitive approach?
   - Does management have special perquisites that separate them from their subordinates, such as special parking or dining facilities?
3. The nature of work
   - Is the work challenging or boring?
   - Are jobs adaptable by the people performing them, or are they rigidly defined so that everyone must do them the same way?
   - Does the organization provide workers with the necessary resources (tools, supplies, information) to get the work done?
4. The focus of support and rewards
   - What gets supported: being warm and friendly to customers or being fast?
   - Are the supports and rewards widely known and shared?
   - Is getting the work done (quantity) or getting the work right (quality) rewarded?
   - On what bases are people hired?
   - To what goals and standards are they trained to obtain?
   - What facets of performance are appraised and rewarded? (Schneider, Brief, and Guzzo 1996, 9–11)

Assess Individuals, Families, Groups, Organizations, and Communities

Assessment and intervention in organizations can be congruent with the person-environment construct (CSWE 2015, 1). Therefore, social workers need to consider multi-level interventions when applying HBSE for organizations.

Five Levels of Assessment

As outlined in Chapter 2, social work practice is an ecological systems phenomenon. Felix Chima (1996) delineated five multilevel factors that are part of the person–environment interaction that occupational social workers may consider in assessment and in the design of interventions:

1. Intrapersonal factors refer to individual dispositions such as self-concept, behavior, attitudes, knowledge, learning history, and skills. EAP workers learn about intrapersonal factors through obtaining a brief client history and asking about strengths such as educational and skill achievement.
2. Interpersonal factors include processes in relationships with formal and informal social networks and social support systems, including family, work groups, and friendship networks. EAP workers may examine how employees get along with other workers and their supervisors. Questions about family stress that may be brought into the workplace are also important.
3. Institutional factors involve cultural characteristics—the formal and informal rules and regulations that guide the workplace. They also involve the customs, habits, skills, technology, values, ideology, science, and religious and political behavior of the larger society in which people live. Because there may be institutional-level difficulties, the occupational social worker may have the organization become the constituency.
4. Community encompasses a large group of people who share certain values, services, institutions, interest, or geographical proximity. Occupational social workers should be aware that all businesses and organizations as well as employees have a place in society. This may become a resource, especially during times of crisis, such as Hurricane Sandy when disaster plans call upon all sectors of society.
5. Public policy factors refer to local, state, and national laws and policies that effect change in the social environment, such as political, economic, environmental, and ideological forces. Occupational social workers should be conversant with these changes, being aware that clients may have stressors related to these social forces, such as the globalization of the world economy (pp. 57–58).

Individual Assessment

At the end of the twentieth century, economic restructuring and changes in social welfare policy had affected workplace culture and climate, bringing about more behavioral health issues (Iverson 1995). Clients often see an EAP social worker when they are stressed by workplace situations. Clients may feel that they are the only ones experiencing this conflict. Therefore, meeting with the EAP social worker becomes a reality check. If the practitioner provides an impartial ear and allows the client's voice to be heard, the client may also test out what he or she thinks about the system in which he or she works. The following questions may facilitate work adjustment:

- What can I expect from my supervisor?
- Am I the right person for the job?

- Do I need to improve my performance?
- What do I need to maintain my job? Is this feasible?
- Do I need additional training?
- What can I change?
- Should I apply for a transfer? (Galambos, Livingston, and Greene 2007)

Family and Work Balance

Workplace stress can be alleviated through the provision of *family-friendly policies* or practices that allow employees to strike a balance between work and home. Benefits of family-friendly workplaces may include flexible work time or, as President Barack Obama advocated at the First White House Summit on Working Families, paid parental leave (*Wall Street Journal* 2013).

Before understanding the needs of employees to coordinate work and family responsibility, it is necessary for practitioners to explore how the employee and family are balancing family and work. To sort this out, the social worker may use the questions provided by the University of Texas–Southwest Employee Assistance Program suggested in Table 8.5.

Organizational Assessment

Self-organizing. Wheatley and Kellner-Rogers (1996) posited ecological systems ideas that organizations may naturally engage in change strategies:

- Living systems learn constantly. They change when necessary, but they adapt by tinkering.
- Living systems are self-organizing. They have the innate capacity to create structures and processes that respond to the needs of the moment. Their organizing tendency shows up as temporary patterns and structures that emerge without plans, supervision, or directive leadership.
- Life is systems seeking. Life seeks to affiliate with other life. Such affiliation makes more life possible. Systems of relationships develop because systems make life more sustainable for their individual members.
- Life is attracted to order, but it uses "messes" to get there. The processes of life have nothing to do with machine efficiencies. They are fuzzy, redundant, and messy.
- Organizations are living systems. As living systems, organizations possess all of the creative, self-organizing capacities of other forms of life. The people within all organizations are capable of change, growth, and adaptation.
- Because we are living systems, most people are intelligent, creative, adaptive, and self-organizing. We want to organize, to learn, to do high-quality work, to contribute, to find meaning. We do not need to impose these attributes on one another (Wheatley and Kellner-Rogers 1996, 11).

Learning organizations. Another theorist who has proposed ideas about openness to and strategies of organizational change is Senge (1990). Senge believed that

Table 8.5.
Inventory: balancing work, family, and personal needs

Answer each question with a number from this scale:

Always	1	2	3	4	5	Never

At home

Does your family complain that you don't spend enough time with them?   _____

Do you often feel anxious about the demands of your family?   _____

Do responsibilities at home make you resentful?   _____

Do you expect your family to adapt to your career needs?   _____

At work

Do you feel frustrated because your income is not enough?   _____

Do you feel guilty about the time spent on your career?   _____

Do you resent having to bring work home?   _____

Do you worry that your work interferes with family needs?   _____

Personal

Do you feel there's never enough time for yourself?   _____

Do you feel guilty about taking a vacation?   _____

Do you wish you got more exercise?   _____

Do you feel you never get to do what you like to do?   _____

Total score _____

A total score of 20 indicates that you have learned to balance family, career, and personal needs successfully.

21–30 indicates a good balance with some room for improvement.

31–40 indicates fair balance.

41–50 shows that you are barely managing the juggling act of home, career, and personal needs.

Note. From the University of Texas–Southwest Employee Assistance Program.

the most successful organizations are those that create a culture and climate that require people throughout the organization to learn, and he called these workplaces *learning organizations.* Such organizations incorporate elements of both organizational culture and climate. In addition, they incorporate a management philosophy closely aligned to MacGregor's Theory Y or a belief in a natural wish to work, discussed previously.

According to Senge (1990), learning organizations are workplaces "where people continuously expand their capacity to create the results they truly desire, where new and expansive patterns of thinking are nurtured, where collective aspiration is set free, and where people are continually learning how to learn together" (p. 3).

Learning organizations tend to be both dynamic and fluid. These are organizations intentionally designed to be adaptable in an environment of continuous change and to continuously learn about themselves in order to survive and thrive in a very fluid contemporary social, economic, and global environment. Learning organizations devote significant resources to continuous learning by all organizational members and consider it to be essential to survival and growth. More specifically, learning organizations

- create a culture that encourages and supports continuous employee learning, critical thinking, and risk taking with new ideas;
- allow mistakes, and value employee contributions;
- learn from experience and experiment; and
- disseminate the new knowledge throughout the organization for incorporation into day-to-day activities ("Learning Organization," n.d.).

In sum, social workers should ask the following about their organizations:

- Does my organization have an intense desire to learn about itself?
- Does it display a strong commitment to generating and transferring new knowledge and technology?
- Does it exhibit openness to the external environment?
- Does it value a shared vision and systems thinking?
- Does it focus on interrelationships among factors and long-term rather than short-term approaches to problems?

Intervene With Individuals, Families, Groups, Organizations, and Communities

EAP Interventions: Individuals and Families

Employees may seek out EAP services on their own or be referred by a coworker or supervisor. Sessions are usually time limited, and social workers may call on individual and family theories discussed throughout this *Handbook*. Interventions include micro-, meso-, and macro-level strategies and may include

- applying information about employment and other aspects of the client's life to make an assessment;
- intervening professionally with a short-term and crisis methodology;
- negotiating between parties such as employee and supervisor;
- attempting to resolve group conflict situations;
- normalizing/stabilizing trauma situations;
- making useful referrals to and developing relationships with community agencies;
- acting as an advocate to gain client entitlements; and
- providing consultation around worker needs and policy situations that move an issue from a single case to a policy cause (Akabas 1995).

Organizational Change Interventions

You have already seen that organizations may have a propensity for self-change (see above). This occurs when systems are more open and adaptable (see Chapter 9 for a discussion of adaptable systems). Learning organizations—those that develop a culture that fosters ongoing employee learning, critical thinking, and risk taking with new ideas—are more likely to agree to and carry out organizational change. Guidelines for the social worker to use to initiate organizational change include the following:

- Knowing and involving stakeholders
- Collecting agency data, such as mission, finances, programs, services, and consumers, characteristics of people served, agency staff, and problems faced
- Understanding possible threats, such as shrinking economic markets
- Keeping planning simple and well coordinated
- Understanding who is affected by changes
- Facilitating information flow
- Gathering information about organizational strengths and weaknesses
- Exploring organizational competition (Sheafor and Horejsi 2012, 245–6)

Using Leadership Theory to Intervene in Organizations

Understanding and critically applying theories of organizations and organization management approaches are critical to effective social work practice in formal organizations. Equally important is an understanding of leadership theory. After a period of direct practice within a human service organization, many social workers move into management and leadership positions within their agencies. A fairly wide range of leadership theories can be helpful to social workers moving into positions of leadership. Although not exhaustive, Tables 8.6 and 8.7 summarize a number of the most common theories relevant to social work practice in organizational management that you may use to configure your own leadership style.

Leadership Styles Congruent With Social Work Values

Servant leadership theory is aligned more closely with social work values than any of the other theories explored here. Perhaps the primary similarity to social work values and principles is the leader's sense of responsibility to society and to those who are disadvantaged (Blanken 2013; CSWE 2015; NASW 2008). Servant leadership requires many of the skills typically used in social work practice. For example, Early and Davenport (2010) listed some of the individual characteristics of a servant leader in addition to an attitude of service to others, including being an excellent listener, having empathy, having a highly developed sense of awareness of context (environment), being a community builder, engendering trust, and being concerned not only with the professional growth of team members but also with their personal and spiritual growth.

Transformational leadership is also in alignment with social work principles. Early and Davenport (2010) asserted that a transformational leader is "an agent of change." Such leaders have faith in their supervisees' abilities, are "value-driven," have "infectious enthusiasm," create a vision for their team members, "anticipate the potential consequences of decisions," and provide "intellectual stimulation" for their subordinates in problem solving and goal achievement (p. 60).

Other Leadership Styles

- *Transactional leaders,* unlike either servant or transformational leaders, reflect a somewhat Theory X perspective in that they use systems of reward and punishment to ensure the achievement of goals by their subordinates. Transactional leaders show or tell the employee exactly what they expect and then hold the employee fully accountable for success or failure. Transactional leaders tend to be "directive, dominating, action-oriented, and task-oriented" (Blanken, n.p.n.d.). They believe in a strong chain of command and expect to have total authority over their employees (Blanken 2013). These leaders "work within the system" and have a "hands-off" approach until they are required to dispense punishment or rewards (Early and Davenport 2010, 60–62).
- *Trait-based leadership theory* posits that leaders are born with characteristics and behaviors that make them suited for leadership. Much research has been conducted over the years, especially in the first half of the twentieth century, to determine whether such traits exist and, if so, what they are. The research has been less than conclusive for two reasons.

    First, traits identified as universal have been elusive. Few such traits have been found, and those that have been are quite general and open to criticism, such as leaders tending to be taller and more outgoing. Such assertions are clearly questionable, as most know, for example, of leaders who are not tall or who are taller than average. To be outgoing, it can be argued, is a characteristic of far more people than those that might be identified as leaders (Fleenor 2006; Zaccaro and Klimoski 2001).

Table 8.6.
Contemporary leadership theories

Theory	Characteristics/assumptions
Servant	The leader has responsibility to the followers.
	Leaders have a responsibility to society and those who are disadvantaged.
	People who want to help others best do this by leading them.
Transformational	People will follow a person who inspires them.
	A person with vision and passion can achieve great things.
	The way to get things done is by injecting enthusiasm and energy.
Transactional	People are motivated by reward and punishment.
	There is a clear chain of command.
	Employees cede all authority to their manager.
	The primary purpose of subordinates is to do what they are told to do.

Note. Adapted from Early and Davenport (2010, 59), Blanken (2013), Leadership styles (n.d.), Johnson (n.d.), and Napier and Gershenfeld (1973).

Table 8.7.
Common leadership theories

Theory	Characteristics/assumptions
Trait based	Leaders are born. Leaders have inherent traits. Situation (context) is not considered.
Positional	Leaders are persons in leadership positions. Leaders rely on their position to justify decisions.
Situational	The best action of the leader depends on a range of situational factors.
Charismatic	Charm and grace are all that is needed to create followers. Self-belief is a fundamental need of leaders. People follow others that they personally admire. Leaders influence others through the power of their personality. Leaders act energetically, motivating others to move forward. Leaders inspire passion.Leaders may seem to believe more in themselves than in the team.
Democratic/Participative	All labor and management have involvement in decision making.People are more committed to actions when they have been involved. People are less competitive and more collaborative when they are working on joint goals. People make better decisions together.
Autocratic	Managers make decisions alone, with no input from others. Managers possess total authority and impose their will on employees. No one challenges the decisions of autocratic leaders.
Laissez Faire	The leader does not supervise employees. The leader fails to provide regular feedback to employees. The leader hinders the production of employees needing supervision. The leader produces no leadership or supervision efforts from managers.

Note. Adapted from Early and Davenport (2010, 59), Blanken (2013), Leadership styles (n.d.), Johnson (n.d.), and Napier and Gershenfeld (1973).

Second, after numerous attempts over the years to identify specific traits, the number of potential traits identified is so large as to render it less than useful as a practical means of choosing leaders. In addition, different traits have been identified by different researchers, resulting in an inability to agree on which traits are universal (Fleenor 2006; Zaccaro and Klimoski 2001).

- *Positional leadership theory* suggests that persons in positions of leadership are thereby leaders. In addition, the person's decisions are justified by fact that the person is in a leadership position. This theory is questionable, as most people can certainly think of persons in positions of leadership who did not perform as leaders (Napier and Gershenfeld 1973).

- *Situational leadership theory* defines a leader as a person who adjusts his or her leadership style to fit the current situation. Situational leaders are flexible enough, for example, to adjust to new members of a team or even a new team based on the problem to be solved as well as the personalities, experiences, and knowledge of the team members. Situational leadership can also emerge based on the requirements of the situation (Napier and Gershenfeld 1973).

  For example, during the World Trade Center disaster on September 11, 2001, many stories emerged of ordinary persons exhibiting extraordinary leadership. Stories included those of janitors who assumed leadership roles in guiding groups of persons on higher floors to stairwells and leading them down many flights to exits. The leadership displayed by such persons was situational, based in part on their knowledge of the buildings' layout and of pathways to get to exits, along with their willingness to accept responsibility for others.

- *Charismatic leadership theory* is based primarily on the personality of the leader. Charismatic leaders have a level of charm and belief in themselves that attract people to them and their ideas. They are energetic and persuasive in their manner and can motivate and inspire their followers. Such leaders are effective in raising team morale. However, if they leave the team may flounder and lose its effectiveness. Charismatic leaders may feel invincible and damage a team by taking on unnecessary risk.

- *Democratic or participative leadership* involves much more than guiding a process of problem solving resulting in a majority vote. Democratic or participative leadership is in some ways antithetical to this simplistic view. Democratic leadership depends on the active involvement of team members in expressing positions and providing evidence to support them. It includes what might be referred to as "respectful arguments" to attempt to persuade other members not with ideological arguments but with arguments based on critical thinking and a willingness both to be heard by others and to listen intently to the positions of other members of the team. Democratic leadership assumes that this process will not only lead to better decisions but also result in more commitment on the part of team members to decisions resulting from active input and engagement by team members.

- *Autocratic leadership* is based on a command and control approach to leadership. The autocratic leader has almost total control of decision making and implementation, with little input from employees. Managers have total authority over employees and can reward or punish performance as they see fit (Blanken 2013).

- *Laissez faire leadership* is almost the opposite of autocratic leadership in that the leader exerts little control and provides little supervision or feedback to team members responsible for implementing decisions. Such leadership does not work well for members who need guidance in the work they are expected to perform. However, members who have significant expertise in the problem at hand often prefer to work autonomously and need little feedback from the supervisor (Blanken 2013; Napier and Gershenfeld 1973).

In conclusion, a number of social work organizations, such as CSWE and NASW have recognized that knowledge for the exercise of leadership within the profession is a lifelong learning objective. Competence in this area is built through years of practice and continuing education. As seen in the following case study, technological innovations are fast becoming part of the tools available to social workers in their practice. For example, according to the report, *Understanding the Costs and Benefits of Health Information Technology in Nursing Homes and Home Health Agencies: Case Study Findings*, available at the website below, technology is now being used to support older adults with chronic disease management, medication management, cognitive and sensory impairment, depression, and decline in functional capacity be able to age in place at home (http://aspe.hhs.gov/daltcp/reports/2009/hitCSF.HTM). You may want to read the report and respond to the case example below.

> ➤ *A social worker at a state Department of Aging and Disability, Carol Gallant, has studied the progress being made using technology to help older adults age in place at home. She is ready to take a 2009 report to Congress to her unit's weekly meeting. What HBSE theory, information about technology and aging, and leadership attributes may help her achieve her goal?*

Critique of Diversity Issues in Social Work Practice

Social workers need to increasingly consider diversity issues in the workplace, especially which style of leadership is most conducive to a pluralistic organization. The significance accorded diversity in the social work profession as reflected in organizational theory, as in all systems, was addressed by Nixon and Spearmon (1991) in their typology of organizational progression to pluralism. Schriver (2014) adapted their model as follows:

- *Level 1: Token equal employment opportunity organization.* Hires people of color and women at the bottom of the hierarchy; has a few token managers who hold their positions only as long as they do not question the organization's policies, practices, mission, and so on.
- *Level 2: Affirmative Action Organization.* Aggressively recruits and supports the professional development of women and people of color and encourages nonracist, nonsexist behaviors; to climb the corporate ladder, women and people of color must still reflect and fit in with policies, practices, and norms established by dominant White men.
- *Level 3: Self-Renewing Organization.* Actively moves away from being sexist and racist toward being pluralistic; examines its mission, culture, values, operations, and managerial styles to assess their impact on the well-being of all employees; seeks to redefine the organization to incorporate multiple cultural perspectives.
- *Level 4: Pluralistic Organization.* Reflects the contributions and interests of diverse cultural and social groups in its mission, operations, and service

delivery; seeks to eliminate all forms of oppression within the organization; the workforce at all levels (top to bottom) reflects diversity; diversity in leadership is reflected in policymaking and governance structures; is sensitive to the larger community in which it exists and is socially responsible as a member of the community (Nixon and Spearmon, as cited in Schriver 2014, 258).

The Nixon and Spearmon model suggests that making the effort to incorporate diversity issues as integral to organizational development is a continuous and unfolding process. The model is perhaps most helpful in providing a mechanism for assessing organizations' effectiveness in incorporating diversity at deeper and deeper levels in the organization. As early as 1990, R. Roosevelt Thomas, Jr., recognized the precarious state of affirmative action in the workplace. He argued that because more than 50% of workers at the time were women, minorities, and immigrants, it was time to move from affirmative action to the celebration of differences and diversity in the workplace.

Glossary

Bureaucracy. An ideal type of formal organization that emphasizes efficiency and effectiveness.

Employee assistance program (EAP). Social services usually at the worksite for workers who may have difficulties that interfere with effective job performance or may be in jeopardy of losing their jobs.

Family-friendly policies. Business practices that allow employees to strike a balance between their work and home lives.

Hawthorne effect. The idea that workers sense that the efforts and presence of researchers in the workplace indicates that management has concern for them and their working conditions.

Human relations theory. A theory that examines organizations based on relationships and noneconomic awards.

Leadership. An activity that provides oversight and direction to meet organizational mission and goals.

Learning organizations. Organizations that are adaptable in an environment of continuous change. They continuously learn about themselves in order to survive and thrive in a very fluid economy .

Organizational climate. The feel of the organization held by those working there, reflected in the experience of people engaging with the organization.

Organizational culture. A way of thinking, behaving, or working that exists in a workplace or organization.

Organizations. Social units deliberately constructed and reconstructed to pursue specific goals.

Organizations as systems. A theory that views organizations as living adaptive groups.

Scientific management theory. A theory that sees science as something to be used in solving the problems faced by industry.

Welfare capitalism. A form of business that embodies welfare services to employees.

References

Akabas, S. 1995. "Occupational Social Work." In *Encyclopedia of Social Work*, 19th ed., edited by R. L. Edwards (Ed.-in-Chief), 685–704. Washington, DC: NASW Press.

Akabas, S. H., and Bikson, L. 2000. "Work and Job Jeopardy." In *Social Work Practice with Vulnerable and Resilient Populations*, edited by A. Gitterman, 841–60. New York: Columbia University Press.

Blanken, R. January 2013. *8 Common Leadership Styles.* The Center for Association Leadership. Accessed October 15, 2015. http://www.asaecenter.org/resources/anowdetail.cfm?itemnumber=241962

Chima, F. O. 1996. "Assessment in Employee Assistance: Integrating Treatment and Prevention Objectives." *Employee Assistance Quarterly* 12 (2): 47–66.

Council on Social Work Education. 2015. *Educational Policy and Accreditation Standards.* Alexandria, VA: Council on Social Work Education.

Culture. n.d. *Merriam-Webster.* Accessed October 15, 2015. http://www.merriam-webster.com/dictionary/culture

Dolgoff, R., and D. Feldstein. 2013. *Understanding Social Welfare: A Search for Social Justice.* Boston, MA: Pearson.

Duden, A. 2011. "Trust and Leadership Learning Culture in Organizations." *International Journal of Management Cases* 13 (4): 218–23. doi:10.5848/apbj.2011.00130

Early, J., and J. B. Davenport. 2010. "Desired Qualities of Leaders Within Today's Accounting Firm." *CPA Journal* 80 (3): 59.

Etzioni, A. 1964. *Modern Organizations.* Englewood Cliffs, NJ: Prentice Hall.

Fleenor, J. 2006. "Trait Approach to Leadership." In *Encyclopedia of Industrial and Organizational Psychology*, edited by S.G. Rolgelberg, 830–2. Thousand Oaks, CA: Sage.

Galambos, C., N. Livingston, and R. Greene. 2007. "Workplace Stressors: A Preventive Resilience Approach." In *Social Work Practice: A Risk and Resilience Perspective*, edited by R. R. Greene, 196–214. Monterey, CA: Brooks/Cole.

Greene, R. and N. Kropf. 2014. *Caregiving and Caresharing: A Lifecourse Perspective.* Washington, DC: NASW Press.

Hansan, J. E. 2011. "Poor Relief in Early America." Accessed October 15, 2015. June 30, 2015 http://www.socialwelfarehistory.com/programs/poor-relief/

Iverson, R. R. 1995. "Occupational Social Work for the 21st Century." *Social Work* 43:551–66.

Jacoby, S. 1997. *Modern Manors: Welfare Capitalism since the New Deal.* Princeton, RI: Princeton University Press.

Johnson, R. n.d. *5 Different Types of Leadership Styles. Houston Chronicle.* Accessed October 15, 2015. http://smallbusiness.chron.com/5-different-types-leadership-styles-17584.html

Karger, H. 1988. *Social Work and Labor Unions.* New York: Greenwood.

Karger, H. 2008. "Unions." In *Encyclopedia of Social Workers*, vol. 4, 20 ed., edited by T. Mizrahi and L. Davis, 308–11. New York: NASW Press and Oxford University Press.

Kotschessa, S. 1994. "Health Issues at Work: Opportunities for Industrial/Organizational Psychology." *American Psychologist* 45:273–63.

Krippner, S. 1994. "Humanistic Psychology and Chaos Theory: The Third Revolution and the Third Force." *Journal of Humanistic Psychology* 34 (3): 48–61. doi:10.1177/00221678940343005

Leadership styles. n.d. *Wall Street Journal.* Accessed October 15, 2015. http://guides.wsj.com/management/developing-a-leadership-style/how-to-develop-a-leadership-style/

Learning organization. n.d. *BusinessDictionary.* Accessed October 15, 2015. http://www.businessdictionary.com/definition/learning-organization.html

Liptak, A. 2010. Justices, 5-4, Reject Corporate Spending Limit. Accessed November 5, 2015. http://www.nytimes.com/2010/01/22/us/politics/22scotus.html?pagewanted=all&_r=0

MacGregor, D. 1960. *The Human Side of Enterprise.* Tokyo, Japan: McGraw-Hill.

Mayo, E. 1933. *The Human Problems of an Industrial Civilization*. Cambridge, MA: Harvard.

Mayo, E. 2007. *The Social Problems of an Industrial Society*. London: Routledge.

Napier, R., and M. K. Gershenfeld. 1973. *Groups: Theory and Experience*. Boston, MA: Houghton Mifflin.

NASW. 2008. *National Association of Social Workers Code of Ethics*. Washingtton, DC: NASW.

NASW. 2011. *National Association of Social Workers Center for Workforce Studies and Social Work Practice*. Washington, DC: NASW.

Nixon, R., and M. Spearmon. 1991. "Building a Pluralistic Workplace." In *Skills for Effective Human Services Management*, edited by R. Edwards and J. Yankey, 142–54. Silver Spring, MD: National Association of Social Workers.

Pugh, D. S., D. J. Hickson, and C. R. Hinings. 1985. *Writers on Organizations*. Beverley Hills, CA: Sage.

Scanlon, E. and S. Harding. 2005. "Social Work and Labor Unions: Historical and Contemporary Alliance." *Journal of Community Practice* 13 (1): 9–30.

Schein, E. H. 1985. *Organizational Culture and Leadership*. San Francisco, CA: Jossey-Bass.

Schneider, B., A. P. Brief, and R. A. Guzzo. 1996. "Creating a Climate and Culture for Sustainable Organizational Change." *Organizational Dynamics* 24 (4): 7–19. doi:10.1016/s0090-2616(96)90010-8

Schriver, J. M. 2015. *Human Behavior and the Social Environment: Shifting Paradigms in Essential Knowledge for Social Work Practice*, 6th ed. New York: Pearson.

Senge, P. 1990. "The Fifth Discipline: The Art and Practice of Learning Organizations." New York: DoubleDay/Currency.

Sheafor, B. W., and C. J. Horejsi. 2012. *Techniques and Guidelines for Social Work Practice*, 9th ed. Boston, MA: Allyn & Bacon.

Sirota, D., L. A. Mischkind, M. I. Meltzer. 2005. *The Enthusiastic Employee – How Companies Profit by Giving Workers What They Want*, 207–8. Upper Saddle River, NJ: Pearson Education, Inc., publishing as Wharton School Publishing.

Taylor, F.W. 1911. *Principles of Scientific Management*. New York: Harper Brothers.

Taylor, F. W. 1947. *Scientific Management, Comprising Shop Management: The Principles of Scientific Management Testimony before the Special House Committee*. New York: Harper.

Thomas, R. R., Jr. 1990. "From Affirmative Action to Affirming Diversity." *Harvard Business Review* 68 (2): 107–17.

Thomas, R. 1996. "Redefining Diversity." *HR Focus* 73 (4): 6–7.

University of Texas–Southwest Employee Assistance Program. *Balance of Family and Workplace Score*. Dallas: University of Texas.

Van Den Bergh, R. 1995. "Employee Assistance Programs." In *Encyclopedia of Social Work*, 18th ed., edited by R. L Edwards (Ed.-in-Chief), 842–9. Washington, DC: NASW Press.

Wheatley, M. 2005. "How is Your Leadership Changing?" Online. Accessed July 2, 2015. http://www.margaretwheatley.com/articles/howisyourleadership.html

Wheatley, M., and M. Kellner-Rogers. 1996. "Breathing Life into Organizations." *Public Management* 78:10–14.

Zaccaro, S. J., and R. J. Klimoski. 2001. *The Nature of Organizational Leadership: Understanding the Performance Imperatives Confronting Today's Leaders*. San Francisco, CA: Jossey-Bass.

9

Human Behavior and the Social Environment Theory: Social Work Practice with Communities

> ➤ This chapter presents human behavior and the social environment theories for social work practice with communities. It traces the historical development of how people relate to one another as members of a society. It then provides an overview of macrolevel social work practice approaches for community assessment and asset-building interventions.

This chapter continues the discussion of human behavior and the social environment theories for macrolevel social work practice with a focus on communities. As best expressed by Schriver (2011), "Community is where the individual and the social environment come together" (p. 490). This notion expands our multilayered theoretical practice context and provides further insight into people's collective identity. The target of the social worker's change efforts expands from individuals, families, and small groups to larger systems and the greater welfare of society.

Community social work practice methods are also broad in scope. Therefore, we have chosen to present an overview of human behavior and the social environment theory that supports macrolevel social work practice approaches for community assessment and asset-building interventions.

> ➤ Community well-being may be linked to sociohistorical factors and changing demographics.

Professional Purpose and Well-Being

Historical Background

Industrialization. Social science researchers became interested in studying community as a distinct component of larger society in the mid- to late 1800s (Table 9.1). The inquiry was part of the English Reform Movement that served as a response to

Table 9.1.
Selected theoretical foundations of community social work practice

Time adopted	Major theorist(s)	Theme	Concepts for practice
1887	Ferdinand Toennies: Sociologist and philosopher	People live in two different types of societies governed by implicit or explicit rules.	Entering a community involves understanding its rules
1905 1922	Max Weber: Sociologist and political economist	Cities must be understood as social and economic entities. Culture allows people to interpret society.	Giving attention to community space and populations
1935	Bertha Reynolds: Social worker	The social work mission should address community-level problems.	Attending to both individual and community welfare
1955 1968	George Hillery: Sociologist	Communities may be virtual.	Attending to clients online
1963 1966 1983	Roland Warren: Sociologist	Communities must fulfill five functions to survive.	Mobilizing communities to solve social problems
1974	Carol Stack: Anthropologist	Communities develop survival strategies.	Entering a community requires acknowledging one's power
1977	Frances Piven: Social economist Richard Cloward: Sociologist	The poor can be organized for mass resistance.	Empowering clients to overcome poverty
1996	William Wilson: Sociologist	The urban poor experience structural racism and poverty.	Combating institutional racism Revitalizing communities
1999	Ralph Anderson, Irl Carter, and Gary Lowe: Social workers	Communities can be understood as a social system.	Assessing a community's functionality

an expanding industrial and factory system with a need for workers (see Chapter 7 on mutual aid groups).

Migration. An interest in community was also driven by a need to understand the migration of people from traditional rural agricultural areas to burgeoning cities. Growing numbers of rural workers were being pushed away from their traditional agrarian roots as a result of social and economic changes such as the dismantling of the tenant farmer method of agricultural production. Tenant farming was increasingly being replaced by mechanization and by what would eventually become large farm-based agribusiness.

The growth of cities in the United States was spurred on by the oppressive Jim Crow era following the emancipation of slaves and reconstruction. Jim Crow policies that were *de jure* discrimination engendered a life of poverty for countless African Americans in the south. Their emancipation and continuing Jim Crow oppression gave many former slaves little hope for a stable and sustainable future in the south. Although the north was clearly not immune to racial discrimination and oppression, it was less extreme, and there was more opportunity for jobs driven by industrialization. The migration to cities was by and large from south to north, especially to the upper Midwest and the northeast. For example, the steel and automobile industries in cities such as Detroit and Michigan, were clamoring for workers to meet the need for factory labor.

> ➤ *Social policy and government activity affected community life.*

Social movements. These and other sociohistorical changes, including the arrival of new Americans, sometimes presented challenges to the community, such as pockets of poverty, substandard housing, and discrimination. Thus, a lower quality of neighborhood life was produced. To counteract this, political activists fought labor abuse and worked to eliminate government corruption during the Progressive Era (1890–1920). This led social worker pioneers such as Bertha Reynolds (1935) to rethink social casework, placing a greater emphasis on how community life influenced individual and families.

However, some of the gains made during the Progressive Era ended because of the 1929 stock market crash and the Great Depression; other progressive actions were taken during the New Deal and World War II. But ironically, the social work profession made a significant turn from social reform to clinical practice. In essence, the profession shifted its emphasis from seeking to address social problems in society to helping to solve the personal troubles of individuals (Schriver 2005; Specht and Courtney 1994).

Urban crisis. It was not until the turbulent 1960s and 1970s and the demands of civil rights activists and leaders of the poor people's movement (Piven and Cloward 1977) that the *urban crisis* (es) was acknowledged. This crisis was brought on by growing anger and resentment over the increasing and systematic deterioration of inner cities. The outcry from people of color and poor people was about long-existing realities such as segregation, discrimination, unemployment, poor schools, health disparities, and police brutality. During this period community organization in social work regained a significant level of importance. The role of social workers in ameliorating or even eliminating social problems and improving social well-being again became an increasing part of the professional mission. Social movements also came about in which working-class people, feminists, LGBT persons (Stonewall riots of 1969), and minorities organized to advocate for their own interests, placing their well-being into their own hands (Piven and Cloward 1977). In addition, social workers acted as a community of interest, organizing to eliminate social justice issues in their own institutions (Tully 1994).

Religion and Community

Social workers have partnered with faith-based organizations to solve community problems for many years. Furthermore, religious institutions have been significant actors in community life for centuries. Faith-based organizations have often worked with communities well beyond their religious role to meet needs not met by other organizations. For example, African American churches were instrumental in moving civil rights forward in the United States by providing a relatively safe place for planning and implementing challenges to slavery, Jim Crow laws, and other oppressive measures. In addition, they often served as centers of community organization through the power of the pulpit.

Many faith-based organizations are also significant providers of goods and services to those community members in dire need of support. They provide for such basic human needs as clothing, utilities, food, and sometimes direct financial assistance.

However, religious institutions can also play a significant role in oppression and intolerance. For example, some religious institutions have organized to defeat or recall community efforts to ensure equal treatment for their lesbian, gay, bisexual, transgender, and questioning members in employment, housing, business services, and accommodations. A common example involves the right of the owner of a bakery to refuse to bake a wedding cake for a gay couple because of sincerely held religious beliefs. A law to this effect was passed in Arkansas in Spring 2015. According to an article in the *Northwest Arkansas Democrat Gazette,*

> House Bill 1228, the so-called Religious Freedom Restoration Act, threatens to coarsen the image of Arkansas as a place that, in 2015, sanctions discrimination. The alleged target this time is gays and lesbians and others who, under the new law, might be refused service by businesses based on the owner's exercise of religious freedom. (Walsh 2015)

Community/Societal Well-Being

Today social workers are expected to understand, support, and implement "strategies designed to eliminate oppressive structural barriers to ensure that social goods, rights, and responsibilities are distributed equitably and that civil, political, environmental, economic, social, and cultural human rights are protected" (Council on Social Work Education [CSWE] 2015, 5). The remainder of this chapter outlines how social workers can achieve community well-being (see case of Blacksburg Village below).

Applying Terms and Assumptions in Social Work Practice

Community Defined

There is no general agreement about how to define community. A community may be thought of as a *place community,* or a geographical location to which people are attached, or a *non-place community,* in which people are dispersed. Non-place communities may be referred to as *communities of the mind; communities of interest,* which include people who share a passion; or *identificational communities,* which encompass friendship groups or ethnic, religious, and cultural groups.

Rather than focusing on physical location, these community perspectives focus on a common interest and social interaction among members (e.g., the profession of social work); a common group identity (e.g., culture; ethnicity; lesbian, gay, bisexual, transgender, and questioning; women); or a more affective notion referred to as a shared "sense of community," a feeling or sentiment that one is a member of a community and his or her membership is recognized and accepted by other members of the community (Rubin in Warren 1966, 56–57). Community members consciously identify with one another and engage in common activities. They also have organizations that allow them to carry out a range of functions (Anderson, Carter, and Lowe 1999).

Communities as a System

Social workers can understand and be change agents in communities by considering the notion of *"community as a social system"*? (Anderson et al. 1999; Warren 1978). Similar to using a social systems perspective to understand other system levels (individuals, groups, families, and organizations), social workers are concerned with how a community maintains effective functioning. This perspective takes into account the assumptions in Table 9.2.

The Analysis of Community Functions

Roland Warren, a noted social work educator and sociologist, refined the social system conceptualization of community. He provided a means of analyzing community functions by asking a series of questions:

1. Of what units is the community as a social system formed?
2. To what extent can the community as a social system be distinguished from its surrounding environment?

Table 9.2.
Community: social systems assumptions

- Communities are macrolevel social systems and part of the person-ecological perspective.
- Communities have boundaries. They can be geographical or intellectual.
- Communities are held together by feeling, sentiment, and purpose.
- Communities have a culture. Members are socialized into that way of life, those values, and those beliefs, sometimes called a *stock of beliefs.*
- Members of a community system relate to one another. They form subsystems sometimes called *networks.*
- Members of communities communicate to exchange information and carry out their goals.
- Members of communities organize to carry out their functions effectively in order to survive.
- Communities use energy (sometimes building infrastructure and institutions).
- To be a community, members must have a sense of "we-ness."
- Members of communities adapt to and accommodate the larger suprasystem.
- Communities have a means of social control (hierarchy, class).
- Communities have relative power vis-à-vis the suprasystem.

3. What is the nature of the structured interaction of units in the community as a social system?
4. What are the tasks that the community performs as a social system?
5. By what means is the structured relationship among the interacting units of a community maintained?
6. Can an external and internal pattern of activities be differentiated in the community?
7. What is the relation of community social system units to other social systems? (Warren 1978, 154)

Navigating subsystems. Perhaps one of the most important activities a social worker can carry out in community practice is to help constituencies navigate subsystems. This practice approach is called *community organization*—a method of bringing agencies and their constituencies together to strengthen service delivery systems within communities at large (Gamble and Weil 2009).

Like all social systems, a community consists of subsystems (school, health care, government, housing, commerce, justice, human services, faith-based organizations, etc.). Together these subsystems form the social system thought of as community. This is not to suggest that simply because the necessary subsystems are in place, a person will have access to entities that will be responsive to and meet their particular needs. Like any other social system, community systems can be dysfunctional. Community-focused social workers must be able both to help individuals navigate existing subsystems and to bring about system change to reduce dysfunction in the system. Like other social systems, community systems cannot survive or fulfill their functions without also being connected to components of the suprasystem (Anderson et al. 1999).

Suprasystems. The suprasystem includes such entities as state and national government; large multinational corporations; national health care; transportation; state systems of higher education; and, increasingly, global systems. Communities' relationships to the suprasystem are not unidirectional. Social workers need to help communities access resources that are available only through interactions with the suprasystem. In turn, the suprasystem needs resources produced at the community level in order to function successfully (Anderson et al. 1999; Warren 1978).

> ➤ *To engage with a community, social workers learn how members relate to one another and how their culture influences constituencies' trust.*

Engage With Individuals, Families, Groups, Organizations, and Communities

Historical Background

Two important groundbreaking theorists provided a way of defining communities and how members interact with one another: Max Weber and Ferdinand Toennies. This community theory can inform social workers about how they can engage with a community. Among the early social scientists to initiate systematic study of community and city life was Max Weber. Weber (1966) postulated a market-driven theory of the emergence of cities. His definition of a *city* was simply a marketplace or market settlement in which people's livelihoods were primarily dependent on trade and commerce rather than agriculture. This was most often driven by a good location, such as the intersection of transportation systems, i.e. a river and a road, allowing movement of goods to and from the market settlement. The emergence of cities as permanent marketplaces still impacts whether city residents have ready access to the goods and services available in society, and issues of privilege and social, economic, and environmental justice still prevail.

Another significant contributor to the systematic study of community was Ferdinand Toennies. In the late 1800s Toennies formulated two quite different conceptualizations of community still pertinent for understanding community relationships today. Both types were based on human volition, or will about the nature of relationships among community members.

Gemeinschaft communities. The first type of community Toennies referred to is *Gemeinschaft communities.* Gemeinschaft community life was structured and conducted according to community member relationships based on natural will. Such communities were driven by shared traditions or ways of life that were passed down from one generation to the next. A driving value underpinning natural will was a sense of mutual and personal responsibility. Such communities, Toennies believed, were most consistent with rural or agrarian life in which community members knew one another well over time (intergenerationally).

In addition, relationships in Gemeinschaft communities were based on a sense of fellowship among equals. They also were marked by patriarchal protective authoritative relationships such as those between a father and child. These community relationships reflected a sense of "I will do this for you because I know and trust you will do something for me when I need your help."

Gesellschaft communities. In contrast, *Gesellschaft communities* were based on rational will. Relationships in these communities were formal or contract-like. In these communities members did things for one another based on the exchange of goods, money, or services. Rational will was reflected in much more impersonal ways of relating. Gesellschaft relationships were driven by the notion that people needed things (food, shelter, and other basic needs) from one another to survive and attained these things through a formal exchange of money, goods, or services. Toennies associated Gesellschaft communities with city or urban life. Gesellschaft relationships could be framed as "I do this for you only if you pay me for it." There was no sense of personal responsibility in these contractual, exchange-based relationships.

Toennies recognized that often communities reflected some combination of Gemeinschaft and Gesellschaft relationships. Such communities, however, tended to reflect a higher degree of one or the other way of relating (Toennies 1935). For example, large Gesellschaft communities or cities often include specific neighborhoods whose relationships are driven primarily by Gemeinschaft. An ethnic neighborhood, such as Manhattan's Little Italy neighborhood in New York City in its early years, is a specific example.

Recent Urban Life

One outcome of the civil rights movements of the 1960s is that theorists began to reexamine urban life. Carol Stack (1974), an anthropologist, wrote *All Our Kin: Strategies for Survival in a Black Community*, a qualitative ethnographic depiction of rural life in a Black community, and William Wilson (1996) authored *When Work Disappears: The World of the Urban Poor*, a sociological account of how racism may precipitate social breakdown and a restriction of economic opportunities. They drew attention to the fact that each community and neighborhood has a culture of its own that may be positively or negatively influenced by the privilege and/or relative power of constituencies (CSWE 2015).

Engagement Factors

A primary interest of social workers engaging a community is the community's culture or way of life. What should social workers know to engage today's cities and communities? The theorists discussed previously suggested asking the following questions:

- Are there several subcultures within the community?
- Should you begin by making contacts within the community to help you enter and build trust?
- How does the community bond together and effectively function?
- Is there strife or discord?
- How are people socialized?
- What are personal responsibilities?
- What are the community's responsibilities to its members?
- How are decisions made?
- How is conflict managed?
- Who is in charge?
- Are rules implicit or explicit?
- What is the nature of community relationships?

> ➤ *Community assessment encompasses an evaluation of personal and collective activities.*

Assess Individuals, Families, Groups, Organizations, and Communities

This section outlines two means of assessing communities: by considering (a) community functions and daily needs and (b) community asset theory. Global indexes and asset mapping are also discussed.

Community Functions and Daily Needs

When assessing community functions, it is helpful to refer to Warren (1978), who defined *community* as "that combination of social units and systems that perform the major social functions having locality relevance" (p. 9). In other words, he saw community as a set locality of relevant functions that provide the necessary services and systems for members to satisfy most of their daily living needs. Therefore, the social worker will want to assess how the following functions are carried out:

- *Participation in production, distribution, and consumption:* A community must be organized in such a way that members have access to means of producing the goods and services necessary to meet the daily living needs of members. Once produced, there must be a means of distributing goods and services to members for consumption. For example, food must be produced (e.g., by farmers), and it must then be made available for distribution to community members (e.g., through a grocery store) for their consumption.
- *Socialization:* Different subsystems contribute to a person learning the knowledge, values, and appropriate behavior patterns for productive membership in the community. Subsystems involved in socialization include families, schools, civic organizations, and faith-based entities.
- *Social control:* This function is carried out through group influences on members' behaviors so that individuals conform to community norms. Social control is accompanied by various sanctions used to hold individuals accountable for conforming to norms. Such subsystems include municipal laws enforced by the police and courts, rules of behavior in public schools, and family-level sanctions for inappropriate behavior.
- *Social participation:* This function provides opportunities for social participation in the life of the community and is carried out by various units of the community. Examples of such units include service clubs, the chamber of commerce, unions, professional associations, political parties, and parent–teacher organizations.
- *Mutual support:* This function provides assistance for community members in times of need. Although a number of community entities facilitate mutual support, social welfare organizations are generally seen as the source of formal means of mutual support. Other more specific mutual support mechanisms include family and kinship groups, public and private human service agencies, and mental health agencies (Warren 1978, 9–11, 170–212).

> ➤ *There is a synergistic relationship between community and individual assets.*

Community Asset Theory

Asset theory is increasingly being used to understand various types of community capital, or assets. Major areas of asset theory include social capital, financial capital, and human capital. This growing body of theory is useful in focusing the types of interventions needed in vulnerable communities. Although these types might seem distinct from one another, their interrelationship is synergistic. In other words, increasing social capital in a distressed community increases community members' capacity to build financial and human capital. And increasing human capital can positively influence the creation of both financial and social capital.

Social capital. Social capital in social work is closely tied to the concept of social networks. According to The Saguaro Seminar: Civic Engagement in America,

> The central premise of social capital is that social networks have value. Social capital refers to the collective value of all "social networks" [who people know] and the inclinations that arise from these networks to do things for each other ["norms of reciprocity"]. ("About Social Capital," n.d.)

According to Briggs (1997),

> Social capital refers . . . to resources stored in human relationships . . . . Social capital is the stuff we draw on all the time, through our connections to a system of human relationships, to accomplish things that matter to us and to solve everyday problems. (p. 112)

The case below provides an example of how personal assets become community assets.

> ➤ Yvette is a senior who will soon be graduating from high school. She aspires to be the first person in her family to attend college. She has been working as a checker in a local grocery store to save money for college. Because no one in her family has gone to college, Yvette cannot rely on her family to provide guidance in applying to and attending college. However, the owner of the grocery store, Ms. Jackson, does have a college degree and has developed a mentoring relationship with Yvette. Ms. Jackson is aware that Yvette is highly motivated to go to college and that she is struggling to understand just how to do this. Ms. Jackson takes time after work to meet with Yvette to assist her in completing the necessary application materials. In addition, Ms. Jackson knows an admissions counselor at the local college, who regularly shops in her store. She volunteers to write a letter of reference to the admissions counselor outlining Yvette's positive qualities. Ms. Jackson even introduces Yvette to the counselor the next time the counselor comes in to shop. Yvette is using the social capital she has accumulated through her positive relationship with Ms. Jackson to receive assistance. Ms. Jackson is willing to use her social capital to support Yvette's college aspirations.

Financial capital. Community well-being also depends on financial capital. The meaning of *financial capital* seems somewhat self-explanatory in comparison to the relationship-driven dynamics of social capital: "financial assets or the financial value of assets, such as cash" (Investopedia, n.d.). It is important to note that "*financial capital* only refers to tangible assets that can be used as money . . . . However assets such as currency in hand, the balances of existing bank accounts, and negotiable instruments such as stocks or bonds do meet the criteria" (wise-GEEK, n.d.).

As simple as these definitions seem, financial capital is a critical asset in social work practice at both the micro- and macrolevels. A foundational principle of social work is social and *economic* justice. In addition, throughout its history the profession has emphasized the centrality of poverty reduction. Although having access to financial capital is critical for both low-income individuals and vulnerable communities, it is only part of the equation. Clearly, social capital, described previously, is also a critical element of poverty reduction that social workers must attend to as well. As indicated, having access to social networks is perhaps equally important for building pathways out of poverty. To attempt more sustainable solutions to poverty, social workers must focus, preferably simultaneously, on the building and use of both social and financial capital.

Human capital. Along with financial and social capital, human capital is a third critical element of the economic justice equation. *Human capital* can be defined as "the collective skills, knowledge, or other intangible assets of individuals that can be used to create economic value for the individuals, their employers, or their community" ("Human Capital," n.d.). Perhaps the clearest example of human capital is that acquired as a result of education. Accumulating knowledge, values, and skill through education is critical—some would say most critical—to building pathways out of poverty. Other aspects of human capital include the talents with which people are born, such as musical or artistic gifts. This is not to say such talents cannot be more finely honed through formal education. Human capital, unlike the other two forms of capital just described, is unique in that once attained, it cannot be taken away. Financial capital can be lost, and the networks on which social capital depends can be severed or lost over time, but human capital remains.

Again, building and accessing methods to increase human capital at both the individual and community levels is a central concern of social work. Such programs as workforce development and training initiatives, Pell grants for higher education, and Head Start preschool programs for low-income children and parents are all intended to increase human capital. This in turn provides increased opportunities to build both social and financial capital.

Global Assessment

The United Nations has provided a means of thinking about community/societal well-being known as the *Human Development Index* (HDI). The HDI is a composite index measuring average achievement in three basic dimensions of human development: (a) a long and healthy life, measured by life expectancy; (b) knowledge, assessed by number of years of expected and achieved schooling; and (c) a decent standard of living, calculated by gross national income. See http://hdr.undp.org/en for details on how the HDI is calculated.

Asset Mapping

Asset mapping is a tool for gathering information that can be used to create a mutual intervention plan between social workers and constituencies (CSWE 2015). Asset mapping allows community members to come together to gather information on their capacity to live effectively in their community. This may include aspects of capital discussed previously, even extending to the number of jazz clubs, community gardens, and murals. When engaging in asset mapping, the social worker

- Asks for community participation
- Takes a proactive stance
- Focuses on capacities
- Seeks collaborators
- Forms partnerships
- Equalizes power
- Cultivates community ownership (Burns, Paul, and Paz 2012)

Intervene With Individuals, Families, Groups, Organizations, and Communities

When intervening with communities, social workers use theory and strategies to improve social, economic, and environmental justice (CSWE 2015). This takes the form of activities to organize and build communities.

Interventions to Organize Communities

In the mid-1970s, Cox et al. (1974) developed and refined a multitype conceptualization of approaches to community organization. The approaches included locality development, social planning, and social action. *Locality development* suggests that community change can come about as a result of participation by a range of different people in the local community. *Social planning* is a more technical process of community problem solving and assumes that the complexity of contemporary communities requires experts to guide the problem-solving process. Such experts may be from inside or outside the community of concern. *Social action* assumes that a disadvantaged group in the community must organize to demand necessary resources from the larger community. This approach attempts to bring about substantive change in community institutions, social policies, or practices of the more powerful parts of the community in order to create a more level playing field for the disadvantaged segment of the community (pp. 5–6). Table 9.3 summarizes the three models in terms of their essence, major themes, and examples.

Interventions to Increase Capital and Reduce Poverty

The forms of capital discussed earlier may seem rather abstract until they are integrated into intervention contexts. In the 1980s and 1990s social work began to develop and use intervention strategies for vulnerable and disadvantaged communities intended to increase social, financial, and human capital and reduce

Table 9.3.
Models of community practice

Key factor	Locality development	Social planning	Social action
Essence	Broad participation of local people in determining and solving their own problems	The need for technical experts (social planners) to guide the solving of complex community problems and get goods and services to people in need	A disadvantaged group in the community is in need of redress from the larger community to achieve social and economic justice
Themes	Democratic processes, voluntary cooperation, self-help, developing indigenous leadership, educating local people	Rational, deliberately planned and controlled change; manipulating large bureaucracies; social policy and program creation and change	Redistribution of power, resources, and decision making to include the disadvantaged group; basic policy change in formal organizations
Examples	Work and training programs, VISTA, Peace Corps, AmeriCorps, Teach for America	Community planning councils, federal planning agencies, housing authority planning departments, mental health planning groups	Civil rights movement; women's movement; lesbian, gay, bisexual, transgender, and questioning rights groups; labor unions; Amnesty International; Greenpeace

Note. Adapted from Rothman (1979, 25–45).

poverty. Two of the important intervention approaches were community building and renewal and people- and place-based strategies.

Community building and renewal theory is a holistic approach to addressing the multiple, complex, and intersecting needs of vulnerable and disenfranchised communities. The theory recognizes the false dichotomy between bricks-and-mortar approaches, often referred to as *place-based approaches,* and program-focused approaches, often referred to as *people-based approaches.* For example, place-based approaches attempt to address such challenges as urban decay or deteriorating infrastructure (streets, utilities, buildings, etc.) by either rehabilitating infrastructure or razing buildings judged to be beyond repair. Such approaches have historically been the terrain of urban planners.

People-based approaches address community problems through creating or enhancing human service programs. These approaches include such programs as juvenile delinquency prevention and intervention (e.g., mentoring programs, employment assistance), services for elders (e.g., Meals on Wheels), children's services (e.g., day care, preschool, or after-school programs), and programs to address basic needs (e.g., food banks, housing assistance, transportation support). These approaches have typically been the purview of social workers and other human services providers.

Community building and renewal theory attempts to integrate place- and people-based approaches to create more collaborative and holistic ways to intervene in vulnerable communities. In the past the two community intervention approaches tended to be implemented independent of each other. The newer approach recognizes that the built environment can directly influence the social environmental outcomes of social programs (i.e., environmental issues such as lead paint in older buildings) and health outcomes (especially of children). In turn, social programs influence the type of physical structures needed (i.e., building accessibility for persons with disabilities, kid-friendly buildings, the size of furnishings, the type and location of restrooms).

According to research by Naparstek and Dooley (1997), community-building initiatives should be guided by the following principles:

- Strategies must be comprehensive and integrated.
- Strategies should be tailored to the individual neighborhood involved and focused on an area of manageable size.
- Strategies should begin not merely with a neighborhood's needs but with an inventory of its assets (see earlier discussion of asset mapping).
- Strategies must involve residents and other local stakeholders in setting goals and priorities and shaping plans to address them (Naparstek and Dooley 1997, 511).

Connell, Kubisch, Schorr, and Weiss (in Naparstek and Dooley 1997, 511) provide additional goals:

- the goal of promoting positive change in individual, family, and community circumstances in disadvantaged neighborhoods by improving physical, economic, and social conditions.
- expansion and improvement of social services and supports such as child care, youth development, and family support health care, including mental health care; economic development; housing rehabilitation and/or construction; community planning and organizing; as well as school reform.

Naparstek and Dooley (1997) also pointed out the significance of a more holistic approach for social work:

> Linking place- and people-based strategies through community building has significant implications for social work, because it means improving the delivery and quality of human services, strengthening community organization, stimulating economic development, and in every possible way improving the quality of life of residents while affecting physical improvements. (p. 510)

Interventions Actualized

Closely associated with the social capital construct are the overlapping concepts of a *civic ethic, civil society,* and *civic responsibility.* These concepts are based on a sense of responsible citizenship in a democratic society and can be the result of interventions that promote the social good (CSWE 2015). A sense of civic ethic and civic responsibility suggests that community members have an ethical and moral responsibility to contribute to the democratic functioning of a community in return for the rights afforded them by the Constitution in a free and democratic system, including rights to freedom of speech, press, religion, and peaceable assembly and the right to petition the government. These rights are accompanied by responsibility for building and maintaining a civil society at a local level. According to the World Health Organization (2015),

> Civil society is seen as a social sphere separate from both the state and the market . . . . the term civil society organizations (CSOs) is that of non-state, not-for-profit, voluntary organizations formed by people in that social sphere. This term is used to describe a wide range of organizations, networks, associations, groups and movements that are independent from government and that sometimes come together to advance their common interests through collective action.

In essence, civil society is the context in which ethical and moral responsibilities of citizenship are carried out. These responsibilities are carried out through voluntary engagement in nonprofit organizations and activities intended to ensure the maintenance of democratic institutions. "Non-profit organizations are considered civic organizations" because they provide a "public or mutual benefit other than the pursuit or accumulation of profits for [their] owners or investors" (Blurtit, n.d.). Such nonprofit activities are perhaps best reflected in the willingness of citizens to voluntarily join and participate in organizations that nourish and teach democratic action to address community rather than individual needs. Such organizations include civic organizations such as the Scouts, Boys and Girls Clubs, the League of Women Voters, Rotary, parent–teacher organizations, social welfare organizations, the American Cancer Society, and many others.

Critique of Diversity Issues in Social Work Practice

Community Oppression

The resources of a community and participation of community members may be said to correlate with its ability to carry out its functions and goals, and achieve a sense of efficacy (Pinderhughes 1989; see Chapter 3 for a discussion of power). Unfortunately, much of social work theory and practice at the community level discussed thus far has been devoted to addressing needs resulting from growing disparities in income, health and educational outcomes, and other social indicators. A primary cause of these disparities is discrimination, oppression, and injustice faced by people of color and low-income persons.

To further understand why such oppression persists in urban communities recently experiencing unrest, social workers must address a number of mechanisms by which such oppression continues:

- *Blockbusting* occurs when people's fears of people different from themselves are inflamed by unethical real estate agents. This dynamic unfolds when a real estate agent sells a house in a White neighborhood to an African American family (or other family of color), sometimes for a reduced cost. The agent then distributes information to the White homeowners in the neighborhood letting them know that an African American family has purchased a home. The information usually includes ominous messages about falling property values, increased crime, and so on resulting from the arrival of the African American family, which is surely to be followed by others. Preying on the racial stereotypes and fears of the White homeowners, the unethical agent then offers to help sell their homes, sometimes offering to buy them outright before the influx happens. Of course, the White families sell or list their homes for less than their real value, and the real estate agent sells the soon-to-be-vacant homes to other African American families at greatly inflated prices. In the process, the neighborhood and tax base is destabilized (Feagin and Feagin 1978).

- *White flight* is the term used to describe the rapid migration of White homeowners out of one neighborhood, often in an urban environment, to another neighborhood, usually an all-White suburb. This migration, often based on the dynamics of blockbusting and racial fears, not only causes instability in the original neighborhood but often results in the deterioration of that community's public services and schools. As in the case of blockbusting, the wealthier Whites taking flight also take with them much of the tax base needed to support civic institutions. Because of income inequality families of color are not able to match the tax generation of the previous White residents.

- *Racial steering* is somewhat similar to blockbusting but differs in some important ways. Racial steering, a practice outlawed by the Fair Housing Act, consists of attempting to limit potential homebuyers to neighborhoods where current residents are predominantly of their race. Racial steering is directed not only at aspiring home buyers but at persons looking for rental properties as well. Its practice is not limited to unethical real estate agents but includes discriminatory property management and rental agencies as well. Racial steering, as the name implies, involves real estate, leasing, or rental agents maintaining existing housing segregation by steering both Whites and people of color to areas in a community that are segregated by race. For example, an agent showing properties to a person of color will say such things as, "You'll be more comfortable in this neighborhood [predominantly occupied by people of color] than in the [predominantly White] one you wanted to look at earlier." Another tactic is not to show properties to clients in neighborhoods other than those segregated according to the client's color at all.

  A 2006 study reported by The Leadership Conference, a national antidiscrimination and civil rights coalition, found that real estate agents in the study racially steered 87% of testers who inquired about purchasing a home. Nearly 20% of African American and Latino testers were refused appointments or offered very limited service. At one agency in Marietta, Georgia, for example, White testers were shown twenty-six houses and African American testers were shown none.

- *Redlining* is another discriminatory practice that is perhaps more pernicious than racial steering, as it is carried out by banking, mortgage, and other lending institutions. Redlining results from a judgment by a local lending company that certain areas of the community are too risky for investment. This judgment is often arbitrarily based on racial composition (African American) rather than income. The area is literally shaded red on a map, and the company will not lend money for home loans, home improvement loans, and loans to small businesses wishing to invest in the neighborhood. Redlining is illegal but is still practiced.

BlackPast.org (n.d.) described redlining as

a discriminatory pattern of disinvestment and obstructive lending practices that act as an impediment to home ownership among African Americans and other people of color. Banks use the concept to deny loans to homeowners and would-be homeowners who lived in these neighborhoods. This in turn results in neighborhood economic decline and the withholding of services or their provision at an exceptionally high cost.

As a consequence of redlining, neighborhoods that local banks deemed unfit for investment are often left underdeveloped or in disrepair. Attempts to improve these neighborhoods with even relatively small-scale business ventures were commonly obstructed by financial institutions that continued to label the underwriting as too risky or simply rejected them outright (BlackPast.org, n.d).

Community Efficacy and Empowerment

In contrast to community oppression, the concept of collective efficacy (Bandura 2002; see Chapter 5) is another means of understanding community social, human, and financial capital. As seen in the research study below, a transtheoretical approach to community development was examined in an electronic Virginia community in meeting the following goals: (1) present itself in ways that increase tourism, (2) greatly improve the roads, (3) improve the quality of life, (4) greatly improve the quality of education, (5) handle mistakes and setbacks, (6) improve quality of community facilities, (7) united in the community vision presented to outsiders, (8) committed to common community goals, (9) work together, (10) resolve crises, (11) enact fair laws, (12) create resources for new jobs, and (13) improve services for senior citizens (Caroll and Reese 2003).

Glossary

Asset theory. A theory used to understand various types of community capital or assets, including social capital, financial capital, and human capital.

City. A marketplace or market settlement in which people's livelihoods are primarily dependent on trade and commerce rather than agriculture.

Community. A social system.

Community building. A means of improving the delivery and quality of human services, strengthening community organization, and stimulating economic development.

Community development. Social work practice to create conditions of economic and social progress for the whole community with active participation and reliance on the community's initiative.

Community organization. A method of bringing agencies together to strengthen service delivery systems.

Financial capital. The financial value of assets, such as cash.

Gemeinschaft **community.** A community in which member relationships are based on shared traditions or ways of life that are passed down from one generation to the next.

Gesellschaft **community.** A community in which member relationships are based on formal or contract-like relationships. Gesellschaft relationships are driven by the notion that people need things (food, shelter, and other basic needs) from one another to survive.

Human capital. The collective skills, knowledge, or other intangible assets of individuals that can be used to create economic value for the individuals, their employers, or their community.

Non-place community. A community that exists beyond the boundary of physical location.

Social capital. The collective value of social networks involving norms of reciprocity.

References

About social capital. n.d. Harvard Kennedy School. Accessed October 15, 2015. http://www.hks. harvard.edu/programs/saguaro/about-social-capital

Anderson, R., I. Carter, and G. Lowe. 1999. *Human Behavior in the Social Environment: A Social Systems Approach.* New York: Aldine.

Bandura, A. 2002. "Growing Primacy of Human Agency in Adaptation and Change in the Electronic Era." *European Psychologist* 7:2–16.

BlackPast.org. n.d. *Redlining (1937-).* Accessed October 15, 2015. http://www.blackpast.org/aah/ redlining-1937

Blurtit. n.d. *What Is a Civic Organization?* Accessed October 15, 2015. http://business-finance.blurtit. com/70259/what-is-a-civic-organization-

Briggs, X. D. 1997. "Social Capital and the Cities: Advice to Change Agents". *National Civic Review* 86 (2): 111–7.

Burns, J. C., D. P. Paul, and S. R. Paz. April 2012. *Participatory Asset Mapping.* Accessed October 15, 2015. http://communityscience.com/knowledge4equity/AssetMappingToolkit.pdf

Caroll, J. and D. Reese. 2003. "Community Collective Efficacy: Structure and Consequences of Perceived Capacities in the Blacksburg Electronic Village." Proceedings of the 36 Hawaii International Conference on systems sciences. January 6–9.

Council on Social Work Education. 2015. *Educational Policy and Accreditation Standards.* Alexandria, VA: Council on Social Work Education.

Cox, F. M, J. L. Erlich, J. L, Rothman, J., and J. E. Tropman, J. E. 1974. *Strategies of Community Organization: A Book of Readings,* 3rd ed., 25–45. Itasca, IL: Peacock.

Feagin, J. R., and C. B. Feagin. 1978. *Discrimination American Style: Institutional Racism and Sexism.* Englewood Cliffs, NJ: Prentice Hall.

Gamble, D., and M. Weil. 2009. *Community Practice Skills: Local to Global Perspectives.* New York: Columbia University Press.

Hillery, G. A., Jr. 1955. "Definitions of Community: Areas of Agreement." *Rural Sociology* 20: 111–23.

Hillery, G. A. 1968. *Communal Organizations: A Study of Local Societies.* Chicago, IL: University of Chicago Press.

Human capital. n.d. Accessed October 15, 2015. http://dictionary.reference.com/browse/human%20capital

Investopedia. n.d. *Capital.* Accessed October 15, 2015. http://www.investopedia.com/terms/c/capital.asp

The Leadership Conference. April 7, 2006. *Report: Racial Steering into Segregated Neighborhoods Most Prevalent form of Housing Discrimination.* Accessed October 15, 2015. http://www.civil-rights.org/fairhousing/laws/report-racial-steering-into-segregated-neighborhoods-most-preva-lent-form-of-housing-discrimination-1.html?referrer=https://www.google.com/

Naparstek, A. J., and D. Dooley. 1997. "Countering Urban Disinvestment through Community-building Initiatives." *Social Work* 42:506–14.

Pinderhughes, E. B. 1989. "Understanding Race, Ethnicity, and Power: The Key to Efficacy in Clinical Practice." New York: Free Press.

Piven, F., and R. A. Cloward. 1977. *Poor People's Movement: Why They Succeed and Why They Fail.* New York: Vintage Books.

Reynolds, B. C. 1935. "Rethinking Social Casework." *Family* 16:230–7.

Rothman, J. 1979. "Three Models of Community Organization Practice, Their Mixing and Phas-ing." In *Strategies of Community Organization: A Book of Readings*, 3rd ed., edited by F. M. Cox, J. L. Erlich, J. Rothman, and J. E. Tropman, 25–45. Itasca, IL: Peacock.

Schriver, J. M. 2005. "Lurie, Harry Lawrence (1892–1973)." In *Encyclopedia of Social Welfare History in North America*, edited by J. M. Herrick and P. H. Stuart, 224–6. Thousand Oaks, CA: Sage.

Schriver, J. M. 2011. *Human Behavior and the Social Environment: Shifting Paradigms in Essential Knowledge for Social Work Practice.* Boston, MA: Allyn & Bacon.

Specht, H., and M. E. Courtney. 1994. *Unfaithful Angels: How Social Work Has Abandoned Its Mission.* New York: Free Press.

Stack, C. 1974. *All Our Kin: Strategies for Survival in a Black Community.* New York: Harper & Row.

Toennies, F. 1935. *Gemeinschaft und Gesellschaft: Grundbegriffe der Reinen Soziologie.* Translated as Communities and Society. Leipzig, Germany.

Tully, C. T. 1994. "Epilogue. Power and the Social Work Profession." In *Human Behavior Theory: A Diversity Framework*, edited by R. R. Greene, 217–44. Hawthorne, NY: Aldine de Gruyter.

Walsh, J. April 4, 2015. *Fayetteville Leaders React to Religious Protection Law.* Retrieved from the *Northwest Arkansas Democrat Gazette.* Accessed October 15, 2015. http://www.nwaonline.com/news/2015/apr/04/fayetteville-leaders-react-to-religious/

Warren, R. L. 1966. *Perspectives on the American Community: A Book of Readings.* Chicago, IL: Rand McNally.

Warren, R. L. 1978/1963. *The Community in America.* Chicago, IL: Rand McNally.

Weber, M. 1905. *The Protestant Ethic and "The Spirit of Capitalism."* London, Unwin Hyman.

Weber, M. 1966. *The Protestant Ethic and "The Spirit of Capitalism."* Los Angeles: Roxbury.

Wilson, W. 1996. *When Work Disappears: The World of the Urban Poor.* New York: Knopf.

wiseGEEK. n.d. *What Is Financial Capital?* Accessed October 15, 2015. http://www.wisegeek.com/what-is-financial-capital.htm

World Health Organization. 2015. *Civil Society.* Accessed October 15, 2015. http://www.who.int/trade/glossary/story006/en/

Asset Mapping website

http://healthpolicy.uclaedu/programs/health-data/trainings/Documents/tw cba20.pdf

10

Risk and Resilience Theory: A Bridge from Neuroscience to the Global Ecology

> ➤ This chapter presents a risk and resilience approach to practice
> with individuals, families, groups, organizations, and communities.
> It suggests that when the risk and resilience approach to social work
> practice is amplified by the ecological perspective and other relat-
> ed theoretical frameworks, the combination of interlocking precepts
> constitutes a human behavior and the social environment theory and
> practice model that bridges the gap between neuroscience and the
> global ecology. The suggested overarching metatheory also presents
> an opportunity for social workers to further incorporate genetic, bio-
> logical, spiritual, and economic concepts into their practice.

This chapter is unlike others in the *Handbook* particularly as it relates to theory building. Other chapters discuss relatively well-established theories that have been applied in social work practice over decades, such as cognitive behavior theory. One chapter presents a model, general systems theory, that is used in conjunction with family therapy schools of thought. This chapter describes a newly emerging theory, pointing out the various elements that contribute to, and are being brought together to form, a metatheory.

The chapter uses a metatheory to describe the risk and resilience approach to social work practice, tracing its development as a branch of developmental psychopathology to its status as a *metatheory*—a discipline that has been combined with others to augment its definitions, assumptions, and terms.

The metatheory explores the following question: What makes some people and communities more capable of self-righting or more resilient than others? The exploration is broad in scope, incorporating, among others, genetic, biological, spiritual, family systems, and economic concepts. In this way, human behavior and the social environment theory provides interlocking intervention strategies for working with individuals, families, groups, organizations, communities, and societies.

Defining a Metatheory

This chapter proposes that when risk and resilience concepts are further elaborated by ecological principles and other related theoretical points of view, the joint assumptions constitute an overarching theory or metatheory (Greene 2014). "Metatheory is concerned . . . with the study of theories, theorists, communities of theorists, as well as with the larger intellectual and social context of theories and theorists" (Ritzer 1988, 188; see also Craig 2009; Weinstein and Weinstein 1993). A metatheory evolves over time as implicit assumptions are made explicit (Dervin 1999) and provides "an opportunity for multiple operations of analysis and synthesis" (Weinstein and Weinstein 1993, 224).

Furthermore, multidisciplinary theoretical frameworks allow for a rich analysis of assessment data from clients and constituencies (Council on Social Work Education [CSWE] 2015). Because a metatheory of risk and resilience encompasses two—or more—theories (Ritzer 2009), it presents an integrating "scaffolding" to bring together "specific theories that conceptually and empirically map different aspects of the phenomena under study" (Anchin 2008, 310). Practitioners can use critical thinking to apply "resilience thinking . . . as a discrete field" (Martin-Breen and Anderies 2011, 5), carrying out comprehensive practice strategies across multiple areas, such as helping people following disasters, reinventing business models for organizational change, developing sustainable agriculture programs to try and address poverty, and mobilizing policymakers for equitable resource distribution (Luthar and Cicchetti 2000).

The Need for a Metatheory

Until recently, the subject matter of risk and resilience has been vaguely defined (Gordon and Song 1994). Theorists interested in risk and resilience have come from various theoretical backgrounds, often using different languages or lexicons—basic terms, assumptions, and practice applications. Research studies have examined various correlates, characteristics, and the etiology of resilience, ranging from genetics to the global economy. In addition, studies have explored how different populations have faced adversity, including children growing up in poverty (Werner and Smith 1992, 2001), adult survivors of the Holocaust (Greene 2010; Moskovitz 1983), and ethnic minorities facing discrimination (Winfield 1991). One might say that the building blocks of the metatheory have been articulated but not yet brought together.

As early as 1987, Elwyn Anthony predicted that these overlapping approaches to the topic of resilience would eventually "coalesce" (p. 3). This appears to be the case as commonalities in definitions of resilience and themes that link risk and resilience principles with ecological systems thinking are increasingly becoming visible in the literature (Martin-Breen and Anderies 2011). Researchers agree more on a definition of resiliency (Chandra et al. 2010); studies are combining multilevel resiliency factors in their designs (Isserman et al. 2014); and social work theorists have joined seemingly divergent frameworks to inform practice with specific population groups, such as returning members of the military (Bowen, Martin, and Mancini 2013; Wooten 2013). Moreover, practice models, aspects of which are discussed here, have recently linked micro- and macropractice phenomena (Greene 2014; Greene and Greene 2010).

As these multiple factors are synthesized as a metatheory (Wallis 2010), they indicate that resilience rests on an ecological systems conceptual base that explains how people adapt to stress and maintain their daily functioning. In addition, the metatheory cuts across theories at the individual, family, group, organizational, and community levels. This knowledge is provided here to "inform intervention strategies for diverse individuals across the life course, for various populations experiencing adverse events, and for systems of all sizes" (Greene 2014, 939).

Professional Purpose and Well-Being

> ➤ *Well-being may be equated with resilience, reflecting an individual and collective ability to adapt to change.*

You have seen throughout the text that each human behavior and the social environment theory addresses social work's professional purpose to promote human and community well-being but starts from a different vantage point. This variation in theory reflects the complex factors of an ever-changing person–environment context, encompassing historical, political, social, economic, organizational, environmental, and global contexts as well as shifts in philosophical and scientific thinking (CSWE 2015). Why has risk and resilience theory emerged at this particular point in time?

Robert Lifton (1973, 1986), a psychiatrist and student of *psychohistory,* or the intersection between psychological, social, and historical change, has given a reason for the growing popularity of the risk and resilience approach. His early work on people's ability to withstand the horrors of Hiroshima and the Holocaust led him to ask how people overcome difficult, if not traumatic, life events. What accounts for their well-being? He suggested that people are more likely to function successfully in their environments if they are adaptable and flexible and meet the future with optimism. He coined the term *protean* to describe such individuals who are comfortable with environments in flux.

In a more recent work, Lifton (1993/1999) described the twentieth century as a period of social uncertainty—an age of a constantly "changing psychological landscape," "daily threats and pulls," "unmanageable historical events," and "personal uncertainties" (p. 28). He went on to explain that some people are better able to manage such daily anxiety, whereas others feel alienated or at odds with the world. He suggested that for the larger part of human history, people lived and behaved in relatively stable environments. However, in more recent eras, the ever-changing person and environment has created major threats to this stability, including the fear of extinction by nuclear war, historical dislocations, a mass media revolution, global warming, and terrorism. He concluded that people who are well grounded, with more of a capacity to withstand stress, disruption, and adversity, are better able to meet these environmental challenges and work with others to seek new life possibilities. That is, Lifton came to equate well-being with resilience. He further contended that resilience as well-being is not limited to individuals but applies to people's ability to connect positively with others, forming cohesive communities and societies.

The premise set forth by Lifton raises questions about social work practice in a changing world: How do individuals and the communities in which they live recover from such disruptions as the 2008 economic crash? Can they meet the challenges of finding new employment and deal with family stress? Can nations deal with global warming, deforestation, and terrorism? Will social workers engage in practices that advance social, economic, and environmental justice (CSWE 2015)?

Applying Terms and Assumptions in Social Work Practice

> ➤ *Multiple disciplines contribute to the lexicon of risk and resilience.*

Historical Background

Several social science movements have contributed to the philosophical approach of resilience:

- *Prevention science,* a research discipline that focuses on risk reduction;
- *Positive psychology,* a psychological approach that emphasizes the power of the human spirit; and
- The *health and wellness movement,* which considers the benefits of positive thinking and continued self-realization.

In keeping with the social work curriculum, theorists coming from both evidence- and strengths-based philosophies have also championed the risk and resilience approach (Begun 1993; Gilgun 1996a, 1996b, 2002; Saleebey 2012). *Evidence-based* practitioners "use theoretical frameworks supported by empirical evidence to understand development and behavior across the life span" (CSWE 2002, 9). They use a process of systematically identifying and using the best available evidence in making practice decisions (Fraser and Galinsky 1997; Gambrill 1999). In contrast, *strengths-based* practitioners generally assume that when people are given positive support, they have the power to transform their lives (Borden 1992). This point of view was well expressed by Saleebey (2012), who contended that social workers should assess people "in light of their capabilities, competencies, knowledge, survival skills, visions, possibilities, and hopes" (p. 17).

Theoretical Background

The risk and resilience metatheory is built on a multitheoretical foundation, or a community of theories, including, among other disciplines, engineering, genetics, developmental psychology, ecology, systems theory, stress theory, economics, and social work (Table 10.1). Examples include the following:

- Erik Hollnagel, an engineer, who called attention to how substances under stress return or bounce back to their original forms—the safety and stability

Table 10.1.
Selected foundations of risk and resilience theory

Time adopted	Major theorist(s)	Theme	Concepts for practice
1968–1974	Ludwig Von Bertalanffy: Biologist	People live in adaptive social systems.	Exploring communication and organization
1967–1968	Walter Buckley: Sociologist	Adaptive systems may run down.	Helping systems regain function.
1973	Crawford Holling: Ecologist	The resilience of ecological systems depends on sustainability.	Understanding the interdependence of human and natural ecologies
1973	Norman Garmezy: Psychologist	Study of both risks and protective factors is needed to understand resilience.	Assessing risks and protective factors
1979	Urie Bronfenbrenner: Developmental psychologist	Human development needs to be understood within the context of ecological systems.	Examining multisystemic influences
1979	Aaron Antonovsky: Medical sociologist	Wellness or salutogenesis is on a continuum from health to disease.	Exploring health, wellness, and strengths
1980	Carol Germain and Alex Gitterman: Social workers	Social workers help to resolve the difficulties of everyday stress.	Working with clients facing stress-related difficulties
1982	Emmy Werner and Ruth Smith: Developmental psychologists	Children who grow up under adverse situations can become resilient adults.	Overcoming risk Developing resilience
1987	Michael Rutter: Child psychiatrist	There is a link between protective factors and warding off mental illness.	Promoting resilience through practice strategies
1988	Erik Hollnagel: Industrial psychologist	Safety in management situations requires a culture of safety.	Exploring preventive measures
1994 2015	Ann Masten: Developmental psychopathologist	Children who overcome risk exhibit competence/ resilience. Interdependent adaptive systems	Fostering the competence of children in clinical practice Treating children in multilevel contexts

(Continued)

Table 10.1 (Continued)

Time adopted	Major theorist(s)	Theme	Concepts for practice
1998	Froma Walsh: Social worker	Family communication, organization, and belief systems are linked to resilience.	Helping families adapt following adversity
1995–1999	James Garbarino: Humanistic psychologist	Violence prevention begins at an early age.	Creating a sustainable society
2004	Michael Ungar: Social worker	Postmodern thinking reveals multiple expressions of resilience.	Providing culturally relevant help
2002	Roberta Greene: Social worker	Resilience assumptions can be made explicit and synthesized.	Translating resilience assumptions into practice strategies
2003	David Godschack: City planner	Hazards undermine sustainable development.	Helping cities mitigate stress
2008	Fran Norris: Social psychologist	Communities need to prepare for disasters.	Mobilizing social supports

of physical materials being the focus of concern (Hollnagel, Woods, and Leveson 1988);

- Norman Garmezy (1974), a psychologist and founder of the study of human resilience, who used the research method of epidemiology to explore which children of mentally ill parents became ill and which did not;
- Emmy Werner and Ruth Smith (1982), developmental psychologists, who were instrumental in defining resiliency in terms of developmental outcomes and traits; and
- Ecologist Crawford Holling (1973), who is known for his idea about how resilience affects the stability of ecological systems.

In addition, social workers have contributed to the elaboration of the risk and resilience approach by providing ideas for practice. For example, theorists Carol Germain and Alex Gitterman (1996), authors of the life model, underscored the role of natural stressors in everyday life, and Froma Walsh (1998) examined the resilience of family systems. More recently, Michael Ungar (2004) emphasized the diverse nature of resiliency contexts, whereas Roberta Greene (2007, 2014) has proposed multisystems practice models.

Furthermore, a resilience-enhancing model takes into account theoretical background that is now seen to be on the periphery of social work practice, including genetics, spirituality, and technology. It is important to point out that neural, biochemical mechanisms are increasingly being understood as influencing resilience (Bryant 2014; Stix 2011). Moreover, spiritual aspects of resilience are believed to be related to the transpersonal aspects of the helping process (see below), and technological interventions can be found in strategies to help older adults and returning military populations.

Assumptions

As the risk and resilience approach expanded, theorists turned to ecological and systems theories to broaden their view of collective resilience (see Chapters 2 and 6 to review what accounts for the functionality of systems). Assumptions have since been made more explicit through a synthesis of the literature (Greene 2012; see Table 10.2), including the following:

- Resilience is a consequence of favorable person–environment "goodness of fit" over time (Richman and Bowen 1997, 104).
- Resilience reflects people's attachments in multilevel social systems (Bronfenbrenner 1979).
- People (at all systems levels) innately respond well to stress through the use of adaptive/coping strategies (Garmezy 1993).
- Systems effectively face environmental demands for growth and change by "structuring, destructuring, and restructuring"—becoming more differentiated or complex (Buckley 1968, 494).

Table 10.2.
Resilience assumptions

Resilience
- involves a dynamic process of person–environment exchanges
- encompasses an adaptational process of goodness of fit
- occurs across the life course with individuals, families, and communities experiencing unique paths of development
- is linked to life stress and people's unique coping capacity
- is a biopsychosocial and spiritual phenomenon
- involves competence in daily functioning
- may be on a continuum—a polar opposite to risk
- may be interactive, having an effect in combination with risk factors
- is enhanced through connection or relatedness with others
- is influenced by diversity, including ethnicity, race, gender, age, sexual orientation, economic status, religious affiliation, and physical and mental ability
- is expressed and affected by multilevel attachments, both distal and proximal, including family, school, peers, neighborhood, community, and society
- is a function of micro-, exo-, meso-, and macrofactors
- is affected by the availability of environmental resources
- is influenced by power differentials
- Resilience at a systems level
- requires the adaptability of systems
- is enhanced by social supports, cohesion, and viable networks
- calls for the building of social capital
- depends on an equitable distribution of resources
- relies on the sustainability of ecosystems

Note. Adapted from Greene (2012) and Martin-Breen and Anderies (2011).

These major assumptions central to risk and resilience thinking have been incorporated into an integrated approach to practice, policy, and research (Greene 2012).

Definitions

There are numerous definitions of resilience, emphasizing individual and collective properties. Definitions of risk and resilience are increasingly congruent with the ecological perspective (Gitterman 1998, 2008). This refers to the extent to which there is a match between people and their environments (CSWE 2015). Resilience is enhanced when people and their environment are well matched. Other definitions of resilience include

- having a good track record of successful adaptation in the face of stress or disruptive change (Werner and Smith 1982);
- adapting well despite (extremely) stressful experiences or experiencing positive patterns of recovery (Masten 1994);
- maintaining the continuity of one's life story (Borden 1992);
- responding well to stress and adversity (Rutter 1987);
- regaining functioning following adversity or extreme stress (Garmezy 1993);
- having a universal capacity that allows the person, group, or community to prevent, minimize, or overcome the damaging effects of adversity (or to anticipate inevitable adversities; Grotberg 1995, 2).

Over time, definitions have been expanded even further to combine what were originally only solitary characteristics. For example, resilience was first studied as a positive trait of children who became successful adults. Today, resilience is understood to be much more—an adaptive systems process. This is reflected in the description of a *resilient socioeconomic system* whose elements include an awareness of hazards and attention to the condition of human settlements and infrastructure. Resilience in socioeconomic systems also encompasses forms of governance that provide supportive public policy and administration, equity in terms of the wealth of the society, and leadership to organize people's abilities in disaster and risk management (Martin-Breen and Anderies 2011). Moreover, business organizations may attract customers who value their generosity and attention to biodiversity and sustainable economies.

Finally, the definition of resilience adopted here offers a holistic view of individual and systems functionality to serve as an overarching means of operationalizing risk and resilience theory: "People have the capacity to successfully reestablish adaptive, functional behavior after experiencing stress. . . . Resilience is an innate ability that allows people to function effectively in their environments" (Greene 2014, 937).

Basic Terms

As mentioned earlier, risk and resilience provide a singular theory evidence-based ideas for social work practice suggested in the CSWE (2015) curriculum statement. The basic terms related to the risk and resilience approach—including *vulnerability, risk factors, protective factors,* and *resilience*—are derived from scientific inquiry and evolved over time. Researchers began by questioning which *risk factors* of children, families, and environments predisposed children to maladaptive behaviors following adverse events. The term *vulnerability* was used to describe children at risk who are more likely to experience undesirable developmental outcomes. Researchers also asked which positive or *protective factors* shielded these children from difficulty (Garmezy 1974, 1993).

A major aspect of the metatheory incorporates Ann Masten's (1994) suggestion that when children overcome risk and exhibit resilience, they display *competence,* or a pattern of *effective functioning* surrounding developmental tasks appropriate for the child's age, culture, and time in history. Thus, as theorists add to the metatheory, one can see a more integrated process of people challenging and meeting their vulnerabilities, overcoming or reducing risk, drawing on their protective factors, and exhibiting competence or the ability to function in their environment.

Another galvanizing idea in the risk and resilience metatheory is that people naturally deal with the *stress* caused by transactions between them and their environment. According to Germain and Gitterman (1996), stress is experienced in an individual's life course at times of *difficult life transitions,* involving developmental and social change; *traumatic life events,* including grief and loss; and *environmental pressures,* encompassing poverty and community violence. The functionality of people and social systems may also be interrupted by war, economic depression, political climate, and natural disasters (Carter and McGoldrick 1999).

Galea (2014) synthesized the idea that resilience is the capability of functioning positively after stress. He said that resilience was bouncing back from something—a process that takes place over time, along a path. This path may lead a few people to chronic dysfunction, but it is more likely to lead to various levels of effective functioning. Galea went on to say that in fact most people "are just fine after something, perhaps more than resilient."

Still another dimension of the risk and resilience metatheory is that all people involved in a stressful event do not experience it in the same way. The idea that the meaning people attach to adverse events is experienced differently was proposed in 1979 by Anton Antonovsky, a medical sociologist. He believed that it is essential for the professional to learn the *meaning* a person or community ascribes to an adverse event. He stated that when an event is *appraised* as *comprehensible* (predictable), *manageable* (controllable), and somehow *meaningful* (explainable), a resilient response is more likely.

Another chapter in the meaning-making literature can be found in the writings of Edward Canda (2006), who espouses transpersonal social work practice. In this instance, resilience is seen as a form of spiritual transcendence (Canda 2006). Although people may go through the appraisal of stress on their own, or with close friends and family members, social workers can be a catalyst in setting in motion this process of finding higher meaning in adverse events.

Another factor that contributes to the conceptual unity of risk and resilience metatheory is relatedness (see Chapter 2 on ecology and attachment). *Relatedness* is a term used to examine interpersonal or collective behaviors involving people's positive interactions. At the individual level, it begins with the child and caregiver's ability to form an intimate human relationship; research has documented that resilient children often have a good, warm relationship with at least one primary caregiver or mentor (Rutter 1987). Collective attachments involve people interacting in multilevel systems, including the family, school, peer networks, neighborhoods, the community, and society (Bronfenbrenner 1979). Because social relationships are a resource for resilience and a buffer against stress, resilience-enhancing interventions are often based on knowledge of these relationships, as social workers connect people with support networks.

Still another resilience process that stems from ecology is *adaptation*. In keeping with the metatheory, adaptation may be thought of as the ability to deal with daily stressors and "adverse critical events, while still maintaining effective functioning" (Greene 2014, 938). According to Martin-Breen and Anderies (2011), the process of adaptation involves cycles of change:

> It is not just adaptation—change—in response to conditions. It is the ability of systems—households, people, communities, ecosystems, nations—to generate new ways of operating, new systemic relationships. If we consider that parts or connections in systems fail or become untenable, adaptive capacity is a key determiner of resilience. Hence in complex adaptive systems, resilience is best defined as the ability to withstand, recover from, and reorganize in response to crises. Function is maintained, but system structure may not be. (p. 42)

Finally, as spelled out previously, resilience needs to be understood as *functionality*. From this vantage point, the social worker is concerned with observable behaviors that may indicate that clients or constituencies are able to carry out their collective tasks effectively. (These terms are used in assessment; see below.)

Use the case of Juan to apply risk and resilience terms to this little boy, his family, and his country, the Philippines, as Typhoon Hagupit hits land.

> ➤ Juan is a six-year-old school boy who was born to a family living in poverty in a seaside location of the Eastern Philippines. Their geographical area was hit by Typhoon Hayjan in 2013 and is scheduled for economic redevelopment by the World Bank in 2017.

> ➤ Juan is an excellent student and receives much praise from his teacher, a committed mentor. But he is malnourished and often misses school to help his parents, who are loggers earning about $2,500 a year. When Typhoon Hagupit hits land in December 2014, Juan and his family are rescued by neighbors and begin to clear the wreckage for survivors. The village Catholic priest arranges for proper burials and a Mass.

> ➤ In critiquing this case study, one can see that Juan and his family are more vulnerable because they live in poverty in an area prone to typhoons. Their risks are considered compounded.

> ➤ A protective factor is Juan's academic ability. However, Juan is less likely to finish school, as he has to help his parents earn a living. Other protective factors include Juan's teacher and mentor, the village priest, the social support of neighbors, and the development plans of the World Bank.

> ➤ The stress of the typhoon affected 650,000 people in the area. However, international efforts from countries such as China, Israel, and the United States illustrate global attempts to restore functionality or resiliency. It remains to be seen whether industry will be restored and employment will become available.

Engage With Individuals, Families, Groups, Organizations, and Communities

> ➤ Engaging the client or constituency begins with providing for basic needs.

Following adversity and/or chronic stress, client and constituency engagement can only occur when health and human service providers ensure them that their basic needs have been met. This global aspiration to guarantee human needs captured in the *Educational Policy and Accreditation Standards* (CSWE 2015) is expressed as a mission of the International Federation of Red Cross and Red Crescent Societies (2012):

> We strive to meet people's basic needs for health, shelter, education, food, water, and security; make every effort to ensure that the social costs and benefits are fairly shared by all and inequities are eliminated; that human rights, human dignity, and local values are understood and respected; and to ensure that nonrenewable resources, biodiversity, and the environment are managed responsibly. (p. 3)

Of course, the provision of basic needs goes hand in hand with empathy. Moreover, the use of the risk and resilience approach in social work practice necessitates "self-reflection" of one's own views about the nature of practice (CSWE 2015, 4). Does the social worker take a resilience-enhancing stance, believing in people's ability to push for self-change and growth? What can the social worker do to marshal clients' and constituencies' strengths and resources (Saleebey 2012)?

Assess Individuals, Families, Groups, Organizations, and Communities

> ➤ Assessment examines the balance among risk, protective, and resiliency factors. It is concerned with the response to stress, human connections, and adaptation. The functionality of systems is key.

According to the *Educational Policy and Accreditation Standards* (CSWE 2015), social workers "collect and organize data, and apply critical thinking to interpret information from clients and constituencies" (p. 7). Assessment from a risk and resilience perspective determines the client's or constituency's relative balance of vulnerability, risk, protective, and resiliency factors. It begins by examining vulnerability. It then establishes the source of stress; explores what risks have been overcome in the past and are now present; addresses how the client has functioned over time; examines the client's goodness of fit with other social systems; and ascertains what support is available from family, friends, the community, organizations, and macrolevel entities. This process is differentiated as the social worker seeks culturally sound solutions.

Assessing Personal-Level Resilience

Several chapters throughout the book have explored theories that emphasize individual functioning (see Chapters 2, 4, and 5). When following a risk and resilience metatheory approach in assessment, it is important to maintain conceptual coherence with the ecological systems point of view (see Chapter 2). This view point helps the social worker understand the interlocking nature of human adaptation for practice with individuals, families, groups, organizations, and communities.

For example, Richardson (2002) described a way to think of biopsychosocial and spiritual processes as a system (Berger and Federico 1982) by illustrating how these processes can be disrupted by stress (Figure 10.1; see Chapter 4). When disruption occurs, a person's system naturally attempts to reestablish its equilibrium. Richardson called this course of action *resilient integration.* Following an assessment of whether resilient integration has occurred, a mutual decision is made between the client and the social worker on whether professional intervention is needed (CSWE 2015).

In addition, if working at the personal level, the social worker will want to learn how and to what degree stress has interrupted client functionality. How has the client managed transitions across the life course? What information about the client's sense of competence emerges? How has his or her generation been affected by sociopolitical events? How does the client perceive his or her support and interaction in the ecological environment? (See the case of the Cohen family.)

Assessing Family Resilience

Chapter 5 presents a general systems model for working with families and offers assumptions and terms, some of which are incorporated into the risk and resilience metatheory. For example, Froma Walsh's (1998) widely known book on family assessment, *Strengthening Family Resilience,* was based on systems theory. In it, Walsh urged social workers to attend to three aspects of family functioning: (a) family belief systems, involving what meaning a family gives to a crisis; (b) *organizational patterns,* encompassing the family's structure and supports; and (c) communication processes, emphasizing problem-solving ability.

Building on the work of Isserman et al. (2014) and Walsh (1998), Greene (2014) synthesized a set of questions for evaluating the extent of (family) systems' functionality (Table 10.3). These questions allow the social worker to explore a range of social system functions—from their nurturing capacity to their relationship with various other social systems. In sum, social systems assessment is concerned with the source of and response to stress, how people have met life transitions as members of a system, people's human connections, and whether a sense of competence or collective efficacy has been achieved. In the case of the Cohens, you can see how a family of Holocaust survivors adapted to life in the United States.

Figure 10.1.

A biopsychosocial resiliency model. (From Richardson 2002, 313).

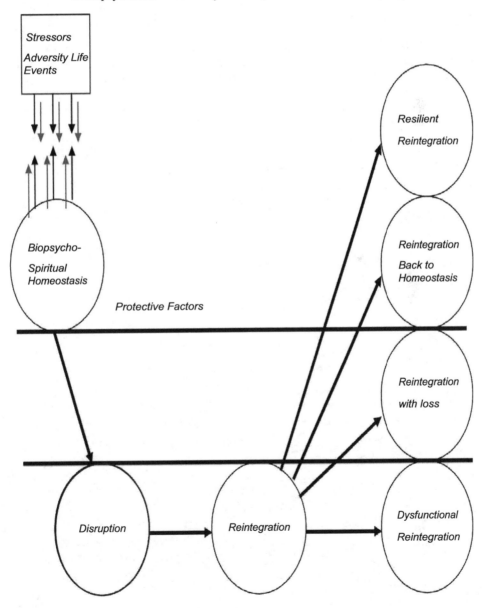

Table 10.3.
Questions for (family) systems assessment

- Does the (family) system have strong bonds?
- Do members nurture one another?
- Do members display empathy?
- Do members provide security?
- Has the (family) system created and recreated an effective structure?
- Is the (family) structure composed of the necessary roles to carry out the functional demands?
- Do (parents) leaders in the system act as executives and providers?
- Are the (family's) system's rules clear?
- Is the system organized in a way that allows for task completion?
- Do members (parents and/or extended family) act as socializing agents connecting children to various social systems?
- Does the system affiliate/connect well with others and other institutions?
- Can the (family) system recognize and accommodate life transitions? Is this reflected in changes in structure, organization, communication patterns, and belief systems?
- Is the system able to use the flow of information to effectively communicate?
- Does communication allow members to find, access, and use resources effectively? For example, are there sufficient resources, such as housing, nutrition, income?
- Can the (family) system map and scan the environment to anticipate, recognize, and identify disruptions and dangers?
- Does the group problem solve effectively?
- Is the group able to make decisions and take action on them?
- Does the group demonstrate collective efficacy, ending in system well-being?
- Can the group resolve internal and external conflict?
- Is the group able to turn to its belief system and culture to establish and maintain resilient functioning?
- Can the system articulate its purpose/goals?
- Is the system able to create and maintain a sense of cohesion/coherence?

Note. Adapted from Greene (2008).

> ➤ The Cohens were a middle-class family living in Berlin before World War II. Mr. and Mrs. Cohen had four children who lived with their grandparents. Joseph, the youngest grandson, aspired to go to the university when the war broke out. The family hoped that the United States and Britain would contain the Nazi invasion of Europe. However, this did not happen soon enough, and the Cohen family was rounded up and sent to Auschwitz. All but Joseph perished.

> ➤ With the help of the Hebrew immigration Aid Society, Joseph immigrated to the United States. He attended night school, opened his own business, and contributed to community causes. He told the social worker, "Family is certainly one [way of rebuilding lives]. My solution was getting involved in American life. I went to work and studied at night. I got married kind of young and my wife has always been supportive."

Assessing Systems Adaptability

Although the social worker may be involved with an individual's ability to adapt to a stressful situation, the adaptability of that person's various social systems is a major focus of resilience assessments. To understand this ability, a social worker performing a risk and resilience assessment will apply the systems theory assumption that the sum of the parts of a system is greater than the whole (Buckley 1968). This reflects the interlinking of the many dimensions of resilience: economic, environmental, political, social, and so forth (Martin-Breen and Anderies 2011).

The adaptability of multilevel, interconnected systems may be assessed using the following checklist:

✓ Is the system organized sufficiently to permit it to discriminate, act on, and respond to the environment?
✓ Has the system developed an adequate map of the environment?
✓ Did an understanding of the environment result in a pool of alternative ideas and behaviors?
✓ Is the system open to change? Are members communicating about what steps they need to take to deal with stress?
✓ Does the system show evidence of past changes requiring modification in role function that were successful?
✓ Do you hear about shifts in structure that will allow the system to act more competitively on the environment?
✓ Has the system produced effective responses to the demands of the environment?
✓ Has the system become increasingly more selectively matched to its environment?

Assessing Community Resilience

An assessment of community resilience may be augmented with further analysis. It requires an examination of the community's pre-event vulnerability to disaster. What is the social and economic well-being and psychological health of the population? Is the community cohesive? By asking these questions, the social worker is incorporating community-based public health questions and economic development assessment questions in the resilience approach (Plough et al. 2013).

A community-based assessment also needs an exploration of the interrelationship of individual, family, and community knowledge and attitudes regarding self-reliance and self-help. Are people relatively vulnerable or self-determined? Furthermore, the assessment necessitates an evaluation of people's capacity to communicate about risks. Moreover, who are the stakeholders? What is the level of social integration of government and nongovernmental organizations in planning, response, and recovery? How will social media be used?

The assessment also depends on the extent of the social connectedness of community members. Are there readily available, viable social networks that the social worker can call into play? If there are no networks, can they be formed quickly? Are there plans and programs that address and support the functional needs of at-risk individuals? Moreover, are post-event and rebuilding plans in place? Finally, what is the community's social capital to achieve recovery goals (Chandra et al. 2010)?

As seen in the true-life case example of Hurricane Katrina below, the recovery in New Orleans required a coordinated approach in which helping professionals considered the total person–environment picture. Case managers helping people who arrive at a hurricane shelter will have a different set of assessment questions in mind than a community planner who is dealing with community-level aspects of emergency preparedness. Examine the following cases to determine the individual and collective nature of resiliency and resources. What policy issue do you observe?

> As Hurricane Katrina is announced in the media, people respond differently to the threat. Sally, who lives in a senior housing building on higher ground, has ridden out storms before. She tells her son, who lives with his family in the suburbs and has a car, to evacuate without her. She later learns that she has to leave her senior housing building and walk to the Superdome, where a shelter has been established. She packs a survival kit with supplies, teams up with another resident, and limps a mile to the shelter, where professionals and volunteers have assembled. She eventually is resettled in senior housing in Texas, where she becomes a participant in the call-a-buddy program.

> John has just been provided housing in a twelve-story Housing and Urban Development low-income building when the storm hits. As John hears about the approach of the storm, he is concerned that he will not be able to get to the HIV/AIDS clinic for his next treatment. But he realizes that residents on the lower floors of his building will have to get to higher floors. He mobilizes them in the move. Recognizing that the electricity will soon be turned off, he borrows a grill from the local fire station to cook communal meals on the rooftop. The social network that is created becomes strong, and all are able to **ride out** the storm.

> Mrs. S. and her son's family live in the Ninth Ward of New Orleans, where poverty is high and the levees are weak. They hope they can ride out the storm, as they have no transportation of their own to evacuate.

> ➤ They first take refuge on the roof of their home. When floodwaters rise, they call 911 but do not get an answer. As the waters reach the rooftop, they decide to take action: They use a mattress as a float for Mrs. S. and the bed of an abandoned, flooded truck as a little boat for the children. They arrive at the Superdome to face armed reserve guards but are able to talk their way into the shelter. Mrs. S., who has diabetes, finds a case manager to talk to about how she can get medication.

> ➤ Change strategies are derived from a synthesis of the risk and resilience literature.

Intervene With Individuals, Families, Groups, Organizations, and Communities

Resilience: The Link Between Research and Practice

In keeping with evidence-based practice, there is a strong link between risk and resilience research factors and the practice strategies they suggest should be carried out. This can be seen in Masten and Coatsworth's (1998) proposal that strategies to promote or enhance resilience depend on whether one focuses on risks, assets, or resiliency processes (Table 10.4). In *risk-focused* approaches, the strategies adopted for practice try to prevent or reduce risk factors. For example, the social worker might work with the rescue team to help Mrs. S. obtain her diabetes medication. *Asset-building* research explores how to improve resource availability and social capital. It may suggest, for example, that a community practitioner's intervention might be to organize the Ninth Ward neighborhood (a poverty-stricken, predominantly African American area) to advocate for a safer levee system (Pyles 2007). Finally, *process-focused* research would lead to interventions that support cultural traditions that foster adaptive, healing rituals, such as musician Wynton Marsalis's visit to the city to lead a New Orleans jazz funeral for the victims (Ungar 2004).

Individual and Group Practice: A Resilience-Enhancing Model

As discussed previously, research explicates intervention strategies for a meta-theory of risk and resilience. Another way of developing practice interventions is through a review and synthesis of the resilience-enhancing literature. For example, Greene and Armenta (2007) created a resilience-enhancing model of intervention to guide an individual or group interview following an adverse event. The process is illustrated here using a case example of people who have learned they must be

Table 10.4.
Strategies for promoting resilience in children and youth

Approach	Goal	Actions
Risk focused	Preventing or reducing risk and stressors	• Prevent or reduce the possibility of low birth-weight or premature birth through prenatal care. • Avoid child abuse or neglect through parent education. • Decrease teenage drinking, smoking, or drug abuse through community programs. • Stop homelessness through housing policy or emergency assistance. • Diminish neighborhood crime or violence through community policing.
Asset focused	Improving the number or quality of resources or social capital	• Make a tutor available. • Organize a Boys and Girls Club. • Create a recreation center.
Process focused	Mobilizing the power of human adaptation systems	• Develop self-efficacy through the graduated success model of teaching. • Teach effective coping strategies for specific threatening situations, such as through programs to prepare children for surgery. • Enhance secure attachment relationships between infants and parents through parental sensitivity training for new parents and their infants at home. • Provide mentoring relationships for children through a program to match children with potential mentors, such as a Boys and Girls Club. • Build friendships for children with prosocial peers in healthy activities, such as extracurricular activities. • Encourage cultural traditions that provide children with adaptive rituals and opportunities for bonds with prosocial adults, such as religious education or classes for children in which elders teach ethnic traditions.

Note. Modified from Masten and Reed (2002, 74–88).

on kidney dialysis. Note that although the steps are numbered here, they are not necessarily sequential. To enhance resilience, social workers do the following:

1. **Acknowledge Client Loss, Vulnerability, and the Future.** When people first learn that they have a need for kidney dialysis, they often feel a sense of loss, a sense of vulnerability, and the notion that they have little future. For clients to make meaning of their diagnosis, they must begin to come to terms with a sense of loss. What can their future hold? How can something positive come of this adverse event?
2. **Identify the Source of and Reaction to Stress.** Each individual with kidney disease and his or her caregiver describe different sources of stress that

accompany the disease. A person's reaction depends on personal factors, such as self-efficacy and problem-solving abilities, as well as on environmental support resources. Clients may indicate that they are most worried about their ability to continue carrying out their work and family responsibilities. Clients may decide that they want to brief their employers and have a family meeting.

3. **Stabilize or Normalize the Situation.** To normalize the situation, clients will eventually need to realize that they are experiencing emotions that many in their situation feel—a combination of anger, sadness, and determination. Affirming these emotions and framing them as positive should help them move forward.

4. **Help Clients Take Control.** Moving forward begins with clients gaining a sense of control. As they begin to make decisions regarding their medical treatment and family responsibilities, they will be initiating a process of growth and transformation.

5. **Provide Resources for Change.** An important role of the social worker is to provide resources for change. For example, there may be a group or a clinic-based program that provides people living with kidney disease with the motivation, skills, and emotional and practical support necessary to deal with life issues and improve their psychological, social, and physical health. Clients can also gain insight and support from a care-sharing group and personal counseling.

6. **Promote Self-Efficacy.** Clients are often able to competently manage their own affairs before they experience a major life stressor. To the extent that a social worker can bolster achievements, such as talking to employers, clients will gain further self-efficacy.

7. **Collaborate in Self-Change.** When dealing with what could at first be disastrous news for clients, the social worker can be helpful by tapping clients' potential for self-change. Do clients believe that they can make life-changing decisions? Are there people in their lives who will be supportive?

8. **Strengthen Problem-Solving Abilities.** Clients' problem-solving capacity becomes stronger during the therapeutic relationship when the practitioner asks reflective questions intended to place them in a reflexive position or trigger the consideration of new options (White and Epston 1990).

9. **Address Positive Emotions.** As the social worker strengthens his or her relationships with clients over time, it is more likely that positive emotions, such as humor and hope, will emerge. Over the course of their therapeutic relationship, clients' sense of humor is helpful in reducing tension and helping them to accept their limitations.

10. **Achieve Creative Expressions.** Letting their imagination soar can put clients on a path to healing. What pleasure can they seek?

11. **Make Meaning of Events.** When clients are diagnosed with kidney disease, they can perceive the event as a major life stressor (a life stressor is something that triggers a person's perception that harm or loss may take place). Through treatment, they can move to a secondary appraisal and consider the coping mechanisms and resources available to help deal with the

situation. By listening to and responding to clients' stories, the social worker can help them decide what is at stake and what can be done. Namely, clients can work to find meaning in the diagnosis and to shape their emotional and behavioral responses to it.

12. **Find the Benefit in an Adverse Event.** Finding a benefit in an adverse life event is closely linked to growth and transcendence. In some cases, clients may make a new start. The process of finding a benefit in an adverse event and growing as a result has been called *posttraumatic growth* (Tedeschi and Calhoun 1996). Clients may decide that they will try and revisit some of their relationships.

13. **Attend to Clients' Spirituality.** As clients review their narratives with the social worker, they learn that one factor contributing to depression is the need for spiritual involvement.

14. **Transcend the Immediate Situation.** As clients progress through therapy, they realize that life is more than survival and that they need not focus solely on their illness. They can become more resilient, looking for new opportunities and discovering new potential.

As seen in the case of Rochelle, the resilience-enhancing model may be used with emergency personnel.

> ➤ Rochelle, who has a master's in social work, was on call for the Office of Emergency Preparedness during Hurricane Katrina. She had to coordinate the efforts of various organizations and personnel. As supplies dwindled and people were left in untenable situations, stress among emergency workers increased. Six months after the storm, Rochelle continues to counsel those with high levels of stress. She has found that after time, some emergency workers have resolved ethical dilemmas involved in their rescue work and that they have found meaning in Katrina. She hopes that a planned tribute to the community's efforts will help others transcend the hurricane's adverse effects.

Interventions and Community Resilience

You have already seen how the adaptiveness of systems is linked to community resilience. However, theorists have offered other concepts for the metatheory. For example, Godschack (2003) has argued that more needs to be done to deal with how cities mitigate urban hazards. Norris et al. (2008) have called on community planners to evaluate their readiness to face disasters, while Adger (2003) has argued that the concept of social capital is required to address these issues:

Collective action requires networks and flows of information between individuals and groups to oil the wheels of decision making. These sets of networks are usefully described as an asset of an individual or a society and are increasingly termed social capital. (Adger 2003, 389)

Interventions and Global Resilience

This chapter has already discussed a few examples of global resilience, such as the case of Juan and the typhoon in the Philippines. Another example of a global resilience initiative is the Rockefeller Foundation's multimillion-dollar Building Climate Change Resilience Initiative announced in 2007. The project is aimed at vulnerable, at-risk populations. The initiative frames resilience as "the capacity over time of a system, organization, community or individual to create, alter, and implement multiple adaptive actions in the face of unpredictable climatic changes" (World Bank 2006, 10). Such a project incorporates economic concepts into the resilience metatheory. It examines such things as the degradation of environments, including deforestation, changes in marginal lands too close to waterfronts, and insufficient infrastructures to support the common good. When social workers have knowledge of the sociodemographics of various regions, they are able to help those who are socially marginalized, thus engaging in "practices that advance social, economic, and environmental justice" (CSWE 2015, 5).

Another global activity involves the World Bank's expectation that nations calculate risk from an economic perspective as the probability of a catastrophic event multiplied by the exposed elements:

$$\text{Risk} = (\text{probability of an event}) \times (\text{exposed elements}).$$

Events may include a tropical cyclone, flooding, extreme heat, drought, or fire. Intervention strategies to reduce these adversities are expected to appear in annual development plans (World Bank 2005, 2006). According to Greene and Greene (2010), who referred to World Bank Independent Evaluation Group (2006),

> This disproportionate effect on developing countries has several possible explanations. One is that developing countries are generally in areas of the world that have harsher climatic conditions, are subject to extreme weather, have unstable geology, or are more difficult to develop; development gains tend to be fragile and easily overwhelmed by the effects of natural events. As a result, disasters can represent a permanent loss of development momentum. It therefore has been recommended that the international community include disaster risk as an integral part of development planning rather than only a humanitarian issue. (p. 1023)

The adaptiveness of larger systems is complex and remains under question. Do such systems regain functioning, or do they become more sensitively attuned to their environment and bounce forward (Davidson 2010)? How can "the multiple levels of human interaction" come together to build resilience and improve the odds of recovery (Masten 2015)?

Critique of Diversity Issues in Social Work Practice

As discussed in detail in Chapter 3, the terms *ethnic minority* or *people of color* generally refer to African Americans, Asians, Latinos, and tribal nations as groups that have historically faced discrimination and been oppressed (Bush et al. 1983). Risk and resilience research has historically included studies of protective factors in these diverse cultures, such as Werner and Smith's longitudinal study in Hawaii and the Civitan International Research Center Project (Grotberg 1995).

The literature on diversity, difference, and resilience is gradually becoming more prevalent (Cross 1998; Genero 1998; Gilgun 2002; Greene et al. 2002). There is also a general agreement that resilience is best understood by examining it within the context of clients' and constituencies' ethnicity and culture (Devore and Schlesinger 1996; Masten 1994; Ungar 2004). In these instances, experts are learning how people share a common story of their beginnings, a sense of history, and a worldview (Green 1995). Therefore, when taking social histories, social workers need to explore the meaning clients and constituencies attribute to being a member of a diverse group.

Social workers also can discover how family culture(s) provides the foundation for child socialization and development. The most important thing about such socialization is that it is often a collective activity and a proactive one. This suggests that families have multiple adults who attempt to teach and "protect" diverse children living within a society of "privilege and power" (CSWE 2015, 4).

For example, the American Psychological Association's Task Force on Resilience and Strength in Black Children and Adolescents (2008) criticized the overemphasis in the literature on disparities in minority families and the insufficient attention to strengths, protective factors, and resilience. It called for socializing children to deal with "pervasive, yet subtle, forms of racialized discrimination and oppression" (p. 1) but within the context of historical racism and institutional barriers.

As a budding theory, the risk and resilience approach to human behavior and the social environment has much to offer, but questions still remain. In addition to whether the theory is culturally sensitive and implies that people should pull themselves up by their bootstraps (Gordon and Song 1994), the question remains whether resilience occurs on a continuum. For example, the U.S. military contends that returning soldiers will regain a relative ability to function and reintegrate into family, community, and society (Meredith et al. 2011), whereas Palmer (1997) has outlined four degrees of resilience: (a) anomic survival, alluding to individuals, families, or groups who are in a constant state of disruption; (b) regenerative resilience, referring to people who make incomplete attempts to attain competence or positive coping strategies; (c) adaptive resilience, involving people, families, or groups who are able to sustain relatively stable patterns of competence and coping; and (d) flourishing resilience, including those who make extensive use of coping strategies and even transform their worldview or life philosophy. Practitioners often tie their interventions to the assumption that resilience is a matter of the degree of daily function, whereas researchers continue to struggle with these questions.

Glossary

Adaptation. A process of modifying how a system functions in order to carry out life's tasks.

Adverse event. An occasion threatening a person's basic assumptions about life.

Appraisal. An internal process that a person or group uses to evaluate a situation.

Competence. The learned capacity to interact positively with the environment; the ability to complete tasks successfully; effective adaptation.

Coping. Changing one's cognitive and behavioral ability to manage specific external and/or internal demands.

Economic sustainability. A method and process of using resources well to support financial viability.

Family belief system. Shared values, beliefs, goals, expectations, and priorities; the meaning a family gives to a (crisis) event.

Meaning making. A client's discovery or reconstruction of the meaning of a (traumatic) event.

Metatheory. A study of theories or community of theories involving the synthesis of knowledge.

Normalization. The process of coming to understand a combination of conflicting emotions following an adverse event.

Positive psychology. An area of psychology that focuses on how people maintain well-being despite adversity.

Prevention science. An area of study that attempts to eliminate or mitigate a problem.

Protean self. Personal attributes that enable some people to remain flexible and see life's possibilities.

Protective factors. Events and conditions that help individuals to reduce risk and enhance adaptation.

Relational resilience. The idea that successful adaptation and dealing with stress depends on relationships with others.

Resilience. Successful adaptation or functioning following stress or an adverse event.

Resilient reintegration. The process of a system returning to equilibrium.

Risk. A factor that influences or increases the probability of the onset of extreme stress.

Self-righting capacity. An individual's natural capacity to heal.

Situational appraisal. A family's shared assessment of a stressor's demands.

Social capital. Networks and assets that enhance societal well-being.

Social cohesion. More closely knit social networks with more reciprocal exchanges of resources. There may be geographical proximity.

Social support. People who are available to rely on and buttress each other against stress.

Stress. An imbalance between an individual's or family's demands and resources to meet those demands.

Stressor appraisal. A family's definition of the severity of its stress.

Transformation. A person's ability to grow and self-actualize in the face of difficulty.

Trauma. A serious or life-threatening situation.

Vulnerability. A person or system that is vulnerable is prone to experiencing an undesirable outcome following risk or stress.

Wellness. Positive regard for oneself as well as others; continuing growth and self-realization.

References

Adger, W. 2003. "Social Capital, Collective Action, and Adaptation to Climate Change." *Economic Geography* 79:387–404.

American Psychological Association, Task Force on Resilience and Strength in Black Children and Adolescents. 2008. *Resilience in African American Children and Adolescents: A Vision for Optimal Development.* Washington, DC: American Psychological Association, Task Force on Resilience and Strength in Black Children and Adolescents.

Anchin, J. C. 2008. "Pursuing a Unifying Paradigm for Psychotherapy: Tasks, Dialectical Considerations, and Biopsychosocial Systems Metatheory." *Journal of Psychotherapy Integration* 18 (3): 310–49.

Anthony, E. J. 1987. "Risk, Vulnerability, and Resilience: An Overview." In *The Invulnerable Child*, edited by E. J. Anthony and B. Cohler, 3–38. New York: Guilford Press.

Antonovsky, A. 1979. *Health, Stress and Coping.* San Francisco, CA: Jossey-Bass.

Begun, A. L. 1993. "Human Behavior and the Social Environment: The Vulnerability, Risk, and Resilience Model." *Journal of Social Work Education* 29:26–36.

Berger, R., and R. Federico. 1982. *Human Behavior: A Social Work Perspective.* New York: Longman.

Borden, W. 1992. "Narrative Perspectives in Psychosocial Intervention Following Adverse Life Events." *Social Work* 37:125–41.

Bowen, G. L., J. Martin, and J. A. Mancini. 2013. "The Resilience of Military Families." In *Families across Time: A Life Course Perspective*, edited by S. J. Price, P. C. McKenry, and M. J. Murphy, 117–28. Los Angeles, CA: Roxbury.

Bronfenbrenner, U. 1979. *The Ecology of Human Development.* Cambridge, MA: Harvard University Press.

Bryant, R. January 2014. "PTSD and Resilience: Evidence from Neuroimaging and Biological Studies." Presentation at the NATO Science for Peace and Security Program, Tel Hai College, Upper Galilee, Israel.

Buckley, W. 1968. "Society as a Complex Adaptive System." In *Modern Systems Research for the Behavioral Scientist*, edited by W. Buckley, 490–511. Chicago, IL: Aldine.

Bush, J. A., D. G. Norton, C. L. Sanders, and B. B. Solomon. 1983. "An Integrative Approach for the Inclusion of Content on Blacks in Social Work Education." In *Mental Health and People of Color*, edited by J. C. Chun, P. J. Dunston, and F. Ross-Sheriff, 97–126. Washington, DC: Howard University Press.

Canda, E. August 2006. "The Transformational Power of Spirituality: Meaning Beyond Breaking Barriers and Creating Common Ground." Paper presented at The First North American Conference, St. Thomas, MN.

Carter, B., and M. McGoldrick. 1999. *The Expanded Family Life Cycle: Individual, Family, and Social Perspectives*, 3rd ed. Boston, MA: Allyn & Bacon.

Chandra, A., J. Acosta, L. S. Meredith, K. Sanches, S. Stern, L. Uscher-Pines, and D. Yeung. 2010. *Understanding Community Resilience in the Context of National Health Security.* Santa Monica, CA: Rand Health.

Council on Social Work Education. 2002. *Educational Policy and Accreditation Standards.* Alexandria, VA: Council on Social Work Education.

Council on Social Work Education. 2015. *Educational Policy and Accreditation Standards.* Alexandria, VA: Council on Social Work Education.

Craig, R. T. 2009. *Metatheory.* Accessed October 16, 2015. http://sage-ereference.com/communicationtheory/Article_n244.html

Cross, T. 1998. "Understanding Family Resiliency from a Relational World View." In *Resiliency in African-American Families*, edited by H. I. McCubbin, E. A. Thompson, A. I. Thompson, and J. A. Futrell, 143–57. Thousand Oaks, CA: Sage.

Davidson, D. 2010. "The Applicability of the Concept of Resilience to Social Systems: Some Sources of Optimism and Nagging Doubts." *Society and Natural Resources* 23:1135–49.

Dervin, B. 1999. "On Studying Information Seeking Methodologically: The Implications of Connecting Metatheory to Method." *Information Processing & Management* 35:727–50.

Devore, W., and E. G. Schlesinger. 1996. *Ethnic-sensitive Social Work Practice*. Boston, MA: Allyn & Bacon.

Fraser, M. W., and M. J. Galinsky. 1997. "Toward a Resilience-based Model of Practice." In *Risk and Resilience in Childhood*, edited by M. W. Fraser, 265–76. Washington, DC: NASW Press.

Galea, S. January 2014. "Trajectories of Resilience Following Mass Trauma." Presentation at the NATO Science for Peace and Security Program, Upper Galilee, Israel.

Gambrill, E. 1999. "Evidence-based Clinical Behavior Analysis, Evidence-based Medicine, and the Cochane Collaboration." *Journal of Behavioral Therapy and Experimental Psychiatry* 30:1–14.

Garbarino, J. 1995. *Raising Children in a Socially Toxic Environment*. San Francisco, CA: Jossey-Bass.

Garbarino, J. 1999. *Lost Boys: Why Our Sons Turn Out Violent and How We Can Save Them*. New York: Free Press.

Garmezy, N. August 1974. "The Study of Children at Risk: New Perspectives for Developmental Psychopathology." Paper presented at the 82nd Annual Convention of the American Psychological Association, New Orleans, LA.

Garmezy, N. 1993. "Children in Poverty: Resilience despite Risk." *Psychiatry* 56:127–36.

Genero, N. P. 1998. "Culture, Resiliency, and Mutual Psychological Development." In *Resiliency in African-American Families*, edited by H. I. McCubbin, E. A. Thompson, A. I. Thompson, and J. A. Futrell, 31–48. Thousand Oaks, CA: Sage.

Germain, C., and A. Gitterman. 1996. *Life Model of Social Work: Advances in Theory and Practice*. New York: Columbia University Press.

Gilgun, J. F. 1996a. "Human Development and Adversity in Ecological Perspective, Part 1: A Conceptual Framework." *Families in Society* 77:395–402.

Gilgun, J. F. 1996b. "Human Development and Adversity in Ecological Perspective, Part 2: Three Patterns." *Families in Society* 77:459–76.

Gilgun, J. F. 2002. "Completing the Circle: American Indian Medicine Wheel and the Promotion of Resilience in Children and Youth Care." *Journal of Human Behavior in the Social Environment* 6 (2): 65–84.

Gitterman, A. April 1998. "Vulnerability, Resilience, and Social Work Practice." The fourth annual Dr. Ephriam L. Linsansky Lecture, University of Maryland, Baltimore.

Gitterman, A. 2008. "Ecological Framework." In *Encyclopedia of Social Work*, vol. 3, 20th ed., edited by T. Mizrahi and L. E. Davis, 97–101. Washington, DC: NASW Press.

Godschack, D. 2003. "Urban Hazard Mitigation: Creating Resilient Cities." *Natural Hazards Review, ASCE* 4 (3): 136–43.

Gordon, E. W., and L. D. Song. 1994. "Variations in the Experience of Resilience." In *Educational Resilience in Inner-City America: Challenges and Prospects*, edited by M. C. Wang and E. W. Gordon, 27–44. Hillsdale, NJ: Erlbaum.

Green, J. 1995. *Cultural Awareness in the Human Services*. Englewood Cliffs, NJ: Prentice Hall.

Greene, R. R. 2002. *Resiliency: An Integrated Approach to Practice, Policy, and Research*. Washington, DC: NASW Press.

Greene, R. R. 2007. *Social Work Practice: A Risk and Resilience Perspective*. Monterey, CA: Brooks/Cole.

Greene, R. R. 2008. *Human Behavior Theory and Social Work Practice*, 3rd ed. New Brunswick, NJ: Aldine Transaction Press.

Greene, R. R. 2010. "Family Dynamics, the Nazi Holocaust, and Mental Health Treatment." *Journal of Human Behavior and the Social Environment* 20:469–88.

Greene, R. R., ed. 2012. *Resiliency Theory: An Integrated Framework for Practice, Research, and Policy*, 2nd ed. Washington, DC: NASW Press.

Greene, R. R. 2014. "Resilience as Effective Functional Capacity: An Ecological Stress Model." *Journal of Human Behavior and the Social Environment* 24:937–50.

Greene, R. R., and K. Armenta. 2007. "The REM Model: Phase II—Practice Strategies." In *Social Work Practice: A Risk and Resilience Perspective*, edited by R. R. Greene, 67–90. Monterey, CA: Brooks/Cole.

Greene, R. R., and D. G. Greene. 2010. "Resilience in the Face of Disasters: Bridging Micro- and Macroperspectives." *Journal of Human Behavior and the Social Environment* 19:1010–24.

Greene, R. R., N. Taylor, M. Evans, and L. A. Smith. 2002. "Raising Children in an Oppressive Environment." In *Resiliency: An Integrated Approach to Practice, Policy, and Research*, edited by R. R. Greene, 241–75. Washington, DC: NASW Press.

Grotberg, E. H. September 1995. "The International Resilience Project: Research, Application, and Policy." Paper presented at the Symposio International Stress Violencia, Lisbon, Portugal.

Holling, C. S. 1973. "Resilience and Stability of Ecological Systems." *Annual Review of Ecology and Systematics* 4:1–23.

Hollnagel, E., D. Woods, and N. Leveson. 1988. *Resilience Engineering*. Burlington, VT: Ashgate-E-Book.

International Federation of Red Cross and Red Crescent Societies. June 2012. "The Road to Resilience: Bridging Relief and Development for a More Sustainable Future." Accessed October 16, 2015. http://www.ifrc.org/PageFiles/96178/1224500-Road%20to%20resilience-EN-LowRes%20(2).pdf

Isserman, N., R. R. Greene, S. Bowen, B. Hollander-Goldfein, and H. Cohen. 2014. Intergenerational Families of Holocaust Survivors: Designing and Piloting a Family Resilience Template." *Evidence-Based Social Work Practice* 30 (1): 62–67.

Lifton, R. J. 1973. *Home from the War: Vietnam Veterans—Neither Victims nor Executioners*. New York: Simon & Schuster.

Lifton, R. J. 1986. *The Nazi Doctors: Medical Killing and the Psychology of Genocide*. New York: Basic Books.

Lifton, R. J. 1999. *The Protean Self: Human Resilience in an Age of Fragmentation*. Chicago, IL: University of Chicago Press. (Original work published 1993).

Luthar, S., and D. Cicchetti. 2000. "The Construct of Resilience: Implications for Interventions and Social Policies." *Development and Psychopathology* 12:857–85.

Martin-Breen, P., and J. M. Anderies. 2011. *Resilience: A Literature Review*. New York: Rockefeller Foundation.

Masten, A. 1994. "Resilience in Individual Development: Successful Adaptation despite Risk and Adversity." In *Educational Resilience in Inner-city America: Challenges and Prospects*, edited by M. C. Wang and E. W. Gordon, 3–25. Hillsdale, NJ: Erlbaum.

Masten, A. S. 2015. "Resilience in Human Development: Interdependent Adaptive Systems in Theory and Action." Paper presented Pathways to resilience III: Beyond Nature and Nurture. Halifax, Nova Scotia, CA, June 18.

Masten, A. S., and J. D. Coatsworth. 1998. "The Development of Competence in Favorable and Unfavorable Environments." *American Psychologist* 53:205–20.

Masten, A., and M. Reed. 2002. "Resilience in Development." In *Handbook of Positive Psychology*, edited by C. R. Snyder and S. J. Lopez, 74–88. New York: Oxford University Press.

Meredith, L., C. Sherbourne, J. Gaillot, L. Hansell, H. Ritschard, A. Parker, and G. Wrenn. 2011. *Promoting Psychological Resilience in the Military*. Santa Monica, CA: Rand.

Moskovitz, S. 1983. *Love Despite Hate*. New York: Norton.

Norris, F. H., S. P. Stevens, B. Pfefferbaum, K. F. Wyche, and R. Pfefferbaum. 2008. "Community Resilience as a Metaphor, Theory, and Set of Capacities and Strategy for Disaster Readiness." *American Journal of Community Psychology* 41:122–50.

Palmer, N. 1997. "Resilience in Adult Children of Alcoholics: A Non-pathological Approach to Social Work Practice." *Health and Social Work* 22:201–9.

Plough, A., J. E. Fielding, A. Chandra, M. Williams, D. Eisenman, K. B. Wells, A. Magana. 2013. "Building Community Disaster Resilience: Perspectives from a Large Urban County Department of Public Health." *American Journal of Public Health* 103:1190–7.

Pyles, L. 2007. Community Organizing for Post-disaster Social Development: Locating Social Work." *International Social Work* 50 (3): 321–33.

Richardson, G. E. 2002. "Metatheory of Resilience and Resiliency." *Journal of Clinical Psychology* 58 (3): 307–21.

Richman, J. M., and G. L. Bowen. 1997. "School Failure: An Ecological-interactional-Developmental Perspective." In *Risk and Resilience in Childhood*, edited by M. W. Fraser, 95–116. Washington, DC: NASW Press.

Ritzer, G. 1988. "Sociological Metatheory: A Defense of a Subfield by a Delineation of Its Parameters." *Sociological Theory* 6 (2): 187–200.

Ritzer, G. 2009. *Metatheory*. Accessed October 16, 2015. www.sociologyencyclopedia.com

Rutter, M. 1987. "Psychological Resilience and Protective Mechanisms." *American Journal of Orthopsychiatry* 57:316–31.

Saleebey, D. 2012. *The Strengths Perspective in Social Work Practice*. Boston, MA: Pearson.

Stix, G. 2011. "The Neuroscience of True Grit." *Scientific America* 304 (3): 28–33.

Tedeschi, R. G., and L. G. Calhoun. 1996. "The Posttraumatic Growth Inventory: Measuring the Positive Legacy of Trauma." *Journal of Traumatic Stress* 9:455–71.

Ungar, M. 2004. "A Constructionist Discourse on Resilience: Multiple Contexts, Multiple Realities among At-risk Children and Youth." *Youth and Society* 35 (3): 341–65.

Wallis, S. 2010. "Toward a Science of Metatheory." *Integral Review* 6 (3): 73–120.

Walsh, F. 1998. *Strengthening Family Resilience.* New York: Guilford Press.

Weinstein, D., and S. Weinstein. 1993. "The Post modern Discourse of Metatheory." *Sociological Inquiry* 63 (3): 224–38.

Werner, E., and R. S. Smith. 1982. *Vulnerable, but Invincible: A Longitudinal Study of Resilient Children and Youth.* New York: McGraw-Hill.

Werner, E., and R. S. Smith. 1992. *Overcoming the Odds: High Risk Children from Birth to Adulthood.* Ithaca, NY: Cornell University Press.

Werner, E., and R. Smith. 2001. *Journeys from Childhood to Midlife.* Ithaca, NY: Cornell University Press.

White, M., and D. Epston. 1990. *Narrative Means to Therapeutic Ends.* New York: Norton.

Winfield, L. 1991. "Resilience, Schooling, and Development in African-American Youth." *Education and Urban Society* 24:5–14.

Wooten, N. R. 2013. "A Bioecological Model of Deployment: Risk and Resilience." *Journal of Human Behavior in the Social Environment* 23:699–717.

World Bank Independent Evaluation Group. 2006. *Hazards of Nature, Risks to Development: An IEG Evaluation of World Bank Assistance for Natural Disasters.* Washington, DC: World Bank.

World Bank Operations Evaluation Department. 2005. *Lessons from Natural Disasters and Emergency Reconstruction.* Accessed October 16, 2015. www.worldbank.org/oed/disasters/lessons_from_disasters.pdf

Index

Page numbers followed by "*f*" indicate figures, and those by "*t*" indicate tables.